LA DATA ANALYSIS
using Microsoft Excel

3rd Edition

Overcoming Crap Data and e

by
Oz du Soleil & Bill Jelen

Holy Macro! Books
PO Box 541731
Merritt Island, FL 32953

Guerrilla Data Analysis 3rd Edition

Authors: Oz Du Soleil & Bill Jelen

Layout: Bronkella Publishing

Copyediting: Kitty Wilson

Cover Design: Shannon Travise

Indexing: Nellie Jay

Published by: Holy Macro! Books, PO Box 541731, Merritt Island FL 32953, USA

Distributed by: Independent Publishers Group, Chicago, IL

First Printing: June 2022

Revision: 202206051010

ISBN: 978-1-61547-074-7 Print, 978-1-61547-160-7 e-Book

Library of Congress Control Number: 2022938519

Dedications

To my mother, Maere Floyd

To all of my followers at Excel on Fire, students who've taken my courses on LinkedIn, and anyone who's learned anything from me about Excel. We're in a battle here, and I appreciate you for being committed to a world free of crap data.

—Oz

To Ron Luther, the first guerrilla data analyst I ever knew.

—Bill

About the Authors

Oz du Soleil was first awarded the Excel MVP Award in January 2015. He's an author, a popular instructor on the LinkedIn Learning Library, and the host of the YouTube channel Excel on Fire. Oz is also a storyteller who's told stories for the *Risk!* podcast and live shows, as well as many shows around Portland, Oregon.

Bill Jelen is the author of 66 books and the host of MrExcel.com. He has been awarded the Microsoft MVP in Excel for more than 15 years.

Acknowledgments

Thanks to Bill Jelen for allowing me to be part of this *Guerrilla Data Analysis* mission that he started in 2002, invited me to update in 2014, and continued in 2022 with this third edition of the book.

Thanks to Helena Bouchez, who coached me in getting the second edition completed. The lessons were with me throughout the writing of this edition.

Oz at Cascade Cigar & Tobacco

Huge thanks to the owners of Cascade Cigar & Tobacco in Happy Valley, Oregon, where much of this book was written over cigars and café mochas—many days from open to close, 10 a.m. to 8 p.m.

Thank you to several people who've been crucial in this happy life that I get to live: Raymond Christian, Deirdre Gruendler, Terri Knight, Mike Land, Happy Little, Andrea Mize, Precious Molyneux, and Charlie Vlahogiannis.

Thank you to the Microsoft MVP community.

—Oz

Thank you, Oz, for being a great co-author and keeping me writing. Thank you, Kitty Wilson, for copyediting. Thanks to Bob Umlas for tech editing. Thank you, Mary Ellen Jelen, for keeping me focused on writing.

—Bill

Table of Contents

Introduction: Welcome to the World of Guerrilla Data Analysis!

Over the years that I've been consulting, teaching workshops, writing a blog, and creating videos for my YouTube channel Excel on Fire, it's gotten clear to me that there are a lot of people who are in data-driven roles but don't have a data background. They aren't sure what Excel can really do, but spreadsheets keep showing up in their inboxes. One of my students complained that she got a promotion, more money, and the title Social Media Strategist. However, instead of getting more social media activity, she got a mountain of data and was directed to "find something interesting in this." She had become an unwitting data analyst who didn't know where to start.

Other students and clients have told stories about taking a week to manually compare lists that were thousands of rows long, retyping data that came to them in ALL CAPS, and spending days creating summaries without knowing that Pivot Tables are designed to make such summaries in seconds.

That is the world of *guerrilla data analysis*: You find yourself in the heat of data conflict, without formal training, and you need to make something happen.

Some aspects of data even blindside people who've been trained to work with data. Consider a person who's studied marketing in college and learned all the analytics and A/B testing and whatnot. He graduates and takes a job in a small boutique marketing firm and *holy moly*! The expensive software that he used in college isn't at the firm, but they have Excel. And the level of data cleansing wasn't part of his formal training. Flattening a file (page 84) wasn't part of the curriculum. He didn't expect to have to break data out of a PDF or compile inconsistent data that's sent to him in Word documents, Excel files, Google Sheets, and pasted into Excel from emails. This is guerrilla data analysis!

If you're reading this book, you're probably a guerrilla analyst, and hopefully you'll get useful tips and insights from this book, as well as solutions that end unnecessary misery. The examples here are practical and cover a wide variety of areas, including nonprofits, accounting, and event planning and retail. The goal is to get your ideas churning by exposing you to a variety of ways to use Excel.

This third edition is more than just an update of the second edition. Yes, it includes the newest brilliant features in Excel, like XLOOKUP, Power Query, dynamic arrays, and LET. But those are just tools, and in and of themselves, the tools don't do anything.

Think about what you set out to accomplish when you pick up a tool—a pen, a roll of tape, a USB cable, a car key, or Excel. You have a mission. You're trying to move something in the real world.

My mission has been to battle crap data in all its forms: duplicate entries, incomplete entries, sloppy cut-and-paste jobs, data in 20 different places needing to be consolidated in a single place … all the ways that data can be messy, wrong, or unusable. The consequences of all this chaos are real, and I want to empower others to use the new Excel tools to minimize and eliminate chaos. Creating this third edition is one way I'm empowering you—by showing you the news tools to continue this mission of ridding the world of the misery caused by crap data.

About This Book

We couldn't include everything in Excel in this book, and we made some hard decisions about what to include and how deep to go on some topics. So, here's what guided the decisions:

What would a person need when they're thrown into the fire and need to work with Excel and data?

When someone needs to do something in Excel, there aren't partitions between beginner, intermediate, and advanced skills. There's data, a need, and people counting on the work to be done and accurate. The user needs *essentials*.

Think about baking a pie. There are easy tasks, like measuring a teaspoon of salt. There are intermediate tasks, such as chopping apples into similar-sized chunks. And there are advanced tasks, like knowing how to roll out the crust.

You need all of those tasks in order to create a tasty pie. You don't need to be an expert or a pastry chef. You need to be functional. It's the same with Excel: You usually don't need to be an expert, but you do need to be functional. This book strives to show you the parts of Excel that'll make you functional in most situations.

- We go beyond the typical standalone Excel parlor tricks in this book and offer warnings, context, and nuance. Most sections of this book are short and designed to give quick insights with practical examples.

Some images in the book do not show entire datasets because they're too large. However, if you want to see a full dataset, you can use the workbooks that accompany the book. In fact, to work along with any of the examples in this book, grab the Excel files from https://www.mrexcel.com/download-center/guerrilla-data-analysis-3rd-edition-71223/.

🐉 What We Mean by Excel Skirmishes

Skirmish

This book is especially meaningful to me because it gives me an opportunity to share stories and insights that we're calling skirmishes.

I've often said that when you have a project, the Excel work can be the easy part, and the hard stuff is outside of Excel. That outside stuff is the skirmishes. Things like:

- Dealing with octopus spreadsheets—where they come from and what to do with them (see page 173)
- Identifying whether your problem is a people problem, a process problem, or a tool problem (see page 224)
- Avoiding working on your source data (see page 215)
- Accepting that data is never 100% clean and determining when it's *clean enough* (see page 163)

These things can make an analyst's work extremely and unnecessarily difficult. Imagine gathering data from five different sources, getting it all compiled, doing all the Pivot Tables, using dynamic arrays, and writing complex calculations. Then you delete some rows you don't need and save the workbook. But then you realize that you needed those rows of data you deleted, and you can't undo your way back. You're deep in a guerrilla data skirmish now!

If you have access to your source data, at least you can start all over again. But, if you originally worked on your source data, *woe be unto you*. The source data is gone. If someone else compiled the data for you, now you've got to go back and humbly request, "ummm … can you get me that data again?"

The skirmishes in this book are included to help you in real-life data situations and circumstances that often can't be ameliorated with extreme Excel sorcery. You'll recognize a skirmish when you see this dragon symbol: 🐉

Blindsided by Data

When we wrote the second edition of this book, big data was a big deal. It isn't such a hot topic anymore (thank goodness). Today's buzzwords include:

- Data-driven decision making
- Data visualization
- Dashboards

Whatever the lingo or fashionable topics, what hasn't changed is the increasing number of unsuspecting people who find themselves working with data and Excel. It might be the person who was trained in college to analyze market trends, or the newbie podcaster who has to manage a budget and review her analytics to determine what listeners like and don't like and with what frequency she should post new episodes. I even met a guy who regularly volunteered to go to a stream and track how many turtles he saw over several hours. That data would be compiled to monitor the turtle population over time, as a measure of the health of the ecosystem.

The turtle tracker, the marketer, and the podcaster can all be blindsided by data. In the case of the marketer, they can be blindsided by the level of data cleansing, and properly structuring the data inside a workbook, that has to be done before all the slick analytics that they were trained to execute.

Small, Stupid Stuff and Big, Complicated Stuff

Data analysis involves both small, stupid stuff and big, complicated stuff. Let us tell you what we mean.

One afternoon in 2005, I needed to print certificates on expensive paper. It was late in the afternoon, and the certificates absolutely had to ship that day. I did the Excel–Word mail merge, and the certificates were coming out of the printer with weirdo numbers instead of dates: 38491, 38464, and 38478 instead of 5/19/2005, 4/22/2005, and 5/6/2005. C'mon! *Really?! Now?!*

It took me two hours to learn that the Short Date formatting in Excel had been changed to General, and I only had to change it back and redo the merge. But the glitch had already cost me at least 50 sheets of fancy paper, the afternoon was gone, and I'd done a lot of worrying that I'd have to tell a lot of already anxious people that the certificates weren't going to ship on time.

That afternoon I didn't really have an analysis problem, but the story is a good example of an analyst having done all the data cleansing, merging, analysis, investigations, etc. to get to a final result—then, BANG! 💣— something weird happens just when it seemed like the hard work was done. Small, stupid details turned the process upside down.

Another reason for telling this story is to let you know that you're not the only one who's been stopped by small things. Students ask about these types of disruptions and start their questions with "This may seem like a small thing, but …" I say it's not small when you're under pressure and a whole process has stopped. Guerrilla data conflict is guerrilla data conflict.

In addition to small, stupid stuff, there is big, complicated stuff. I had a client who hired me several times to build prototypes that his in-house team would convert into web-based applications. I asked him, "Why pay me when you've already got the developers?" He described how he knew a little Excel and could guide me in creating what he was looking for, but, he said, "when those guys open their editors and I see all that code, I don't know what the 😵 is going on. So, I get you to build what I want, in Excel, with all the calculations working right, and then I can tell them, 'Here. Build this.'"

One time he and I spent two hours on a video call, working on a single formula while I shared my screen and took his instructions as he watched. Some of the formula details:

- His clients would pay quarterly fees based on their annual revenue. My formula had to use the annual revenue to retrieve the fee from a fee schedule.
- If a client started mid-quarter, the formula had to prorate the fee. If they started one-third into the quarter, the fee would be two-thirds.
- If a client left within a year, the full fee for the quarter was due. If the client left after a year and left mid-quarter, the fee would be prorated. This meant my calculations had to look at the client's start date and exit date to determine if a full fee or prorated fee was due.

All this might sound like a pretty small task, but my client was dealing with millions of dollars from his clients. So, I felt the pressure to get it right. I asked lots of questions about possible scenarios, and that spurred him into thinking of even more scenarios that we then tested. We tweaked the formula until the results were accurate.

Big and complicated can be a complex project that takes months to complete. It can also be the pressure of writing a single formula that accurately reflects a contractual agreement between multi-million-dollar businesses. Pressure is pressure. Guerrilla data conflict is guerrilla data conflict.

Note: If you have any questions, notice errors, or want to share how the book has helped you, please be in touch. I would love to hear from you. Find me at Oz@DataScopic.net.

Chapter 1: Reviewing the Basics

This book assumes that you have some basic knowledge of Excel. However, even seasoned Excel users may need a refresher on some of the basics, so let's start with some fundamentals to get a running start on the rest of the content. You might need this information when you're battling crap data and things get hot.

Overview of Excel Functions and Formulas

There is a difference between a formula and a function.

A function is a feature in Excel that is programmed to perform a specific task. Functions have names like MAX, COUNTA, SUMIFS, NOW, TOCOL, TEXTAFTER, KURT, and CHAR. There are hundreds of Excel functions grouped in several categories. You don't need to know all of the functions. Getting the most from Excel requires using resources like online forums, tutorials, and books—and just asking people if they can help answer questions.

A formula starts with = and does not always include a function. For example:

- =3+2 is a formula without a function. It adds 3 and 2.
- =B3+E3 is a formula without a function. It adds the values in cells B3 and E3.
- =SUM(3,2) is a formula that uses the SUM function to add 3 and 2.
- =B1*MAX(A3:C20) is a formula that uses MAX to find the maximum value in the range A3:C20 and multiply that value by the value in B1.

Excel Formula Notation

Here is a list of some of the notation that you'll see in formulas and what it means:

Notation	What It Means
A2=B2	Cell A2 equals cell B2
A2>=B2	Cell A2 is greater than or equal to cell B2
A2>50	Cell A2 is greater than 50
A2<>B2	Cell A2 does not equal cell B2
""	Nothing/empty
A2=""	Cell A2 equals empty
A2<>""	Cell A2 does not equal empty
AND(C2=B2,A2<=50)	Cell C2 is equal to cell B2 and cell A2 is less than or equal to 50
"Paris"	Treat the word Paris as text
OR(A2="Lima",A2="LIM")	Cell A2 is either Lima or LIM
$	Absolute reference
A3#	Return all values from the array that starts in A3
&	Concatenate
:	Range
!	Refers to another worksheet
{ }	1. Surrounds a legacy array formula 2. Used as an array constant within other functions such as the CHOOSE function
[ ]	1. Table reference 2. Reference to another workbook

Excel Error Notation

Here is a list of some of the errors that you'll see in Excel and what they mean:

Error	What It Means
#REF	An invalid cell reference was used.
#N/A	A lookup is being attempted for a value that doesn't exist.
#NULL	Cell references aren't separated properly.
#DIV/0	The formula is trying to divide by zero.
#NAME?	Excel doesn't recognize text in a formula.
#VALUE	The wrong type of formula argument was used.
#CALC!	FILTER is returning no results. Excel does not (yet) support empty arrays.
#######	The column isn't wide enough for cell contents or a negative time value calculated.
#SPILL!	There isn't enough room for the spilled array.

Relative, Absolute, and Mixed References

PAY ATTENTION! This is an area of spreadsheet development that causes too many problems. Excel defaults to relative references. Using absolute and mixed references will make formulas simpler to write and make organization easier.

Which would you rather do?

1. Spend a few seconds writing a formula once and dragging it over thousands of cells.

2. Spend hours manually manipulating data or rewriting minor variations of the same formula.

If you enjoy peaceful sleep, then you probably chose option 1. Option 2 will ruin your sleep in the form of taking up too much time and causing nightmares associated with all the errors and tedium.

The key to option 1 is understanding relative and absolute cell references.

By default, when you build formulas, the cell references are relative. For example, this figure shows the formula =B2*C2 in cell D2, which was dragged down the column so it made the calculation in each cell. This is a relative cell reference.

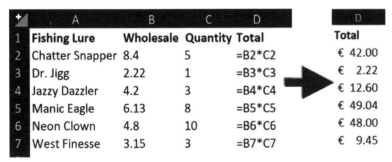

Now let's get into absolute cell references. In the image below, the goal is to have the markup in F2 applied to every one of the totals.

	A	B	C	D	E	F
1	Fishing Lure	Wholesale	Quantity	Total		Markup
2	Chatter Snapper	€ 8.40	5	€ 42.00		1.8
3	Dr. Jigg	€ 2.22	1	€ 2.22		
4	Jazzy Dazzler	€ 4.20	3	€ 12.60		
5	Manic Eagle	€ 6.13	8	€ 49.04		
6	Neon Clown	€ 4.80	10	€ 48.00		
7	West Finesse	€ 3.15	3	€ 9.45		

But look what happens if all of the cell references are relative and the formula in D2 is dragged down. The reference to F2 isn't locked down, and D4 is multiplying by the empty cell, F4.

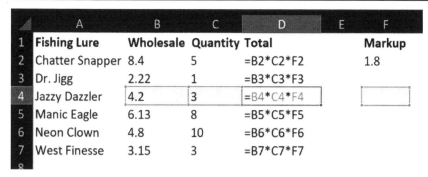

	A	B	C	D	E	F
1	Fishing Lure	Wholesale	Quantity	Total		Markup
2	Chatter Snapper	8.4	5	=B2*C2*F2		1.8
3	Dr. Jigg	2.22	1	=B3*C3*F3		
4	Jazzy Dazzler	4.2	3	=B4*C4*F4		
5	Manic Eagle	6.13	8	=B5*C5*F5		
6	Neon Clown	4.8	10	=B6*C6*F6		
7	West Finesse	3.15	3	=B7*C7*F7		

The you-know-what has hit the fan! The formulas in D2:D7 are wrong because they're capturing empty cells—but you're not in the business of giving away free fishing lures.

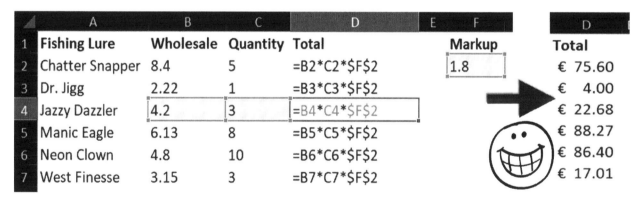

F2 needs to be locked down, so you need an absolute cell reference.

$F$2 allows you to drag the formula in D2, and it will always refer to cell F2. $F locks the column reference to column F; $2 locks the row reference to row 2.

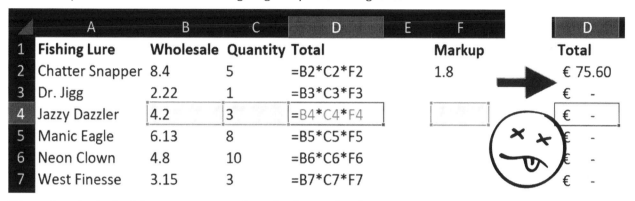

You can use a mix of relative and absolute references, but mixed references get a little tricky. Let's look.

The next challenge is to create a matrix so that it's easy to review possible markups. Rather than use a reference to a single cell, the goal is to drag the formula down and to the right while still referring to the wholesale prices in column B and the markups in row 2—the result being, for example: Cell E3 must multiply E2*B3.

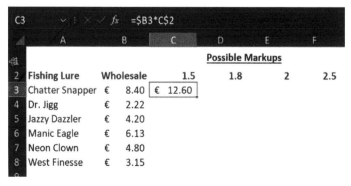

To get this result, you write the following formula just one time, in cell C3:

```
=B$2*$A3
```

Next, drag the formula down and right, so that this happens:

- B$2 changes to C$2, D$2, E$2, and F$2.
- $A3 changes to $A3, $A4, $A5, $A6, and $A7.

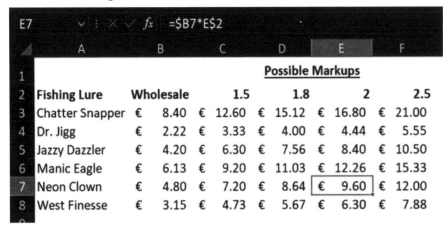

> **Tip:** When using absolute cell references, you can type the dollar signs or press the F4 key. You can press F4 multiple times to toggle through the reference types:

Keystroke	Resulting Formula	What happens when the formula is dragged to other cells
Enter	=B1	Relative changes
Press F4 once	=$B$1	Absolute reference: no changes
Press F4 a second time	=B$1	Column changes, row reference does not change
Press F4 a third time	=$B1	Column reference changes, row changes
Press F4 a fourth time	=B1	Back to the original relative reference

Text Manipulation Functions

These are examples of formulas using functions that clean, flag, or extract text:

Formula	What It Does
=LEFT(A1,2)	Returns the two leftmost characters in cell A1.
=RIGHT(A1,2)	Returns the two rightmost characters in cell A1.
=MID(A1,3,2)	Returns the third and fourth characters of cell A1; the 3 denotes the character starting position, and the 2 denotes how many characters (moving to the right) to return.
=LEN(A1)	Counts the number of characters in cell A1.
=TRIM(A1)	Removes any spaces from in front of or behind the value in cell A1, as well as any extra spaces between words, so that only one space remains between any words.
=LOWER(A1)	Copies and converts text in A1 to all lowercase.
=UPPER(A1)	Copies and converts text in A1 to all uppercase.
=PROPER(A1)	Copies and converts text in A1 to all proper case (that is, capitalizes just the first letter of each word).
=FIND("x",A1)	Returns the position of the character x in cell A1.

Caution: TRIM is a tricky function because it helps clean leading and trailing spaces. However, there are times when it looks like there are spaces but TRIM isn't doing anything. In those situations, there might actually be a tab, carriage return, or line-feed character. In web data, there might be a non-breaking space— in HTML or character 160 in ASCII. TRIM can't handle any of these special characters. Also, PROPER isn't perfectly proper. It will convert McDonald into Mcdonald, AAA to Aaa, and PO Box to Po Box. You will have to go in and manually correct these issues.

IF Statements

The IF statement is the number-one function to get comfortable with! Whatever you're doing with your data, you'll need to work with data based on conditions, like this:

```
= IF(Check for a condition, If the condition is met do X, If the condition is
not met do Y)
```

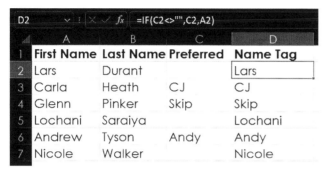

Say that you're preparing nametags for an event and some people want to be called by a name other than their given name. The formula in D2 chooses the preferred name:

```
=IF(C2<>"",C2,A2)
```

This tells Excel that if C2 is not empty, it should use the value in C2; otherwise, it should use the value in A2.

Note: You can nest up to 64 IF statements. However, if you are nesting more than a few IF statements, it is likely that a lookup table and an XLOOKUP or a join in Power Query can solve your problem much more easily.

I cannot overstate how important IF is to anyone working with data. Years ago I wrote a monster formula that had 25 IFs. It was huge and ugly. It was torture to build and modify. But guess what? It worked.

Basically, the formula said: Check for this criterion, and if that's okay, then do this thing; if that's okay, then look at this other thing … on and on 25 times. If the formula failed at any point before the 25th IF, then it would return an X.

At the time, I didn't have the skill to do any better, and Power Query didn't exist.

The takeaways:

- Use the tools that you are comfortable using and can be responsible for. You can implement new, more refined techniques and strategies as you learn them. But don't apologize if your solution isn't fancy. It just needs to work.

  When I built that 25-layer beast, several people on online forums offered me some solutions (including VBA code), but they made no sense to me. They were too far over my head—at the time—for me to be responsible for them, so if my client needed a modification, I would have been dependent upon the strangers online who'd made the solution.

- IF can take you a long, long way. As my friend and data visualization superstar Ann K. Emery has said:

  The most powerful tool that you can develop is your brain.

  Excel and all its functions are tools. Tools alone don't get a job done. Your mind builds solutions. For several years, all I could do in Excel was sort, filter, write IF statements, and drag cells around. Those were the sole ingredients in plenty of effective solutions. They worked.

Using an IF Statement with AND

Time for some IF action!

Say that you have a list of homes that you're considering. You've decided that your future home needs at least three bedrooms, and the walkability score is important. Walkability scores above 80, you've decided, are neighborhoods that are too congested, and values below 55 mean the house is in the middle of nowhere.

The functions IF and AND will be combined to result in an x if a property is worth visiting and result in a blank if not.

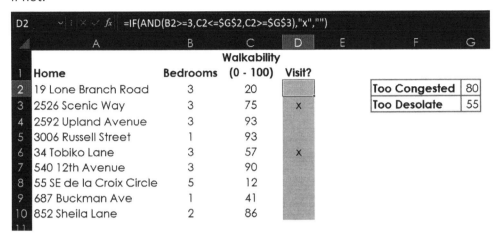

The formula used in the Visit? column is:

```
=IF(AND(B2>=3,C2<=$G$2,C2>=$G$3),"x","")
```

The AND checks if all three criteria are met. If they are, x is the result. If any of the criteria are not satisfied, the result is an empty cell.

IF, COUNTA, and XLOOKUP

In this example, members were required to attend at least two meetings. In the Call column, anyone who attended two or three meetings has the desired result, OK. For those who attended zero or one meeting, their phone number needs to be retrieved from column H.

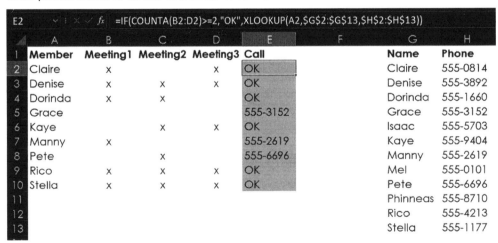

The formula in E2:

```
=IF(COUNTA(B2:D2)> =2,"OK",XLOOKUP(A2,$G$2:$G$13,$H$2:$H$13))
```

- COUNTA counts the number of attendances.
- If COUNTA results in ≥2, the result is OK, and the formula is done.
- If that criterion was not met, XLOOKUP is engaged and retrieves the phone number.

IF Nested in IF

Let's change the previous example such that Meeting2 was most important, thus:

- If a person attended Meeting2: OK.
- If a person attended ≥2 meetings: Y (they're fine).
- Anyone else: PROBATION.

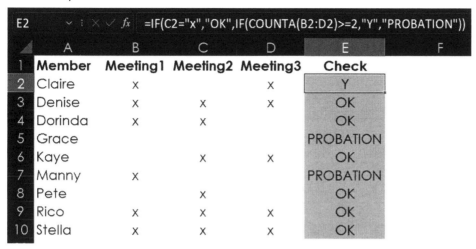

The formula in E2:

```
=IF(C2="x","OK",IF(COUNTA(B2:D2)>=2,"Y","PROBATION"))
```

See how it works? Pete shows OK even though he only attended one meeting because he attended Meeting2.

IF with Wildcards

IF doesn't support wildcards, but COUNTIFS nested inside an IF helps with this example. Here, if a dish has *soup* in the title, the result should be a checkmark.

The formula in B2:

```
=IF(COUNTIFS(A2,"*soup*"),"P","")
```

The wildcard * is used.

COUNTIFS is checking for the word *soup*. Having the wildcard before and after allows the formula to find *soup* anywhere inside the string of text. If you use "*soup", it will only flag text where *soup* is at the end.

And what's with the P in the formula? I'm glad you asked. 😁

Cells B2:B11 are formatted with the font Wingdings2, and that converts the P to a checkmark.

More on wildcards on page 58.

Developing Dynamic Spreadsheets

What is *dynamic*, as in *dynamic objects* or *dynamic spreadsheets*? *Dynamic* means that as your data changes, the changes are reflected throughout your formulas, your calculations. So if a change in a value impacts five calculations, you don't have to make the change in five different places.

Dynamic spreadsheet development offers several major benefits:

- A spreadsheet automatically updates with changes in the data. If you make one change to your data, the change will ripple throughout the spreadsheet, and all relevant changes will be made.
- It maintains the integrity of calculations.
- It lets you know where data and calculations came from.

In the next figure, the total in D2 isn't dynamic. Someone typed in the 65, and it's wrong. The total number of employees in B2:B6 is 63.

You can see that the 65 in D2 is a number and not a formula by selecting that cell and then looking in the formula bar. There's a 65 instead of a formula.

Someone may have calculated the total in their head or on a scrap of paper, then typed the number in (the dreaded crime of hard-coded values). Maybe the 65 was right, and then the numbers in B2:B6 changed, but the 65 didn't change.

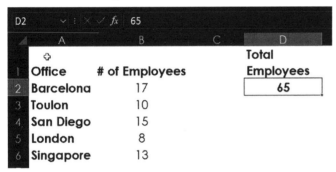

The image below shows a dynamic solution. There's a formula in D2 that calculates the total, and if any of the values change, the Total Employees number will change.

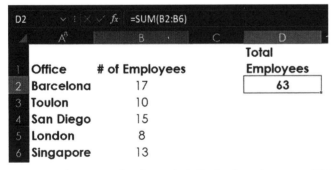

However, because the formula is limited to the range B2:B6, it doesn't work when the rest of the data comes in for Toronto, Lagos, and Hong Kong.

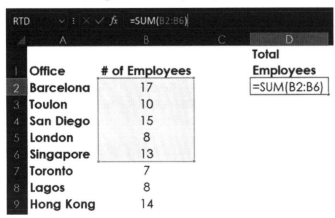

This problem with static ranges shows up as a concern if the data changes. And if any Pivot Tables or graphs are tied to a static range that changes, those can be tougher to correct than a formula. Therefore, get in the habit of asking yourself, "How dynamic does my spreadsheet need to be?"

You face very different tasks if your data changes a lot than if it rarely changes or if it is a one-time dataset that will never change. In some cases, making a spreadsheet dynamic will really save you a lot of hassle. In other cases, it's just not necessary. The next figure shows two versions of the same spreadsheet—one static and the other dynamic. If you know you'll need to add offices and employee counts with this dataset, then you can see that making the spreadsheet dynamic will save you some errors and problems later on.

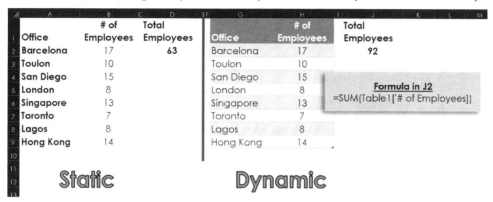

Throughout this book, you'll learn about a number of tools and features that help you create dynamic spreadsheets:

- Pivot Tables
- Slicers
- The OFFSET function
- The INDEX function
- Tables

Concatenating Names and Changing Formulas to Values

Here's a must-know: It's important to use formulas in Excel when you want everything live and dynamic. There are other times when the underlying formulas have done their work and need to go away before they cause problems.

Say that you've received a report that has names that are in separate cells, but they need to be put together as full names. In the image below, the original data had columns A, B, and C. Column D was empty, and that's where the formulas were added to create the full names.

	LAST NAMES	FIRST NAMES		FULL NAMES	Formulas in Column D
1					
2	Lee	Terese		Terese Lee	=B2&" "&A2
3	Konda	Margarita		Margarita Konda	=B3&" "&A3
4	Abosede	Efe		Efe Abosede	=B4&" "&A4
5	Senn	Dior		Dior Senn	=B5&" "&A5
6					
7	Last Name	First Name	Middle		
8	De Luca	Kelsi	E.	Kelsi E. De Luca	=TEXTJOIN(" ",TRUE,B8,C8,A8)
9	Nolan	Desiree	Simone	Desiree Simone Nolan	=TEXTJOIN(" ",TRUE,B9,C9,A9)
10	Kawai	Makaio		Makaio Kawai	=TEXTJOIN(" ",TRUE,B10,C10,A10)
11	Dawes	Smokey	L.	Smokey L. Dawes	=TEXTJOIN(" ",TRUE,B11,C11,A11)

BEWARE! We're going all-in with this example. Just like in the real world, the data and tasks don't show up all nice and clean.

There are twists in this example:

- The last names are in column A, and the first names are in B.
- In rows 8:11 some names have a middle component, though row 10 doesn't.

I'm showing you two ways to get these names put together:

- Concatenate using the & symbol
- Concatenate using the TEXTJOIN function

Concatenating Using the & Symbol

Notice the formula =B2&" "&A2 is being used in D2. You have to include the space between the first and last names. (To see for yourself, set up a similar spreadsheet and use the formula =B2&A2 instead.)

Concatenating with TEXTJOIN

TEXTJOIN's syntax:

```
TEXTJOIN(delimiter, ignore_empty, text1, [text2], …)
```

In D8 the function TEXTJOIN is being used to simplify the concatenation task:

```
=TEXTJOIN(" ",TRUE,B8,C8,A8)
```

> **Note:** The TRUE in the TEXTJOIN tells the formula to ignore an empty cell; i.e., if there's a blank or an empty cell, don't leave a blank space.

Deleting the Underlying Formulas and Keeping the Data

Once you have the names in one cell, your work is done, and you no longer need columns A, B, and C. Can you just delete them?

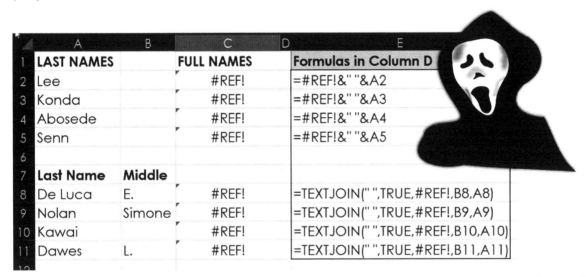

In the image above, the First Name column (column A) was deleted, everything slid to the left, and the #REF! error shows up because the formulas are looking for data that no longer exists.

You need to undo the deletion with Ctrl+Z or the undo arrow in the ribbon and get your data back.

There are several ways to delete the underlying formulas and keep the data. Here's one:

1. Highlight the range that contains underlying formulas and right-click.

2. In the context menu that pops up, select Copy.

3. Right-click again and select Paste As Values, which is designated by the clipboard icon with the 123, as shown in the image below.

Now the formulas are gone. Check to be sure!

In the image below, D4 has the name Efe Abosede, and it matches in the formula bar. No more formula.

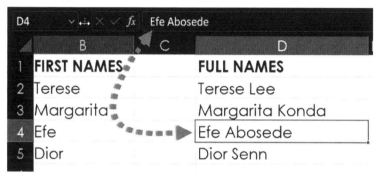

SUCCESS!

You have actual data in the FULL NAMES column, and you're free to delete columns A:C.

Another way to get rid of the formulas:

1. Highlight the range.
2. Hover the mouse over one of the edges.
3. When the cursor turns into a four-way arrow (as shown in the circle in the image below), right-click.
4. While holding the right mouse button down, slide the range slightly out of position.
5. Slide the range back to the original position.
6. When the options pop up, select Copy Here as Values Only.

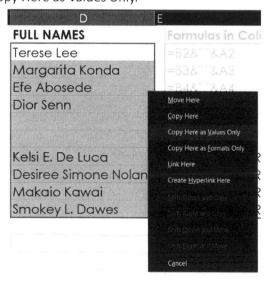

Transposing Columns and Rows

The data in the image below is musicians who'd be great to work with. Scrolling left and right is a hassle. It'd be so much easier to work horizontally, with the names as row headers instead of column headers.

Here's the fix:

1. Highlight the range and press Ctrl+C (or right-click and select Copy) to copy the data.

2. Select the cell where you want the vertical data to start. The following figure shows the cursor in cell A6.

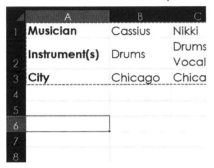

3. On the Home tab, in the Clipboard group, select the arrow below Paste.

4. From the menu that appears, select the clipboard icon with the two-way arrow (as shown circled in the following image).

BOOM!

	A	B	C
6	Musician	Instrument(s)	City
7	Cassius	Drums	Chicago
8	Nikki	Drums, Vocals	Chicago
9	Mark	Singer, Guitar	Evanston
10	Dezembro	Cavaquinho, Guitar, Bass	Chicago
11	Rudy	Bass, Guitar, Keys	Naperville
12	Cat	Bass, Drums	Chicago
13	Phoenix	Singer	Oak Park
14	Boots	Percussion, Bass, Vocals	Maywood
15	Tanya	Bass	Chicago
16			

Much better! No more scrolling.

Linking Worksheets and Workbooks

One thing that is mysterious to Excel beginners is how to write formulas across multiple worksheets and whether it's possible to link to different files.

If you don't know how to do this, put on your glasses, and let's go through it in several ways.

> **Note:** The examples throughout the book tend to keep data on a single sheet to simplify the learning objectives and screenshots. In real life, however, well-organized and intelligible workbooks have data on multiple sheets.

In the image below, your job is to fill in the range B2:F4 on the Summary sheet with the appropriate data.

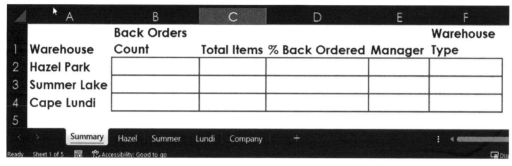

Workbook details:

- Each warehouse has a worksheet.
- There is a Company worksheet where you can find the managers' names.
- Each dataset has entries for Back-Ordered, Low, and Available.

Following are snapshots of the worksheets.

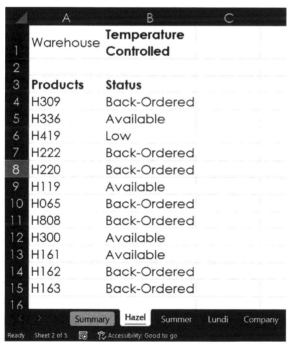

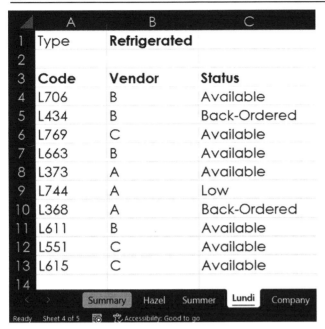

Notice: For Hazel and Lundi, the Warehouse Types are in cell B1 (Temperature Controlled and Refrigerated, respectively); for Summer, the Type is in A2 (U.S. Custom Bonded). Also, the datasets have different columns. It would help if the sheets were uniform, but these inconsistencies are not big problems.

Linking One Cell to a Cell on a Different Worksheet

The first link you can make is a link between the warehouse types. To do so, follow these steps:

1. On the Summary sheet, in cell F2, type = so that Excel is ready to accept a formula.
2. Click on Hazel's worksheet tab to move to it.
3. Select cell B1. In the formula bar, you can see that the formula is being built: =Hazel!B1.
4. Press Enter.

Repeat these steps for cells F3 and F4.

The image below shows F3 has retrieved U.S. Custom Bonded and the formula is:

```
=Summer!A2
```

The ! tells you that the formula in F3 is linked to another worksheet—in this case, the worksheet named Summer.

Those are basic links. No work is being done other than retrieval of whatever content is in another cell. The next section will show how to write a formula that does the work of looking for and retrieving data from another sheet.

Using XLOOKUP with References to Another Worksheet

In cells E2:E4 on the Summary sheet in the previous example you need the name of each manager/director, and XLOOKUP is going to do the dirty work.

One twist is that the company data is in a table—which you'll learn about soon. Right now I just want you to see the table and table nomenclature.

To begin, select cell E2.

You build the XLOOKUP as you did earlier in this chapter (page 8), except that here you go to the Company sheet and highlight the range A2:B14. This is the formula in E2:

```
=XLOOKUP(A2,Directors[Department],Directors[Director])
```

This time you don't see a !. Instead:

- Directors[Department] means the XLOOKUP is looking for the directors' names in the table named Directors in the Department column.
- Directors[Director] means the XLOOKUP is returning the appropriate value in the Director column in the table named Directors.

The image below shows the formulas used to retrieve the manager names in column E.

	E
1	Manager
2	=XLOOKUP(A2,Directors[Department],Directors[Director])
3	=XLOOKUP(A3,Directors[Department],Directors[Director])
4	=XLOOKUP(A4,Directors[Department],Directors[Director])

The Completed Grid

Hopefully the previous examples were enough to show how to link between sheets. Thus, I won't go through linking the cells in B2:C4. They are the same steps but just use different functions. COUNTIFS is used to retrieve the back orders count, and COUNTA retrieves the count of total items.

	A	B	C	D	E	F
1	Warehouse	Back Orders Count	Total Items	% Back Ordered	Manager	Warehouse Type
2	Hazel Park	7	12	58.33%	Julian Butler	Temperature Controlled
3	Summer Lake	2	9	22.22%	Mariam Chang	U.S. Custom Bonded
4	Cape Lundi	2	10	20.00%	Mariam Chang	Refrigerated

The next figure shows the underlying formulas.

	A	B	C	D	E	F
1	Warehouse	Back Orders Count	Total Items	% Back Orde	Manager	Warehouse Type
2	Hazel Park	=COUNTIFS(Hazel!B4:B15,"Back-Ordered")	=COUNTA(Hazel!A4:A15)	=B2/C2	=XLOOKUP(A2,Directors[Department],Directors[Director])	=Hazel!B1
3	Summer Lake	=COUNTIFS(Summer!D5:D13,"Back-Ordered")	=COUNTA(Summer!A5:A13)	=B3/C3	=XLOOKUP(A3,Directors[Department],Directors[Director])	=Summer!A2
4	Cape Lundi	=COUNTIFS(Lundi!C4:C13,"Back-Ordered")	=COUNTA(Lundi!B4:B13)	=B4/C4	=XLOOKUP(A4,Directors[Department],Directors[Director])	=Lundi!B1

Linking Workbooks

It is possible to link completely separate Excel files, which are called workbooks. To do it, you follow the same steps of typing the formula you want and then selecting the cell or range in the workbook that you want to target, finishing the formula, and pressing Enter. You'll end up with a formula that looks like this:

```
=SUM('C:\Users\Owner\Desktop\[LinkingSheets.xlsx]Summary'!$B$2:$B$4)
```

Here are the parts of the formula explained:

- **SUM:** The function that's being applied to the range B2:B4
- Worksheet name: Summary
- **Workbook name:** LinkingSheets.xlsx

- Path to the LinkingSheets file: C:\Users\Owner\Desktop\
- By the way, don't worry about having to type such a formula. Excel will create it for you.

Caution: Linking between workbooks can lead to a lot of misery. If workbook Big Cities.xlsx has a live link to Traffic Data.xlsx, and someone wants you to email them Big Cities.xlsx, you have to remember to email *both* workbooks. If Big Cities.xlsx is no good anymore and is replaced by Bigger Cities.xlsx, that reference needs to be changed in Traffic Data.xlsx. And, of course, moving Big Cities.xlsx to another folder will cause problems in Traffic Data.xlsx. So, yes, you can link workbooks, but you need to be extra careful if you do, and you should have a good reason for doing it.

Linking data between cells, worksheets, and workbooks enables you to make data dynamic. If you change a value in one cell, it will update everything and everywhere that it has an impact. Linking can also help you keep your data better organized. If you don't link between worksheets, you'll have everything on one massive, clumsy, hard-to-understand worksheet.

Caution: When you are linking to external workbooks, you cannot refer to more than 10,000 cells in a closed workbook. You can quickly reach this limit by doing a VLOOKUP or XLOOKUP that references a range such as A1:T501.

Helper Columns

Helper columns aren't an Excel feature, but using them is actually a good strategy for dealing with complex formulas. When you need multiple calculations in a formula, you can break the actions into several steps or multiple formulas rather than try to write a massive formula all at once.

In the image below, it's time to contact these customers and let them know the amount due on their custom-made hats. To get the final totals, consider:

- A deposit has already been paid.
- Discounts may be applied.
- Shipping is $30.
- Orders ≥$400 (after discounts are applied) get free shipping.

The Order Total and After Discount columns were not part of the original data. They are the helper columns being used as intermediate steps toward calculating the amount due.

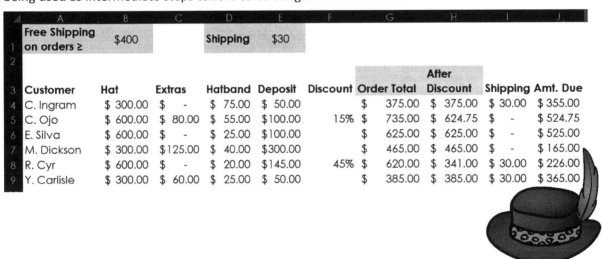

	A	B	C	D	E	F	G	After H	I	J
1	Free Shipping on orders ≥	$400		Shipping	$30					
2										
3	Customer	Hat	Extras	Hatband	Deposit	Discount	Order Total	After Discount	Shipping	Amt. Due
4	C. Ingram	$ 300.00	$ -	$ 75.00	$ 50.00		$ 375.00	$ 375.00	$ 30.00	$ 355.00
5	C. Ojo	$ 600.00	$ 80.00	$ 55.00	$100.00	15%	$ 735.00	$ 624.75	$ -	$ 524.75
6	E. Silva	$ 600.00	$ -	$ 25.00	$100.00		$ 625.00	$ 625.00	$ -	$ 525.00
7	M. Dickson	$ 300.00	$125.00	$ 40.00	$300.00		$ 465.00	$ 465.00	$ -	$ 165.00
8	R. Cyr	$ 600.00	$ -	$ 20.00	$145.00	45%	$ 620.00	$ 341.00	$ 30.00	$ 226.00
9	Y. Carlisle	$ 300.00	$ 60.00	$ 25.00	$ 50.00		$ 385.00	$ 385.00	$ 30.00	$ 365.00

For the first two orders, here are the underlying formulas:

	A	B	C	D	E	F	G	H	I	J
1	Free Shipping on orders ≥	400		Shipping	30					
2										
3	Customer	Hat	Extras	Hatband	Deposit	Discount	Order Total	After Discount	Shipping	Amt. Due
4	C. Ingram	300	0	75	50		=B4+C4+D4	=G4-(F4*G4)	=IF(H4>=$B$1,0,$E$1)	=I4+H4-E4
5	C. Ojo	600	80	55	100	0.15	=B5+C5+D5	=G5-(F5*G5)	=IF(H5>=$B$1,0,$E$1)	=I5+H5-E5

It would be entirely possible to calculate the amount due in a single formula, but notice it takes four formulas to determine that C. Ingram owes $355. In case you really want to see that behemoth formula, here it is:

```
=SUM(B4:D4)-(F4*SUM(B4:D4))+IF(SUM(B4:D4)-(F4*SUM(B4:D4))>=$B$1,0,$E$1)-E4
```

Because helper columns do take up space, you can hide them and get them out of the way, as shown in the image below. Here's how:

1. Highlight the columns you want to hide.
2. Right-click | Hide.

The arrow in the image below shows that the visible columns jump from F to I. G and H are hidden, doing their work behind the scenes.

Other Benefits of Helper Columns

Helper columns (and rows) have other benefits:

- If you know your calculation is wrong, helper columns make it easier to spot where it went wrong. It's much harder to troubleshoot a monster formula with a labyrinth of parentheses.
- If you're planning to create a single formula, helper columns can aid you in thinking through all necessary components and ensure that they work. Then you can build the single behemoth and delete the helper columns.
- If you have to modify the final calculation, it's easier to add, remove, or alter helper column components than wade through a single string of parentheses, absolute references, cell references, operators, and functions.
- If your data needs to keep a certain order that Excel won't recognize, use a helper column and have Excel sort by the helper column content. The image below shows project and personnel data. The Index column was not part of the original data. It was added as a helper column to keep the overall structure of the data. Now, it's possible to sort by first name, last name, manager, or email, and the Index column will aid in getting the rows back where they belong.

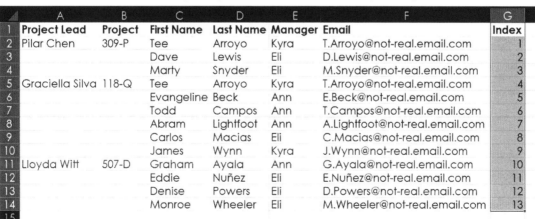

One Downside to Helper Columns

If helper columns are scattered hither and yon on other sheets, in hidden cells or on hidden sheets, troubleshooting can get frustrating. Use of helper columns requires staying organized.

Given the benefits and drawbacks, use of helper columns needs to be strategic in anticipation of auditing or modifying work in the future.

🦎 Slick, Fancy Solutions vs. Effective Solutions

Skirmish

Does your solution work, and does it employ good practices like no hard-coded values in formulas and use of absolute and relative cell references?

That's what matters.

Don't get mired in trying to use exotic functions or really long formulas. Don't be ashamed if you have to use helper columns.

Use what you know how to use and can be responsible for.

You and the people you build solutions for are the only ones who matter. If you aren't comfortable with XLOOKUP (yet) but you have a way of achieving an accurate result without XLOOKUP, use your solution.

When I was in bands and playing bass, it took a long time to realize that I and a lot of other bassists worried too much about what more experienced bassists might say. I know they could hear it if I missed a note or bungled a chord progression or got lost in a song. But what are the things that really matter?

- Did the music sound good?
- Were people dancing?
- Did my bandleader pay me at the end of the night?

Those more experienced folks are worthy of aspiring toward. They've got enviable techniques and a swagger that makes you gasp. Some can be pompous jerks. But you have to take time … slow down … do what you can do … continue to develop. Your swagger is taking shape.

Sorting and Filtering

One key skill in working with data is the ability to separate, isolate, rearrange, and group a dataset in different ways. Sorting and filtering can get you a long way. Sometimes a job requires nothing but sorting and filtering. Sometimes you can't figure out what formulas to write to complete a task, but if you can sort and filter with confidence, you have these as a last resort.

Please don't get caught out in the world not knowing how to sort and filter.

Basic Sorting

In the dataset below, if you want to sort by the speaker names, ascending, place your cursor anywhere in column A within the dataset, then Data | Sort & Filter AZ.

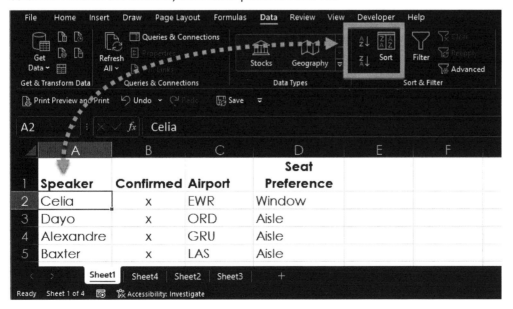

Result:

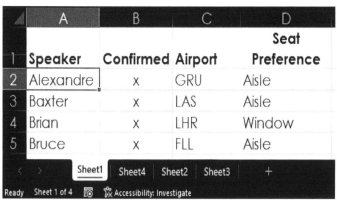

Two-Level Sorting

To sort by airport and then by speaker:

1. Place your cursor anywhere inside the dataset | Data | Sort & Filter | Sort icon.

2. Click OK.

Now you see the speakers flying out of GRU (São Paulo), MEX (Mexico City), and ORD (Chicago) grouped together and sorted alphabetically.

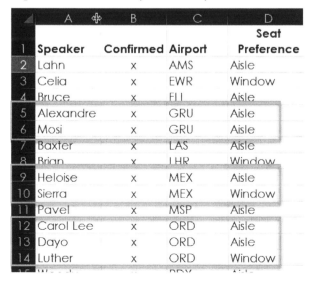

Sorting Rules and Workarounds

In order for sorting to work, you have to follow some rules.

The following sections describe some helpful uses of sorting. But before we dive in, let's go over some important rules you need to follow to get Excel to cooperate with you. These sorting rules really get into the fundamentals of good spreadsheet development because they not only apply to sorting but also Pivot Tables, VBA coding, and other features of Excel that can make your work easier.

The Data Range Must Be Contiguous (No Empty Rows or Columns)

In this figure, if you sorted by column B with the dataset as it is—with column C empty—only columns A and B would be included in the sort:

What if you're in a situation where someone insists that there be an empty column C? There are several options:

- **Highlight the whole range:** In this image, the entire range of data was highlighted before attempting to sort. And notice that the Sort interface doesn't recognize the headers in row 1. Instead, it only recognizes Excel's column headers. So, to sort by the Airport column, you'd have to sort by column D.

Caution: This would be a dangerous move because you'd have to remember to highlight the range every time. If your data looks like this—with columns C, G, and J empty—copying the whole range of data every time you sort would be a tedious and risky proposition.

Speaker	Confirmed		Airport	Seat Preference	Booked		Hotel	Booked		Contract Signed
Celia	x		EWR	Window	x		Gold Pines	x		x
Dayo	x		ORD	Aisle			Block 77	x		x
Alexandre	x		GRU	Aisle	x		Block 77	x		
Baxter	x		LAS	Aisle	x		Block 77	x		x
Sierra	x		MEX	Window	x		Augustus	x		x
Woody	x		PDX	Aisle			Block 77	x		

- **The hidden character trick:** Another option is to make the data contiguous by placing a character—any character—in column C and coloring it white. Excel will read the dataset as one solid range, even though the dataset will still appear to be separated.

- **Single accounting formatting:** Sometimes people use blank columns to make small gaps between columns, as shown in the next figure. They simply want the column heads to have some space between them.

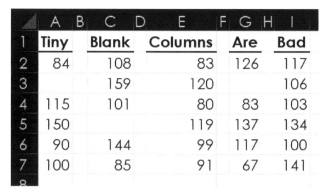

	A	B	C	D	E	F	G	H	I
1	**Tiny**		**Blank**		**Columns**		**Are**		**Bad**
2	84		108		83		126		117
3			159		120				106
4	115		101		80		83		103
5	150				119		137		134
6	90		144		99		117		100
7	100		85		91		67		141

In this case, there's another workaround. You can get the same space-between-columns effect by leaving the dataset in contiguous columns but replacing the bottom borders of those heads with a Single Accounting underline. Press Ctrl+1 to display the Format Cells dialog, choose the Font tab, and select Single Accounting.

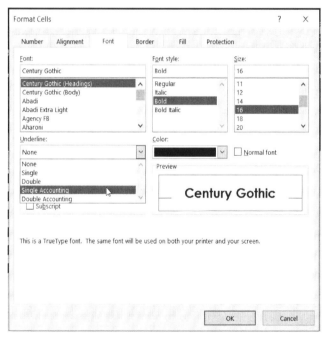

The result is an underline under each heading, with small gaps between the columns:

	A	B	C	D	E	F
1	**Accounting**	**Underline**	**Does**	**The**	**Same**	**Thing**
2	84	108	83	126	117	123
3		159	120		106	105
4	115	101	80	83	103	100
5	150		119	137	134	112
6	90	144	99	117	100	108
7	100	85	91	67	141	108

Headings Must Be Only One Cell Tall

In the image below, C1:C2 and D1:D2 represent Nearest Airport and Seat Preference, respectively. If you try to sort, Excel sees row 2 as the headers. Thus, in the Sort interface, the Preference option appears twice.

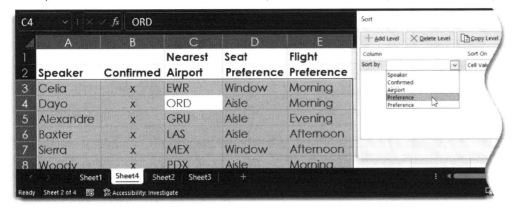

The headers should be in one cell. Typically, the problem that's being addressed is that the header names are long and make a column unnecessarily wide. There are two solutions:

- Wrap text (using the icon circled below).

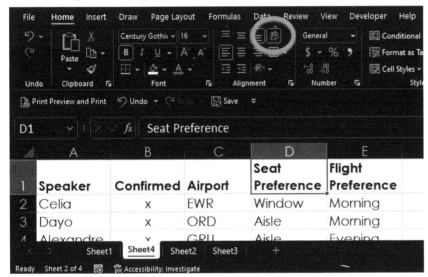

- Place your cursor between the words that need to be split and press Alt+Enter. That starts a new line—inside the cell—for everything after the cursor. This is also good if you want to control where the break happens.

The image below shows both options. If you change the column widths, in G1 the line break will always be after Preference. In H1, Word Wrap will constantly adjust where the wrap happens.

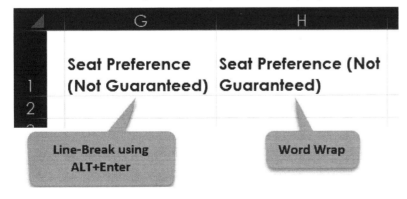

No Merged Cells

In this situation, Baxter is driving rather than flying, and C5:E5 are merged as a single cell to include a note. When attempting to sort, this triggers the error message shown below.

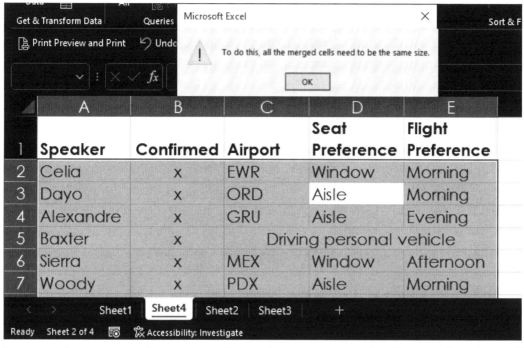

In general, it's best to avoid merging cells, but the error message is telling you that it's possible to sort merged cells—if and only if every row has the same columns merged.

To Use the Quick Sort Icons, Headers Must Be Distinguishable

The quick-sort icons (the ones with AZ or ZA) only require that your cursor is in the data range and in the column that you want to sort by. Excel sorts as soon as you click one of these icons. Therefore, everything has to be set up properly before you click the icon. If your columns do have headers, **be sure that they are distinguishable**. Otherwise, Excel will assume you have no headers and will sort the entire column.

In this example, the three columns were sorted separately, ascending. Column A has the bold header font, and column E has the header in all caps. Those sorted fine. However, in column C the header looks like the column entries, and it ended up in C3.

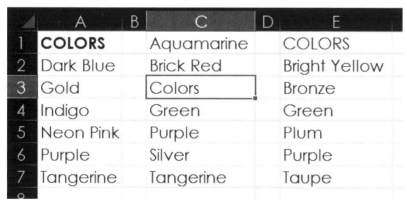

> **Note:** These sorting rules really get into the fundamentals of good spreadsheet development because they not only apply to sorting but also Pivot Tables, VBA coding, and other features of Excel that can make your work easier.

Horizontal Sorting

In this dataset, there are students and their scores. The goal is to get the students in alphabetical order, left to right:

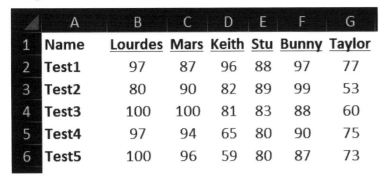

Name	Lourdes	Mars	Keith	Stu	Bunny	Taylor
Test1	97	87	96	88	97	77
Test2	80	90	82	89	99	53
Test3	100	100	81	83	88	60
Test4	97	94	65	80	90	75
Test5	100	96	59	80	87	73

1. Highlight B1:G6.

2. Data | Sort & Filter | Sort. The Sort interface opens.

3. Options | Sort Left to Right | OK.

Note: Only after you click OK will you be able to select Row 1 in the Sort By field in the Sort interface.

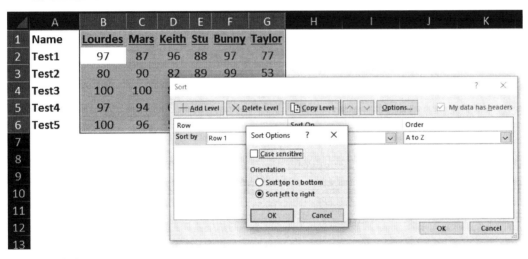

4. Click OK.

There you have it! The names are in alphabetical order, and the scores are still connected to the right people.

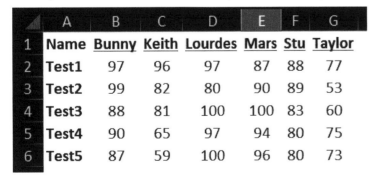

Name	Bunny	Keith	Lourdes	Mars	Stu	Taylor
Test1	97	96	97	87	88	77
Test2	99	82	80	90	89	53
Test3	88	81	100	100	83	60
Test4	90	65	97	94	80	75
Test5	87	59	100	96	80	73

Custom Sorting (Monday to Sunday)

Excel takes sorting literally. For example, because *F* comes before *M* in the alphabet, Friday shows up before Monday in an Excel sort. This is a problem if you need to sort chronologically by day of the week or by month. An ascending sort in Excel will result in:

```
Friday, Monday, Saturday, Sunday, Thursday, Tuesday, Wednesday
```

To have the days of the week sort in chronological order, as people expect:

1. Sort by: Day.

2. Open the Order dropdown and choose Custom List.

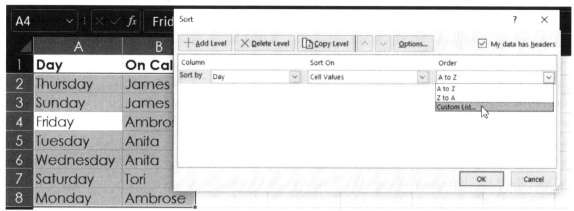

3. Select Monday, Tuesday, … from the Custom Lists dialog.

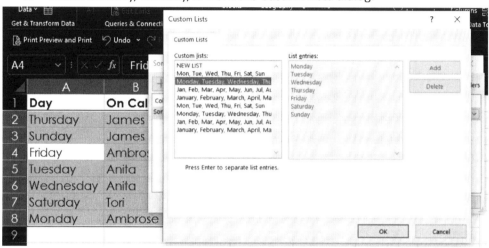

The result:

> **Note:** Many years ago, I regularly had to sort a dataset containing PTC-710, PTC-960, and PTC-1100. An alphabetical sort would always put PTC-1100 before PTC-710. To solve the problem, I came up with a workaround: Type the list in the proper sequence, then used File, Options, Advanced. On the Advanced tab of Excel Options, scroll all the way to the bottom and choose Edit Custom Lists. Select the cells with the proper sequence and import a new custom list. You can then use that list for sorting the products into the proper sequence.

Explore the sorting options. They are very helpful. You can even sort horizontally as well as vertically. Dig in there and get some ideas about what's possible.

Sorting with the Aid of a Helper Column

Sometimes sorting alone isn't enough, and you have to be clever.

Here, we have 12 employees who were to complete three training programs. Instead of looking at the list in alphabetical order, by name, it'd be great if we could easily see who's completed 0, 1, 2, or 3 requirements.

In this example, the source data had columns A:D. The dataset was formatted as a table, and then the Count column was added as a helper column for sorting.

The formula in E1:

```
=COUNTA(Table1[@[Training A]:[Training C]])
```

The table sent the formula down the column, counting all of the non-empty cells in each row. The dataset was then sorted by two levels:

1. Descending, by Count

2. Ascending, by Employee

Now you can see that neither Jay nor Mozelle has started any of the required training, and Dudley, Mallory, and Naveen are done.

	Employee	Training A	Training B	Training C	Count
1	Employee	Training A	Training B	Training C	Count
2	Dudley	x	x	x	3
3	Mallory	x	x	x	3
4	Naveen	x	x	x	3
5	Aaliyah	x		x	2
6	Anita	x	x		2
7	Rock	x	x		2
8	Salome	x	x		2
9	Damien			x	1
10	Jasmine			x	1
11	Sarah		x		1
12	Jay				0
13	Mozelle				0

Filtering

Filtering, like sorting, is an Excel feature that can take you a long way whether you know just a few Excel functions or you're a bona fide Excel beast. Working with data requires being able to isolate, rearrange, delete, insert, group, and modify what's been handed to you. That's what filtering and sorting are about.

You also need to be able to investigate what's in a dataset, assess the size of the job that you're taking on, and create a strategy. Again, more filtering and sorting.

The rules for filtering are similar to those of sorting (see page 22):

*   Header rows must be one cell tall.

*   A dataset must be contiguous; no empty rows or columns are allowed.

*   Cells can't be merged.

Filtering Data to Explore Data Quality

Let's start this filtering section with something that you should get into the habit of doing. When you receive an unfamiliar dataset, dig into it before you dive in. (See the Don't Just Dive In skirmish on page 198.)

Here is data about people—their start dates, advisors, regions they live in, and the status of their annual fees.

	A	B	C	D	E	F	G	H	I
1		First Name	Last Name	Start Date	Advisor	Region	Annual Fee	Paid	Due
2		Harmony	Jordan	14-Jan-20	Benedict Matsuno	North	$3,200.00	$1,600.00	$1,600.00
3		Rifky	El-Maleh	24-Feb-19	Marilyn Grainger	North	$3,200.00	$2,176.00	$1,024.00
4		Ketzia	Truth	27-Jun-21	Lyndsey de Bruijn		$3,200.00	$2,496.00	$704.00
5		Carla	Woods	8-Jul-18	Marsha Iqbal	Far West	$3,200.00	$1,984.00	$1,216.00
6		Penny	Navarro	27-Feb-19	Honore Green	Central	$3,200.00	$3,200.00	
7		Kit	Acosta	2-Mar-21	G. Nelson Hart		$3,200.00	$1,920.00	$1,280.00
8		Zakwan	Sahimi	2-Mar-21	Brandice Fleming		$2,300.00	$1,932.00	$368.00
9		Roseanne	Spears	21-Mar-18	Collin Hashemi	West	$3,200.00	$3,200.00	
10		Sienna	May	30-Jun-20	Brandice Fleming	Central	$3,200.00	$2,144.00	$1,056.00
11		Leilana	Van Dale	21-Oct-22	G. Nelson Hart		$3,200.00	$2,976.00	$224.00

Sheet1 Sheet2 +

Ready Accessibility: Investigate

By scrolling through the data, you can confirm that there are no empty rows or columns, and row 96 is the final row.

Looking at the first 10 records (rows 2 through 11), you can see that there are entries missing in the Region section. So, start exploring the data in that column. With the cursor anywhere within the dataset:

1. Data | Sort & Filter | Filter (the funnel icon in the Sort & Filter group).

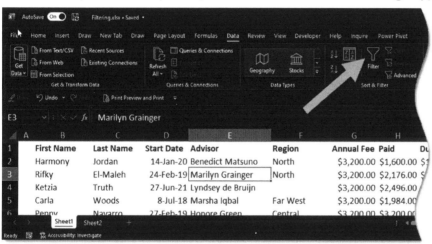

This will toggle on the filter arrows in your headers, as shown in the image below.

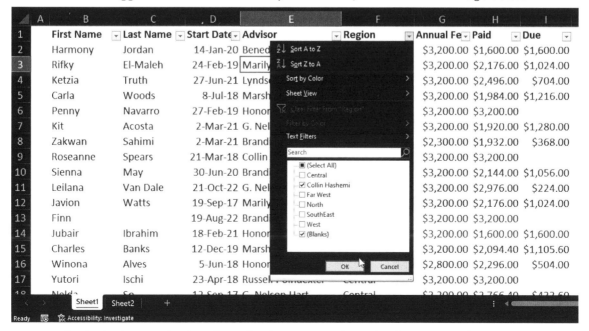

Also in the image, the dropdown for the Region column has been opened, and I've unticked the boxes except for Collin Hashemi and (Blanks).

In this example, Collin Hashemi is an advisor, not a region. You want to see whose record has this errant entry and how many records have a blank cell instead of a region.

2. Click OK.

The result: Nine records have missing or errant data in the Region field.

	A	B	C	D	E	F	G	H	I
1	First Name	Last Name	Start Date	Advisor		Region	Annual Fe	Paid	Due
4	Ketzia	Truth	27-Jun-21	Lyndsey de Bruijn			$3,200.00	$2,496.00	$704.00
7	Kit	Acosta	2-Mar-21	G. Nelson Hart			$3,200.00	$1,920.00	$1,280.00
8	Zakwan	Sahimi	2-Mar-21	Brandice Fleming			$2,300.00	$1,932.00	$368.00
11	Leilana	Van Dale	21-Oct-22	G. Nelson Hart			$3,200.00	$2,976.00	$224.00
23	Sarahi	Sohn	20-Jun-19	Collin Hashemi			$3,200.00	$1,600.00	$1,600.00
70	Savannah	Hall	17-Oct-20			Collin Hashemi	$3,200.00	$3,200.00	
83	Christine						$3,200.00	$3,200.00	
90	Andrea	So	15-May-19	Marsha Iqbal			$3,200.00	$2,272.00	$928.00
93	Jin	Fujisawa	28-Feb-19	Collin Hashemi			$3,200.00	$2,944.00	$256.00

Notice the row numbers on the left and how they jump 1, 4, 7, 8, etc. Excel has hidden the rows that don't fit the criterion that was filtered for.

Also notice in row 83 that Christine has no Last Name, Start Date, Advisor, or Region details. But Christine has paid the full annual fee. Very odd. In the real world, you'd investigate all nine of these records. But let's move on to some more filtering.

You can clear a filter in three ways:

• Click on the funnel again to clear all filters and get rid of the filter arrows.

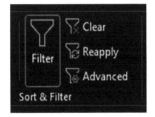

• Click the Clear icon (the funnel with the red x) to clear all filters but leave the filter dropdowns available.
• If you have several filters applied, clear a single filter by selecting the dropdown arrow, opening the filter options, and clicking the funnel icon with the red x.

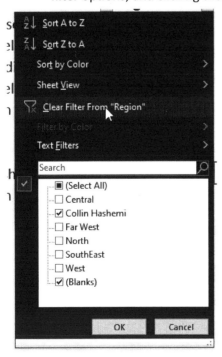

After clearing the Region filter, open the Advisor filter. (You are not going to filter here; the point is that you can use filtering to just look and see what you're dealing with in the dataset instead of scrolling up and down your worksheet.) More strange entries:

- G. Nelson Hart and Gordon N. Hart. Same person, but if there were any analysis done on this data, these two entries would be treated as two different advisors.

- Excel sees Marsha (no last name) and Marsha Iqbal as two different people.

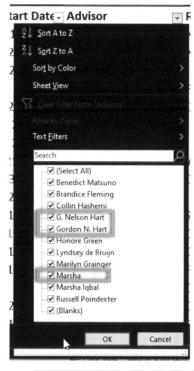

Note: The filter list is limited to showing the first 10,000 unique items. If you see a warning triangle at the bottom of the list with the message "Not All Items Showing," then you know that some checkboxes are missing. You can access the hidden items by typing them in the Search box.

Text Filtering

Let's say there's someone you want to look up, and all you remember is that their last name ends with an *x*. Filtering can help you find the person:

1. Open the Last Name filter | Text Filters | Ends With.

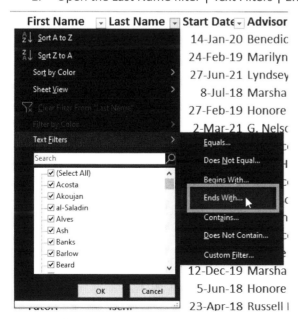

The Custom AutoFilter interface opens. Ends With is already selected on the left.

2.   Input an x on the right and click OK.

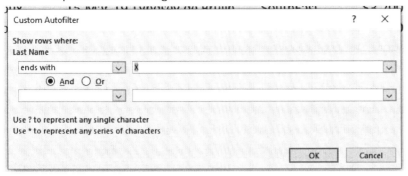

The result:

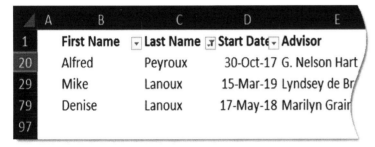

And now you remember it's Denise Lanoux you're looking for.

> **Note:** Before moving on, notice the other options that are available in the text filter: begins with, contains, does not equal, etc. They might come in handy for you.

Number Filtering

Let's see who:

- Has a balance due that's between $500 and $1000 **and**
- Has either Honore Green or Collin Hashemi as an advisor

Here's how:

1.   In the Due column, open the filter dropdown | Number Filters | Between. The Custom Autofilter interface opens.

2.   Input 500 and 1000 and click OK.

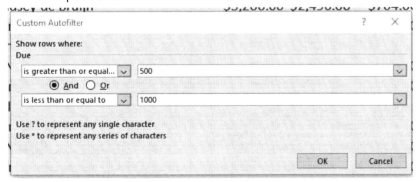

3.   Open the Advisor filter, select Honore Green and Collin Hashemi, and click OK.

Here are the four people who fit the criteria:

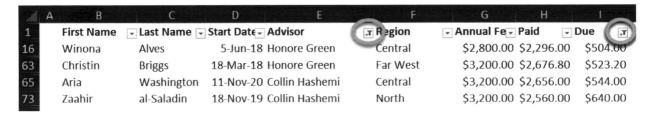

First Name	Last Name	Start Date	Advisor	Region	Annual Fee	Paid	Due
Winona	Alves	5-Jun-18	Honore Green	Central	$2,800.00	$2,296.00	$504.00
Christin	Briggs	18-Mar-18	Honore Green	Far West	$3,200.00	$2,676.80	$523.20
Aria	Washington	11-Nov-20	Collin Hashemi	Central	$3,200.00	$2,656.00	$544.00
Zaahir	al-Saladin	18-Nov-19	Collin Hashemi	North	$3,200.00	$2,560.00	$640.00

In the image, the circles highlight funnel icons, which tell you that a filter is being applied to each column. If you ever worry that some of your rows of data have disappeared, look on the very left side to see if any rows are collapsed or look in your column headers to see if any filters are on. Your data may not have disappeared; the rows might just be filtered from view.

> **Caution:** AutoFilter has some limitations. You cannot have more than one AutoFilter on a worksheet unless you use Tables. If you have product details in the range A1:F1100 and vendor details in H1:M45, you can only AutoFilter one or the other, not both at the same time. With tables, you would move H1:M45 to row 1102 or below. Format both ranges as a table with Ctrl+T.

Other Filtering Options

There are many other options for filtering. In a date column, you can filter for entries like Yesterday, Next Quarter, Between, Before, This Week, or Last Week. You can also filter for the top or bottom number of values that you specify. You can even filter by color if you have colored cells or conditional formatting applied. I urge you to explore the various options.

Say that you are using the dataset used in the filtering examples and need to segment it into four separate datasets:

- People whose fees are paid
- People who owe <$100
- People who owe $100 to $500
- People who owe >$500

You have options:

- Write formulas to flag the records accordingly. Then copy and paste each segment onto one of four separate worksheets.
- Use Power Query to import and separate the data.
- Filter for a segment, then copy the results and paste them on their own worksheet. Do the same for the other segments.

Filtering can help you get what you need to get from your data. It might not be fancy or quick, but it can work. The bottom line is: Does it work?

Chapter 2: Excel Tables: The Glue in Dynamic Spreadsheet Development

If you work with datasets that grow and shrink and formulas that need to adjust with the changes, you must make friends with Excel tables. They will make your life easier and your data more trustworthy.

Unfortunately, tables remain one of the most underused features in Excel. Research suggests that just 1% of Excel users use tables. Please, help expand the 1% by learning and using tables. Avail yourself (and your reluctant friends) of the benefits:

- Formulas that reference a table are easier to read and troubleshoot.
- Formulas automatically extend through the height of a table column. You don't have to remember to drag the fill handle.
- A Pivot Table that's tied to data in a table is easy to update.
- Items in a dropdown list that are tied to a table can be added or removed instantly.

Converting a Data Range to a Table

The following figure shows the first few hat orders in a dataset of 12 orders. The note up top, in the text box, says that we keep only 50% of hatband sales; the other half goes to the talented artisan who makes them.

Ordered	Customer	Hat	Extras	Hatband	Style
		We keep 50% of the cost of hatbands			
12 Jan 22	Crimson	$400.00	$100.00	$ 65.00	Porkpie
19 Jan 22	Suzie	$400.00	$ 50.00	$ 65.00	Porkpie
25 Jan 22	Leone	$400.00		$ 90.00	Fedora
25 Jan 22	Leone	$400.00		$ 70.00	Porkpie
25 Jan 22	Clay	$400.00		$ 40.00	Fedora
1 Feb 22	Suzie	$425.00			Gambler

To convert the range to a table, place your cursor anywhere inside the range. Then: Home | Styles | Format as Table | pick the style of your preference.

The image below shows two ways that you can tell a dataset is in a table:

- When your cursor is in the dataset, the Table Design tab is available in the ribbon.
- You can see the hard corner in the lower-right corner.

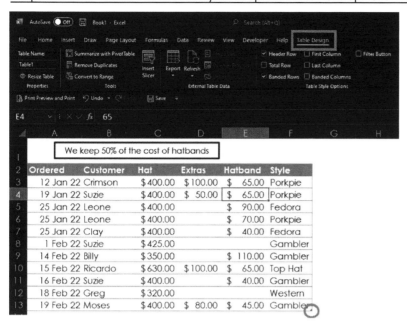

Tip: You can do a few interesting things with the Table Design tab, including:
- Modify the color scheme of a table
- Toggle the filter buttons off and on
- Convert the table data back into a normal range

Have a look at it. Dig around.

Next, a column needs to be added to calculate the total for each order. (Later, a Revenue column will be added to account for the 50% revenue share.) Type Total in G2. As soon as you press Enter, the table automatically expands to include the new header.

In G3, this formula calculates the total cost of each order:

```
=[@Hat]+[@Extras]+[@Hatband]
```

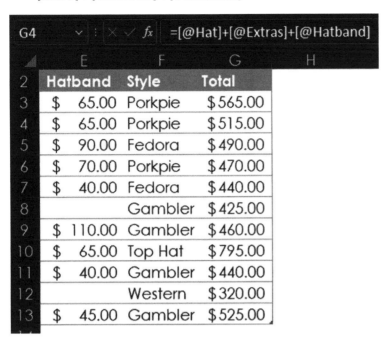

Note: In table notation, [@Hat] retrieves the value in the Hat column, and the notation is the same for the other columns. Thus, table formulas can be easier to read than =C3+D3+E3.

Also note: You can build the formula in any cell in the column, and the formula will be applied in the whole column—top to bottom.

Next, the revenue share. Type Revenue and create the formula:

```
=(0.5*[@Hatband])+[@Extras]+[@Hat]
```

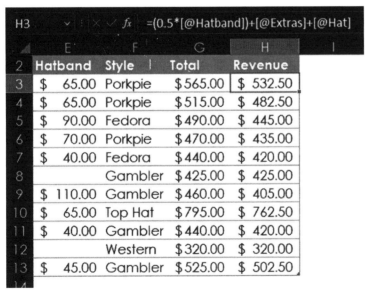

WOW! Another order just came in on 19FEB22 and needs to be added to the table.

Type the new date in A14, and the table expands. Also, the dashes in G14 and H14 show that the formulas are in place and ready to start calculating when the new data is entered.

See ... the flexible glue is in effect!

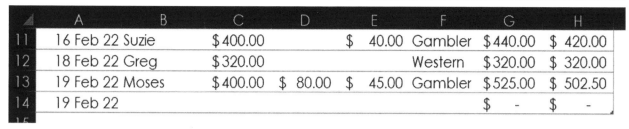

	A	B	C	D	E	F	G	H
11	16 Feb 22 Suzie		$400.00		$ 40.00	Gambler	$440.00	$ 420.00
12	18 Feb 22 Greg		$320.00			Western	$320.00	$ 320.00
13	19 Feb 22 Moses		$400.00	$ 80.00	$ 45.00	Gambler	$525.00	$ 502.50
14	19 Feb 22						$ -	$ -

Fill in the rest of the data for the sexy top hat that Faraz just ordered.

	A	B	C	D	E	F	G	H
11	16 Feb 22 Suzie		$400.00		$ 40.00	Gambler	$440.00	$ 420.00
12	18 Feb 22 Greg		$320.00			Western	$320.00	$ 320.00
13	19 Feb 22 Moses		$400.00	$ 80.00	$ 45.00	Gambler	$525.00	$ 502.50
14	19 Feb 22 Faraz		$455.00	$ 65.00	$ 100.00	Fedora	$620.00	$ 570.00

Using a Total Row

One helpful feature in tables is the total row. To get a total row, place your cursor anywhere in a table and then: Table Design | Table Style Options | tick the box for Total Row.

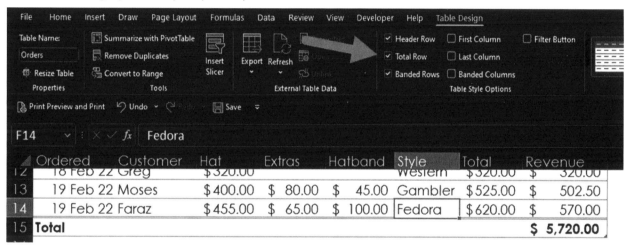

Now you can see the total.

Each of the cells in the total row has several options, including Count, Minimum, and Standard Deviation. The image below shows the result for Average.

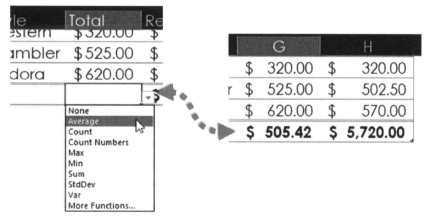

Naming a Table

In the Table Design tab, you can name a table. In this image, you can see that I've named the table Orders.

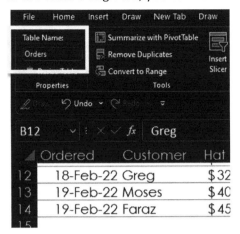

Naming a table makes formulas look even more different from the type of formulas that only use cell references, but table formulas are easier to read. For example, in the next section, you'll see this formula:

```
=SUMIFS(Orders[Hat],Orders[Style],[@Style])
```

Orders[Hat] is a reference to the Hat column in the Orders table.

What's the difference between Orders[Style] and [@Style]? Orders[Style] refers to the Style column in the Orders table. You write this when you're writing a formula in another table—not in the Orders table. [@Style] refers to the Style column in the table that you're in.

Using Tables to Make Dynamic Dropdown Lists

Dropdown lists help control entries and keep them accurate and consistent, preventing nonsense entries like misspellings (Feddora), hats that you don't sell (Beret), common alternatives (Tophat instead of Top Hat or Cowboy Hat instead of Western).

The image below shows a summary table with the total orders for each style of hat.

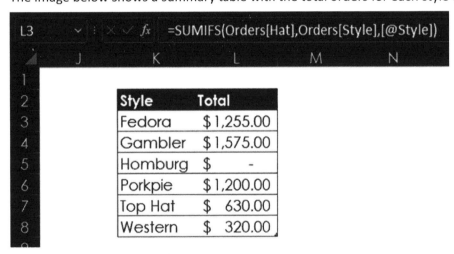

The formula in the Total column:

```
=SUMIFS(Orders[Hat],Orders[Style],[@Style])
```

You're going to use the Style column for the entries in the dropdown list:

1. Start by highlighting the Style column in the Orders table because this is where the dropdown lists will be applied.

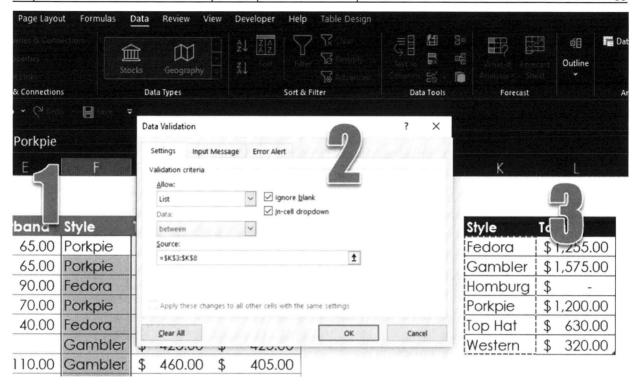

2. Data | Data Tools | Data Validation | Allow: List | Tick: In-cell dropdown.

3. Highlight the Style column in the Summary table. This will provide the acceptable entries for hat styles in the Orders table.

4. Click OK.

To see what makes this table dynamic, add Derby to cell K9.

The image below shows that the dropdown list is in place, and Derby is now available as a legitimate choice.

	Hatband	Style	Total	Revenue
3	$ 65.00	Porkpie	$ 565.00	$ 532.50
4	$ 65.00	Porkpie	$ 515.00	$ 482.50
5	$ 90.00	Fedora	$ 490.00	$ 445.00
6	$ 70.00	Porkpie	$ 470.00	$ 435.00
7	$ 40.00		$ 440.00	$ 420.00
8			$ 425.00	$ 425.00
9	$ 110.00		$ 460.00	$ 405.00
10	$ 65.00		$ 795.00	$ 762.50

Dropdown list: Fedora, Gambler, Homburg, Porkpie, Top Hat, Western, Derby

Style	Total
Fedora	$1,255.00
Gambler	$1,575.00
Homburg	$ -
Porkpie	$1,200.00
Top Hat	$ 630.00
Western	$ 320.00
Derby	$ -

Tables Functions and Cell References

Remember the importance of absolute, relative, and mixed cell references (see page 4)? Tables simplify references for you.

In this example, today is the day for cleaning the parking lot at the apartment complex. Residents were notified not to park in a certain area today, and a few didn't cooperate.

In this image, on the left is a list of tenants who need to be contacted to move their cars or get towed. On the right side is the full list of tenants and their license plate numbers.

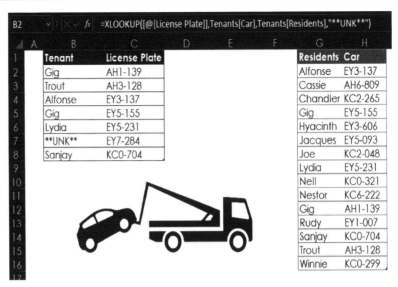

The data started with the list of license plate numbers in column C. To retrieve the names from the Residents column to fill in the Tenant column, XLOOKUP was used:

```
=XLOOKUP([@[License Plate]],Tenants[Car],Tenants[Residents],"**UNK**")
```

As stated earlier, the references apply to entire columns. Even though the formula was written in B2 and traveled down to B8, the references to the Residents and Car columns didn't also travel down. You'd have to worry about that with regular data ranges and relative references.

> **Note:** **UNK** indicates a car that might be a guest, a tenant's car that hasn't been listed with management, or someone who's illegally parking on apartment complex property.

Some Warnings About Working with Tables

Tables can be peculiar. Here are a few things you need to know.

Absolute Cell References in Table Nomenclature

Creating absolute values with table nomenclature is different from pressing F4 in a regular formula. Actually, it's messy and calls for manual steps.

In this image, you have the Bldg and Unit numbers for each tenant. In columns M:O you want a count of tenants for each building.

Cell M2 uses the following formula to count the number of tenants in building A:

```
=SUM(COUNTIFS(M1,Tenants4[Bldg]))
```

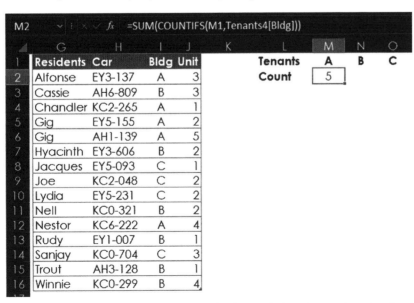

To get a count for buildings B and C, the formula in M2 needs to be dragged to the right, but the reference to Tenants4[Bldg] will also shift to the right and capture the wrong data. You need Tenants4[Bldg] to stay put.

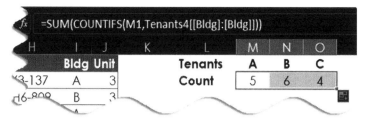

Manually modifying the formula so it looks as shown below allows you to drag the formula and keep the reference to the Bldg column:

```
=SUM(COUNTIFS(M1,Tenants4[[Bldg]:[Bldg]]))
```

You have to use the colon, repeat the column reference, and enclose them both in square brackets. Here are the two formulas, side by side:

Relative Reference	Absolute Reference
=SUM(COUNTIFS(M1,Tenants4**[Bldg]**))	=SUM(COUNTIFS(M1,Tenants4**[[Bldg]:[Bldg]]**))

Mixing Formulas in a Column

It's good practice to keep formulas in a column consistent, and that's what tables help ensure. But there are exceptions. Let's says that you want to calculate a 15% discount for the first order in the Hats Order table by applying this formula:

```
=[@Total]*0.15
```

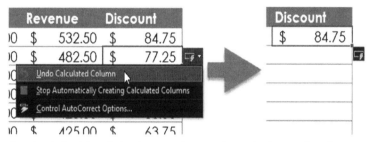

On the left side of the image above, the calculation has been applied to the whole column. But notice: After typing the formula and pressing Enter, a small dropdown box appears. Click on it, and you get these options:

- Undo Calculated Column
- Stop Automatically Creating Calculated Columns

The right side shows the result after selecting the Undo Calculated Column option. The discount in the first cell remains, and if you want to apply discounts to any other entries in the column, you can write the formula, and it'll stay only in that cell.

Adding New Data to a Table

Another important consideration is that new data must be added to the next contiguous row or column in a table. Watch the fill handle at the lower-right corner of a table. It lets you know if your data is inside or outside the table.

In this image, the entries in rows 14:17 are outside the table. To bring them inside, simply use your cursor to grab the handle in the lower-right corner of the cell in row 13 in the End column and drag it down to capture the other four entries.

	Name	Date	Start	End
10	George Boston	23 May 22	LAX	DFW
11	Lee W. Jackson	11 Apr 22	ATL	ORD
12	Florence Z. Singh	2 Jun 22	PHX	DFW
13	Hal Cannon	13 Jun 22	DME	ORD
14	Pedro V. Catania	17 Jun 22	SYD	SBA
15	George Boston	2 Jun 22	ORD	EWR
16	Gisele M. Stark	11 Jun 22	DEL	ATL
17	Vince Sosa	13 Jun 22	SBA	ATL
18				
19				

Sheet Protection: Tables Must Be Completely Protected or Completely Unprotected

Yet another issue is that tables cannot be partially protected with sheet protection. You can protect either all or none of a table. This drives a lot of people crazy because tables are so useful, and sheet protection limits what a user can see, modify, or corrupt. A table on a protected sheet would be fabulous. Alas … it ain't possible. ☺

Excel Tables Conclusion

Excel tables allow you to maintain the integrity of spreadsheets that need to flex as users add and remove data. With tables, you don't have to write the volume and complexity of delicate formulas that you had to write back in the olden days.

You will see tables used a lot in the free templates that Microsoft provides. (Find them by selecting File | New.) One of the guys Microsoft hired to create many of those templates became such a fan of tables that he cowrote an entire book about them: *Excel Tables: A Complete Guide for Creating, Using, and Automating Lists and Tables* (by Zack Barresse and Kevin Jones, 2014).

🐉 "How Do I Master Excel?"

Skirmish

Let's address this question before we get too far. It's a question that's asked by people who start working with Excel and find intense joy with what they're able to do.

Short Answer

No one masters Excel, and there's no reason to. Excel is a tool—not a life's purpose, solution, or objective.

BUT, you use Excel as a tool to whoop crap data into shape, end misery, stave off confusion, and be the hero for the people the data is connected to. That, my friend, is a venerable mission.

Longer Answer

Think about Excel as a development platform. It's not just a spreadsheet. When you add in VBA, Power Query, Power Pivot, and Power BI, Excel can do way more than many imagine.

Excel has countless features and more than 500 functions across the categories listed below:

- Compatibility
- Cube
- Database
- Date & Time
- Dynamic Array
- Engineering
- Financial
- Information
- Logical
- Lookup & Reference
- Math & Trigonometry
- Matrix
- More
- Statistical
- Text
- Web

Very few people will ever use all of these categories, much less all of the available functions. In 20+ years of working with Excel, I've never needed the ARCTANGENT or RTM functions or a radar plot. However, I've used IE.readyState when writing VBA code because of several projects that involved importing web pages into Excel.

Nuanced Answer

Here are a few points about mastering (or getting good with) Excel:

- You get good at—and can master—what you need to be good at: tasks, not a tool. If you have to battle crap data in the form of marketing, logistics, website analytics, scheduling, inventory, or financial modeling, those are the tasks that you strive to master.
- Give yourself permission to say "I don't know" and then go look for solutions in Excel.
- See a lot of uses for Excel over a long period of time.
- Study the spreadsheets of people who are better at Excel than you.
- Always ask: "Is there a better way?"

I used to get nervous when meeting a new client or helping someone who'd implored, "I need your help!" I was worried about being asked something I didn't know, worried that my mastery would be exposed as fraudulent. Eventually I learned the real value is in the ability to know where to look to find solutions if I don't know the solution immediately.

As an example, one morning a desperate call came in. At a small office, 10 people had been trying for 3 days to troubleshoot a workbook that they knew was wrong. I was able to find and correct the problem in 45 minutes. Mastery? No. It was possible through years of experience and an instinct for where to look.

Chapter 3: Collaboration Tools

If everyone on your team is using Microsoft 365, you can now collaborate on the same worksheet at the same time. Microsoft was forced to improve the collaboration tools in Excel to keep up with Google Sheets.

In order to collaborate on a workbook, it must be saved in OneDrive or SharePoint Online. You don't have to work on the spreadsheet in Excel Online! Everyone can be working in Desktop Excel.

Collaboration is dramatically easier if everyone on your team is part of the same tenant. If you all work for the same company and all have emails that end in something like MyCompany.OnMicrosoft.Com, then you are all part of the same tenant.

Many of the MVPs who write about Excel are in single-person companies, and they don't have anyone to collaborate with. When two people from different companies try to collaborate, it is difficult. Microsoft has made it easier in the past five years, but it is definitely an experience that works better when everyone is on the same tenant.

How to Share a Workbook

To share a workbook:

1. Use File | Save As and choose to save to either SharePoint Online or OneDrive.

2. Click the Share button at the top right of the worksheet.

3. If you are sharing with someone at work, you can enter their name. Otherwise, enter their email.

4. Click Send, and they will receive a link in Outlook.

But I hate this method because the link in Outlook opens Excel Online. 99% of the people outside of Redmond, Washington, would never choose to use Excel Online over Desktop Excel. The people inside Redmond are living in some strange bubble where Excel Online is good enough.

> **Tip:** When I receive a notification that someone has shared something with me, I don't click the link in the email! Instead, provided that the person works for my company, I simply open Excel and choose File | Home | Shared with Me to see a list of all workbooks that have been shared with me. The advantage here is that the workbook will open in Desktop Excel, and I don't have to touch Excel Online.

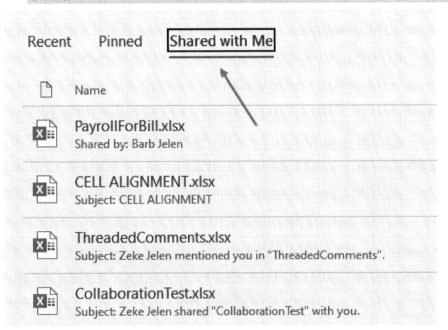

You can also share a workbook with someone in your company by @Mentioning them in a comment.

Guidelines for and Limits of Sharing

Everyone who is to share a workbook should be on the latest version of Microsoft 365. If you are sharing with that one guy who has been here for 80 years and won't upgrade from Excel 2007, he will screw everything up.

Everyone should have AutoSave turned on for the shared workbook.

It is fine if people are using a mix of Desktop Excel, Excel for Mac, Excel Online, and/or Excel for iPad or a phone.

Microsoft is really comfortable with five simultaneous collaborators all being in the same sheet at the same time. They are really comfortable with a megabyte of data of input cells changing at once. You can go beyond these limits, but you increase the chance of the dreaded "veto" (discussed next). Microsoft is working hard to make vetoes less common even when you go beyond five users or with more data.

When Something Goes Wrong: The Veto

Let's start with a simple example. You and a co-worker are both editing the same workbook. Here are the steps that are supposed to happen:

1. You select cell A1. Your co-worker sees a blue box around A1 with your initials in a circle to the right of the box.

2. You start typing 123 but don't press Enter. Your co-worker sees your initials replaced by an animated three dots.

3. You finish typing 123 and press Enter. Your cell pointer moves to A2. Your co-worker sees the blue box move to A2.

4. The 123 is AutoSaved to the OneDrive file. The 123 is pushed to your co-worker's computer.

This is a simple example. Now imagine that four co-workers each select 100,000 cells. They each type something and press Ctrl+Enter to enter that value in 100,000 cells. They all do this at the same time. There are now one-half million cells being sent to the server and pushed back out to five computers.

If Excel can't manage this, you get a message on your computer that the data could not be synced. It suggests doing a Save As and then trying to copy and paste back into the real version of the file. I hate when this happens. I pretty much close Excel, say a few choice words, and start over again.

Is it comforting to know that vetoes are happening 90% less than before? I suppose so. No. Not really. We are working in Excel. We don't expect to get stabbed in the heart. For decades, it was one person in one workbook, and there were few problems. Now we have many people in a worksheet. When someone stabs me in the heart, it doesn't help to hear that this used to happen 10 times more frequently for the early adopters.

The Awesome Part of Collaboration: Sheet Views

Many years ago, I was one of the very early adopters of collaboration. I set up a common to-do list for one co-worker and myself. I thought it would work great. Within two minutes of my sharing the file, my co-worker filtered the list to see only his records. That change happened on my computer. I couldn't see any of my tasks. It was a complete failure that was abandoned three minutes after it started.

When I asked the Excel team if we could each have our own filter, they pointed out that =SUBTOTAL and =AGGREGATE calculate based on hidden vs. visible rows, and if they allowed each person to have a different filter, then the results of the formula would not match on both computers.

Seven years later, they finally decided that we could live with different results for AGGREGATE and SUBTOTAL, and sheet views allow each person to sort and filter their data without those changes being visible to anyone else.

Consider the workbook shown below.

If multiple people are working in the workbook, and I sort column D descending or filter column B to Bill, I will be presented with a dialog that asks if I want this change to affect everyone's view of the data or just mine. As you can see below, Excel asks this question in a strange way. It basically asks whether you want to see just your changes or everyone's. I really think the honest way to write this question is "Do you want to see this change only on your computer, or do you want to force this change on everyone else's computer?"

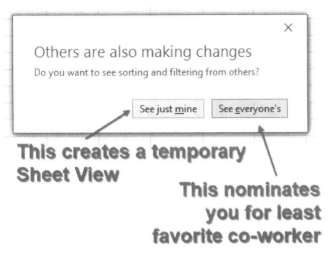

This creates a temporary Sheet View

This nominates you for least favorite co-worker

The correct answer here is See Just Mine. When you choose See Just Mine, you have created a temporary sheet view called Temporary View. The row headers and column numbers now have a dark background to alert that you are not seeing the "official" version of the worksheet. Even though you aren't seeing the official version of the worksheet, any data that you type in this view will be synchronized back to the official version of the worksheet.

Let that sink in for a moment. In the figure below, row 3 shows Bill / Kiwi / 9692. In the "real" version of the spreadsheet, Bill / Kiwi / 9692 is in row 18. Make a change to D3 below, and that change is synchronized back to cell D18 in the official version. How does Excel do this? I can't figure it out.

Close sheet view

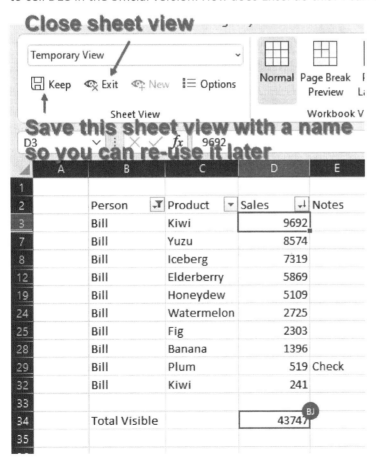

Save this sheet view with a name so you can re-use it later

Caution: Notice the Notes column above. It is not part of the filtered range—and this is dangerous. If someone sorts using the filter dropdown, the data in column E will not be sorted with the rest of the data.

Excel Help tells you that the first time you create a sheet view, the current state of the sheet is saved as a view called Default View. In January 2022, this was not working for me, and I'd had reports from others that it was not reliable for them either. So, my new strategy for sheet views goes like this:

1. Make sure to turn on the filter dropdown arrows using either Data | Filter or Home | Filter as Table.

2. Make sure the workbook is saved to OneDrive or SharePoint Online.

3. Make sure the AutoSave switch is turned on. This is the switch in the top-left corner of Excel.

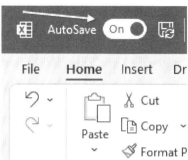

4. Start with the normal view of the data with all rows visible. On the View tab, in the Sheet View group, click the New icon. Excel calls the new view Temporary View. Change the name to Show All or See All. This extra step replaces the Default View, which is currently unreliable.

5. Click New to create your own sheet view. Give it a name immediately. For this example, I will call it Bill's View.

6. While Bill's View is the active view, any changes that you make to sorting or filtering become a part of the sheet view. Perhaps filter Person to Bill and sort Sales descending.

> **Tip:** I've never fully understood what is saved in a view. Clicking the Save icon or giving the view a name is not like clicking Save for a workbook. It is **not** saving a snapshot of your view. Once a view is displayed, if you move on and want to see all records and you clear the filter, this will become part of the sheet view definition.
>
> If your co-worker needs to use your view and you nicely say, "Hey! Select Bill's View. It is exactly what you need," you are inviting trouble. Because even though your co-worker did not author the Bill's View sheet view, once they have it as their sheet view, if they then move on and filter to someone else while Bill's View is active, they will change the definition of Bill's View to something else.

Hiding Columns with a Sheet View

As of January 2022, Excel Help said that hiding columns works in Excel Online but not in Excel Desktop. Both halves of this sentence are incorrect. Hiding columns only partially works in Excel Online. The part that works can still be useful. And the part that works will work equally well in Desktop Excel.

Say that you and a co-worker want to share the same workbook. You are both working in Desktop Excel. You want to see the columns for Q1 and Q2. Your co-worker wants to see the columns for Q3 and Q4. Here are the steps:

1. Save the workbook to OneDrive and turn on AutoSave.

2. Even if you have no intention of filtering rows, you must turn on the filter in the range where you will be hiding columns.

3. Before hiding any columns, one of you should create a view called See All Columns. This view will be available to both of you and will be effective in getting all of the columns back.

4. Both people should open the workbook.

5. On your computer, go to View | Sheet Views | New to create a new view. Click into the Name box and call the view Q1 and Q2.

6. Your co-worker goes to View | Sheet Views | New to create a new view. They click into the Name box and call the view Q3 and Q4.

7. Your co-worker selects cells that are part of the filtered range whose columns need to be hidden by using Home | Format | Hide & Unhide | Hide Columns.

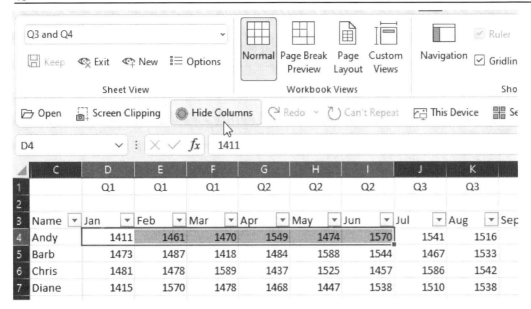

8. On your computer, with the Q1 and Q2 view active, select J4:O4 and hide those columns.

Now, you will be able to work on January through June, while your co-worker will see only July through December. When you close and reopen the workbook, it will remember that you were in the Q1 and Q2 view and bring you back to that view.

> **Caution:** The part that is not working, though: If you ever switch to another view, the hidden columns will correctly unhide. However, the columns will never re-hide when you return to this view. While this is a disappointing limitation, it does allow a team to work in the same workbook together and see different columns.

> **Note:** You might know the archaic Custom Views command, which has been on the View tab forever. Custom Views remembers which columns are hidden. However, selecting a custom view while collaborating is currently something that causes the other collaborators to lose their changes. So, if you are collaborating, custom views are not an option.

🐢 The Role/Purpose of an Analyst

Skirmish

If you work with data, you're an analyst. It may or may not be in your formal title, but **you are an analyst**.

What an analyst does is defined by the role. An analyst isn't a generic person who crunches numbers, makes graphs, creates forecasts, and advises the company—though that can be an analyst. Other analysts monitor turtle populations. Some analysts write a lot of formulas and never build graphs.

Consistently, however, I believe:

Your role as an analyst is to be the hero for the people who rely on what you do—or don't do—with the data.

It's easy to get wrapped up in Excel features and functions and to stand up and joyfully scream after you've completed a challenging task using XLOOKUP, an anti join, SUMIFS, and mixed cell references. That's definitely worth celebrating, but this is really about the people who want their reimbursement accurate and on time; accurate accounting of where expenses are vis-à-vis the budget; accurate accounting of legally required continuing education; details of how a $50,000 grant was spent (or they won't get another grant); accurate accounting of court-mandated hours of community service.

The person who might have to go back to jail if their community service hours are wrong doesn't care if you used Power Query or your fingers and toes.

Don't forget the people. We use Excel to battle crap data and endure skirmishes to make life civil.

Excel is your weapon, and you get to pick. Is Excel your sword? Magic wand? Tow truck? Soldering iron? Or, is Excel the web you shoot from your wrist to ensnare miscreants?

Good, honest people are counting on us.

Chapter 4: Summing and Counting with Criteria

Generating sums and counts gets complicated when there's a need to consider certain criteria. Maybe you want a count of employees who aren't in the Far West region or a sum of expenses where:

- The expense is ≥$250 **and**
- The category is Computers & Accessories **and**
- There's no approval code

Here are a few other needs and criteria:

Need	Criteria1	Criteria2	Criteria3
Count of employees	Region <> Far West		
Sum of expenses	≥ $250	Category = Computers & Acccessories	Missing approval
Sum of donations	Payment method = Online	Status = Member	Years: 2017 and greater
Count of schools	County = Lake	Has a wrestling team	Has a gymnastics team
Count of students	Registered	Did not attend	
Sum of fees paid	Session = Summer	First-time attendees	

Note: The table above shows only 3 criteria but, you can use up to 127 criteria with COUNTIFS and SUMIFS.

Let's return to the question of unapproved Computers & Accessories transactions. This time, the goal is to get a sum and count based on the following criteria:

- Category: C&A
- Amount: ≥$250
- Approval: empty

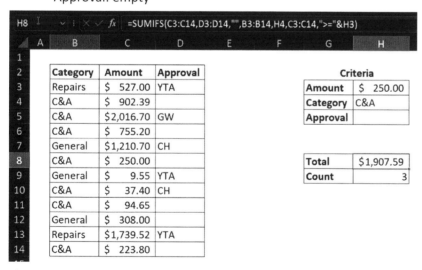

The formula in H8:

```
=SUMIFS(C3:C14,D3:D14,"",B3:B14,H4,C3:C14,">="&H3)
```

This formula says to sum the dollar amounts in C3:C14 *only* for entries that meet the following criteria:

- In the range D3:B14, where the cell is empty (equals: "")
- In the range B3:B14, where values are equal to the value in H4, which is C&A
- In the range C3:C14, where values are greater than or equal to the number in H3, which is 250

Result: $1907.59.

Here's the formula in H9:

```
=COUNTIFS(D3:D14,"",C3:C14,">="&H3,B3:B14,H4)
```

This formula says to count the number of entries where:

- Values in the range D3:D14 are empty
- Values in the range C3:C14 are greater than or equal to the value in H3, which is 250
- Values in the range B3:B14 equal the value in H4, which is C&A

Result: 3.

To verify the result, you can see that the entries that could be included are rows 4, 6, and 8:

```
902.39 + 755.20 + 250 = $1907.59
```

You should know that there are a few more functions that aid you in working with data based on multiple criteria: IFS, MAXIFS, and AVERAGEIFS. (I won't go through them here, but I urge you to make up some data and play with these functions to see what they do.)

> **Tip:** The mixture of SUMIFS, COUNTIFS, and AVERAGEIFS can provide useful insight into what you're dealing with. For example, if you received a sum of $2,036.00 in donations, you might want to know if that was from 5 donations averaging $407.20 each or 55 donations averaging $37.02 each. That's real analysis, and it goes beyond getting a formula to work. You could go even deeper into the numbers and calculate the median, the highest and lowest donations, etc., but the point is that having more details paints a more vivid picture of the data.

Chapter 5: VLOOKUP and XLOOKUP

With the introduction of XLOOKUP, it's tough to know how much to say about VLOOKUP. However,

- VLOOKUP still works.
- In addition, many Excel users cite their comfort with VLOOKUP as the moment they got comfortable and confident with Excel and working with data.

Why does VLOOKUP represent a turning point for so many users? First, VLOOKUP has four pieces in its syntax. Consistently getting them right takes a lot of time. Second, VLOOKUP forces a person to think about their data in a way that IF, OR, and SUM don't demand. VLOOKUP requires the data to be set up a certain way, and its purpose isn't immediately clear to new users.

So, when you get comfortable with VLOOKUP, you're getting comfortable in how you think and work with data and how you apply strategies.

VLOOKUP: What Does It Do?

In this example, VLOOKUP is going to be used to look at rep IDs and retrieve the names associated with those IDs. Ultimately, this data will be shared with your director, and she doesn't know anyone named F2C5724, but she does know Mei.

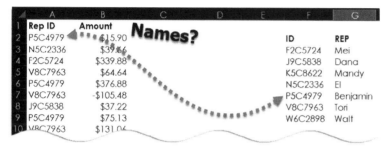

In the image above, you see the first 9 of 246 transactions in columns A:B. In columns F:G there are the ID numbers and rep names.

The arrow shows P5C4979 is Benjamin. You want Benjamin's name to populate C2 and every other cell in column C that has P5C4979 as the rep ID.

This is VLOOKUP's syntax:

```
VLOOKUP(lookup_value, table_array, col_index_num, [range_lookup])
```

One way to think about VLOOKUP's syntax:

Argument	Translation
lookup_value	What do you want me to look for?
table_array	Where do you want me to look?
col_index_num	What data do you want me to return?
[range_lookup]	Do you want an approximate match or an exact match? • Approximate match = TRUE or 1 • Exact match = FALSE or 0

This is the formula that returned Benjamin's name to C2:

```
=VLOOKUP(A2,$F$3:$G$9,2,FALSE)
```

Double-click the fill handle and send the formula down all of the 246 rows, and every transaction has an identifiable name or an error.

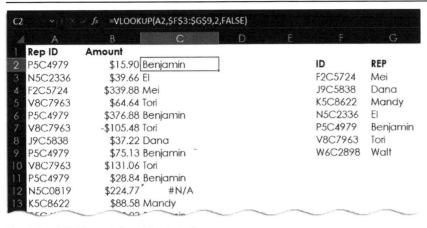

The VLOOKUP explained in detail:

Part of the Formula	Explanation	Detail
=VLOOKUP(	Opens the VLOOKUP	
A2	The value to look for	
$F$3:$G$9	• Look in the range F3:F9 for a value that matches A2. • The entire range F3:G9 is the lookup range that includes the data you want to retrieve.	The $ sets the absolute cell references in anticipation of dragging the formula down. You don't want the lookup range to also move down.
2	Starting with column F, if the value is found, which column do you want?	This lookup range has two columns, and you want the second column.
FALSE	FALSE = look for an exact match	You can use either 0 or FALSE
)	Closes the VLOOKUP	

Notice in C12 the #N/A error was returned. It tells you that the VLOOKUP could not find N5C0819. Maybe that rep ID is wrong. Maybe whomever N5C0819 is no longer works for the company. **You have to know your data and the larger context in order to interpret if the error is expected or if it's pointing to a problem.**

A Brief VLOOKUP Story

I had a job in customer service, where I would take monthly transactions and retrieve the names of the reps who processed the transactions in order to pay bonuses. One report had the transactions and IDs, another had the IDs and names of the reps within customer service. VLOOKUP allowed me to match thousands of transactions with the rep names. When #N/A was returned, instead of a name, I knew those were tied to employees who were not in customer service and irrelevant to my objective.

So, when I did the VLOOKUP to match transactions with customer service rep names, the bottom line for me was: Anything that returns #N/A is a transaction that I can delete. But **it took a few months to develop a relationship with the data** such that I was safe deleting those entries.

How VLOOKUP Works

In order for VLOOKUP to work, the lookup array needs to have the lookup values to the left, and what you want to retrieve must be to the right.

In our current example, if the columns in the lookup array are reversed— with the REP column first and ID second (as shown here)—you cannot use a VLOOKUP because the VLOOKUP would have to find the ID and then look leftward. Nope. Can't do it.

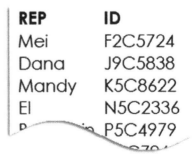

In these situations, you'd have to implement any number of workarounds, including:

- Switch the columns.
- Use INDEX/MATCH.
- Nest a CHOOSE inside the VLOOKUP.

When I used VLOOKUP regularly, if the lookup array was to the left of the data that I wanted to retrieve, I would sometimes modify the dataset so that the VLOOKUP could look rightward. The image below shows original column headers where the goal is to look up the ID and retrieve the name, requiring a lookup to the left.

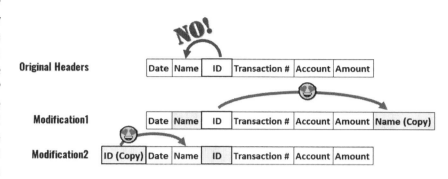

Modifications 1 and 2 show two ways to get the rightward-looking VLOOKUP to work. Modification1 is a copy of the Name column to the right of ID. Modification2 shows a copy of the ID column.

The ultimate would be to use XLOOKUP or an outer join in Power Query (page 107) because the position of the columns doesn't matter.

Let's do one more VLOOKUP before moving on to XLOOKUP.

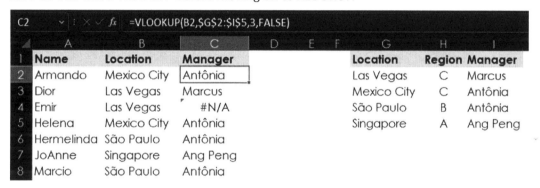

In column C, the managers were retrieved from column I using:

```
=VLOOKUP(B2,$G$2:$I$5,3,FALSE)
```

The formula was dragged down the column, and there are two errors:

- For Miguel in row 10, the VLOOKUP is looking for exact matches, and São Paulo ≠ Sao Paulo.
- For Emir in row 4, the problem is invisible on paper, but in the spreadsheet, you could dig into this and discover a trailing space. In the image below, the LEN function is used to count the characters in cells B3 and B4.

Leading and trailing zeros are sneaky. You see Las Vegas with your own eyes, but the formula is erroring out. Here are two ways to investigate:

- Select a cell that's in question and place your cursor in the formula bar. OUCH! There's a trailing space.

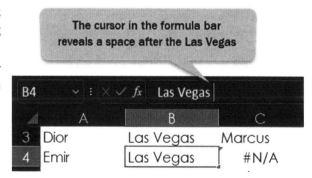

The cursor in the formula bar reveals a space after the Las Vegas

- Use the LEN function to count the characters in the cells, and there is a clue: B3 has 9 characters, and B4 has 10 characters.

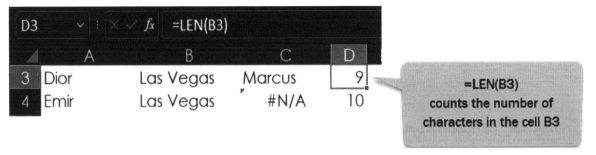

	A	B	C	D
3	Dior	Las Vegas	Marcus	9
4	Emir	Las Vegas	#N/A	10

=LEN(B3)
counts the number of
characters in the cell B3

The next move is to go in and remove the trailing space in B4 and correct B10 to show São Paulo instead of Sao Paulo.

XLOOKUP

'Twas a grand day at the Microsoft MVP Summit when the Excel development team showed us a preview of XLOOKUP! It was agonizing to keep the preview a secret until XLOOKUP was released to the general public a full 17 months later.

XLOOKUP brings an end to the feud over VLOOKUP vs. INDEX/MATCH.

XLOOKUP has three mandatory and three optional components:

```
=XLOOKUP(lookup_value, lookup_array, return_array, [if_not_found],
[match_mode], [search_mode])
```

In this dataset, XLOOKUP is being used in column D to retrieve the room assignments in column J.

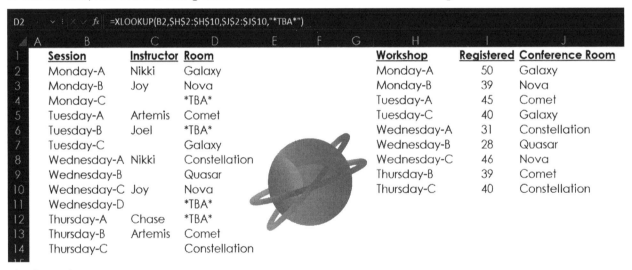

D2   fx   =XLOOKUP(B2,$H$2:$H$10,$J$2:$J$10,"*TBA*")

	A	B	C	D	E	F	G	H	I	J
1		**Session**	**Instructor**	**Room**				**Workshop**	**Registered**	**Conference Room**
2		Monday-A	Nikki	Galaxy				Monday-A	50	Galaxy
3		Monday-B	Joy	Nova				Monday-B	39	Nova
4		Monday-C		*TBA*				Tuesday-A	45	Comet
5		Tuesday-A	Artemis	Comet				Tuesday-C	40	Galaxy
6		Tuesday-B	Joel	*TBA*				Wednesday-A	31	Constellation
7		Tuesday-C		Galaxy				Wednesday-B	28	Quasar
8		Wednesday-A	Nikki	Constellation				Wednesday-C	46	Nova
9		Wednesday-B		Quasar				Thursday-B	39	Comet
10		Wednesday-C	Joy	Nova				Thursday-C	40	Constellation
11		Wednesday-D		*TBA*						
12		Thursday-A	Chase	*TBA*						
13		Thursday-B	Artemis	Comet						
14		Thursday-C		Constellation						

The formula in D2:

```
=XLOOKUP(B2,$H$2:$H$10,$J$2:$J$10,"*TBA*")
```

The XLOOKUP is looking for Nikki in the lookup range $H$2:$H$10 and retrieves the value in $J$2:$J$10. Those are the required components. In this example, the [if_not_found] component is being used to input *TBA* for to be assigned.

If VLOOKUP were being used, you'd have to nest the VLOOKUP inside IFNA, as such:

```
=IFNA(VLOOKUP(B2,$H$2:$J$10,3,FALSE),"*TBA*")
```

VLOOKUP vs. XLOOKUP

Here's a comparison of VLOOKUP and XLOOKUP:

VLOOKUP	XLOOKUP
The return array must be to the right of the lookup array.	The positions don't matter.
For values that aren't found, the error #N/A is returned. If you want to replace the error, wrap the VLOOKUP in IFNA.	XLOOKUP has a built-in component for "if not found." There's no need for another function.
The return array is expressed as the number of columns to the right of the lookup array. This is a hassle if you have more than a few columns.	Select the return column that you want.
To find approximate values, the lookup array must be sorted ascending.	To find approximate values, the lookup array does not need to be sorted.
If you insert a column between the lookup array and the return array, the VLOOKUP will return corrupted results.	You can insert a column between the lookup array and the return array.
Cannot do a horizontal lookup. You'd have to use HLOOKUP.	XLOOKUP can look up vertically or horizontally.
Most VLOOKUPs are used for exact matches. VLOOKUP defaults to an approximate match. Therefore, you **must** include FALSE in the *lookup_range* part of the syntax.	XLOOKUP defaults to exact matches.

Two-Way Lookup

In this example, in D5:D9 the prices of the fishing lure orders need to be retrieved from the lookup grid in columns H:J. The client wants 31 Big Whips. Look over on the right and see that 31 is between 15 and 50, so the price is €16.50.

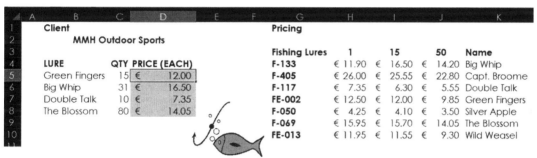

This is the XLOOKUP that's doing all of the dirty work:

```
=XLOOKUP(B5,$K$4:$K$10,XLOOKUP(C5,$H$3:$J$3,$H$4:$J$10,,-1))
```

An XLOOKUP has been nested inside an XLOOKUP. No VLOOKUPs, INDEX, or MATCH. XLOOKUP handles both the horizontal and the vertical.

Lookup from the Bottom Up

You have a fleet of vehicles and want to know the last time vehicle 8GJ-T6 was in for maintenance. Prior to XLOOKUP, this was a tough task to accomplish. With XLOOKUP, the [*search_mode*] argument offers several options (and in this case, the lookup range does need to be sorted ascending):

[*search_mode*] Value	Description
1	Perform a search, starting at the first item. This is the default.
-1	Perform a reverse search, starting at the last item.
2	Perform a binary search that relies on *lookup_array* being sorted in ascending order. If not sorted, invalid results will be returned.
-2	Perform a binary search that relies on *lookup_array* being sorted in descending order. If not sorted, invalid results will be returned.

To retrieve 8GJ-T6's last documented maintenance, -1 is the search mode to use:

```
=XLOOKUP(A2,$C$2:$C$15,$D$2:$D$15,,,-1)
```

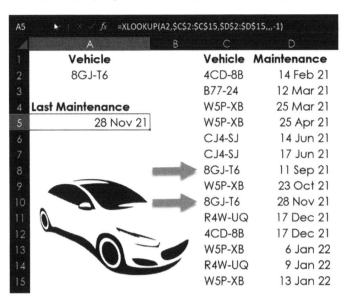

XLOOKUP's Equivalent to VLOOKUP-True and XLOOKUP as a Dynamic Array Formula

I've always been irritated about VLOOKUP-True being described as an *approximate* match. What it really does is match entries with tiers or levels.

You could say that 74 is *approximately* 75. However, if a situation means that values ≥75 are passing, and <75 is failing, 74 is more *approximate* to 3 than to 75 because they both fail.

XLOOKUP makes this easier to think about and apply with the [*match_mode*] argument in the XLOOKUP:

[*match_mode*] Value	Description
0	Look for an exact match. If none found, return #N/A. This is the default.
-1	Look for an exact match. If none found, return the next smaller item.
1	Look for an exact match. If none found, return the next larger item.
2	Look for a wildcard match, where *, ?, and ~ have special meaning.

In this example, column B contains scores, and the results are being retrieved from the lookup table in columns E and F, using the formula in C2:

```
=XLOOKUP(B2:B8,Table1[Score],Table1[Result],,-1)
```

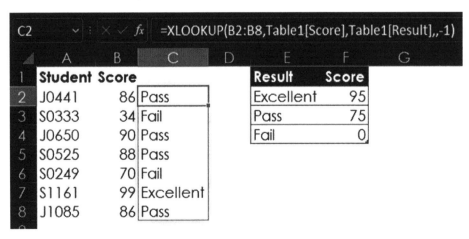

First, the line around C2:C8 shows that the XLOOKUP is being used as a dynamic array formula—retrieving multiple results with a single formula. Second, the lookup value B2:B8 is being used rather than just referencing B2 and dragging the formula down the column to C8.

Here, each item in the list is located in a zone in the warehouse. The webcam in cell A2 is located in zone C. But what zone is that in? The XLOOKUP retrieves values from the lookup table in columns F:H.

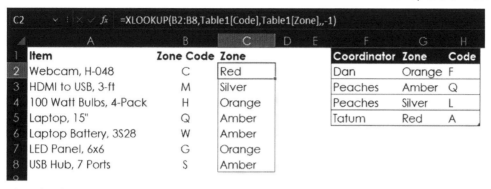

There's a lot to observe here:

- Zone codes:
    - A through E are in the Red zone.
    - F through K are in the Orange zone.
    - L through P are in the Silver zone.
    - Q through Z are in the Amber zone.
- The lookup table is sorted by the coordinator's name—not by the codes.
- The codes are to the right of the zones.
- The blue line around the data in C2:C8 shows that a single dynamic array formula is being used:
  `=XLOOKUP(B2:B8,Table1[Code],Table1[Zone],,-1)`

Retrieving the zones using XLOOKUP instead of VLOOKUP is better in the following ways:

- With VLOOKUP the lookup values need to be sorted. With XLOOKUP that isn't necessary. The -1 in the formula finds the exact match or next smaller. Thus, a search for code H finds the next smaller, F, which is the Orange zone.
- In this example the coordinator dataset is sorted alphabetically by the coordinator names. Maybe this is the preferred way of looking at the data vs. sorting by the Code column. XLOOKUP allows you to have your data set up the way you want to see it.

  The point might be clearer this way. In the image below, books are assigned codes, but you can see that the data is sorted first by the area, second by the genre. Now, if you have a book with a code 605, XLOOKUP can be used to tell you 605 is in the Dystopian genre. With VLOOKUP you'd need to sort the Codes ascending—and ruin the structure of the dataset.

Area	Genre	Codes
Fiction	Dystopian	500
	Horror	800
	Romance	300
	Sci-Fi	1500
Non-Fiction	Art & Photography	1050
	Cooking	1350
	History	100
	Technology	650
	Travel	1200

XLOOKUP with Wildcards

Excel offers wildcards for when you need to look up a partial string of text.

In this example, you want to retrieve the phone number for MJ. But you don't remember if her actual name is Missy, Milly, or Misty. It's definitely not Marny.

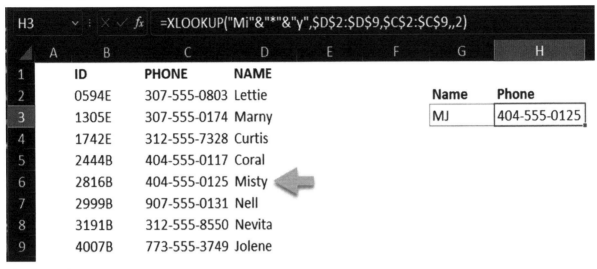

The formula in H3:

```
=XLOOKUP("Mi*y",$D$2:$D$9,$C$2:$C$9,,2)
```

Notice that the wildcard and text have to include double quotes. It can be concatenated as shown above or a single text string. This part of the formula finds any cell value that starts with Mi and ends with y:

```
"Mi*y"
```

The * is a wildcard for any number of characters in between. Therefore, you have to be confident that the list doesn't include names like:

- Micky
- Miley
- Michelle Ray

Wildcards overview:

Wildcard	Description	Examples
? (question mark)	Finds any single character	**g?re** finds *gore* and *gyre*. It won't find *glare* or *galore* **???f** returns all four-letter words that end with f (clef, half, hoof)
* (asterisk)	Finds any number of characters	***owl*** finds *bowler*, *acknowledge*, and *slowly*
~ (tilde) followed by ?, *, or ~	Tells Excel to treat a ? or * like text or punctuation, not as a wildcard	**part?** treats the **?** as a wildcard and finds every instance of *party* and *parts* ***part~?** treats the **?** as text, finding any sentence that ends with *part?*, such as: *You liked that part?* or: *They tore it apart?* It won't find: *They tore it apart.*

Note: The IF function does not accept wildcards. The commonly used functions that accept wildcards include:

AVERAGEIFS	MATCH	SEARCH
COUNTIFS	MAXIFS	SUMIFS
HLOOKUP	MINIFS	VLOOKUP

To count values that end with *part?*, the example below use the formula:

```
=COUNTIFS(B2:B7,"*part~?")
```

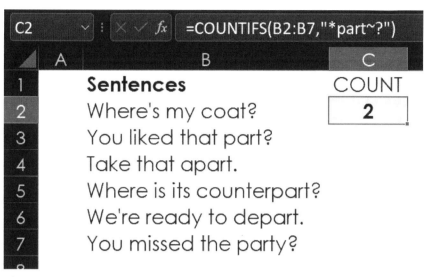

The 2 in C2 is counting the values in B3 and B5.

Chapter 6: Pivot Tables: The Turning Point!

Pivot Tables are among the spookiest of Excel's features because I often hear from people who've heard of Pivot Tables and how amazing they are, but they can't recall ever having seen one or why they're supposed to be so helpful. In my workshops, when I show how easy it is to create a Pivot Table and what it does, I hear a disappointed groan. That disappointment quickly turns to outrage as users realize how handy Pivot Tables could have been to them over the years.

What I eventually realized was:

- New Excel users aren't sure *when* a Pivot Table would be useful.
- The source data for a Pivot Table is rarely ready to go into a Pivot Table.

Years ago I was visiting a small family-owned company that was struggling with data. They had all the necessary information in reports they'd downloaded, but the reports weren't useful as is. I showed them a Pivot Table and created a report of sales—by month and by product. One of the owners, shocked, said, "Dude, you did in 30 seconds what took me a whole weekend."

What do I mean by "the reports weren't useful as is"? The company subscribed to a service that, for a hefty annual fee, provides specific reports: monthly revenue, forecasts, accounts, etc. It's also possible to export a data dump—a raw file with columns and rows of data, and no formulas, summaries, or graphs … just a big mountain of data. Of all the existing reports, none of them provided the data broken down by products. Hence: "the reports weren't useful as is." However, when I noticed that the owner had a data dump, and there was a product field, it was easy to see the potential for a Pivot Table instead of dragging cells around and writing formulas.

This isn't magic and it shouldn't be spooky. We're only talking about Pivot Tables. You won't be turned into a toad. But Pivot Tables do require that you shift your thinking a bit.

What Is a Pivot Table, and What Can It Do?

Pivot Tables do so much that it's hard to say exactly what a Pivot Table is. Let's just jump in, and I'll explain along the way.

The image below shows the first 13 of 375 rows of records. Take a moment. Look at the data.

	Registration Date	Student	Class	Paid	Month	Coordinator
1						
2	1 Jan 22	Feven	Advanced Pastry	150	Jan	Skylar Shiro
3	1 Jan 22	Angelo	Artisan Bread	150	Jan	Peliah Mercado
4	1 Jan 22	Abenezer	Perfect Pizza	200	Jan	Zoe Asadi
5	2 Jan 22	Bianca	Event Planning	200	Jan	Reymundo Silva
6	2 Jan 22	Léonie	Event Planning	200	Jan	Reymundo Silva
7	4 Jan 22	Alix	Artisanal Chocolate	150	Jan	Peliah Mercado
8	4 Jan 22	Homer	Event Planning	200	Jan	Reymundo Silva
9	4 Jan 22	Kaye	Mixology	0	Jan	Blue Chaisson
10	4 Jan 22	Cookie	Mixology	200	Jan	Blue Chaisson
11	6 Jan 22	Rufus	Artisanal Chocolate	200	Jan	Peliah Mercado
12	6 Jan 22	Evan	Event Catering	200	Jan	Reymundo Silva
13	6 Jan 22	Nanami	Event Catering	200	Jan	Reymundo Silva

Here are some question that can be asked about this data:

- What are the totals that were paid, by month and by class?
- What are the totals paid, by month and by coordinator?
- Which students, if any, took three or more courses?
- Did any students take the same class more than once?
- Which students paid $0.00, and which courses did they take?
- What are the monthly dollar amounts, by coordinator?
- Which months had ≥70 total registrations?

A Pivot Table can give you instant summaries that answer all of these questions from this raw data. No formulas required because this is what a Pivot Table is designed to do.

The Pivot Table interface (including the field list) makes it easy to rearrange data and get different views. Next we'll look at a few examples that show just what Pivot Tables can do, and then you'll learn how to create Pivot Tables.

Example 1: Summing Values with a Pivot Table

As you can see here, a Pivot Table can help you sum values.

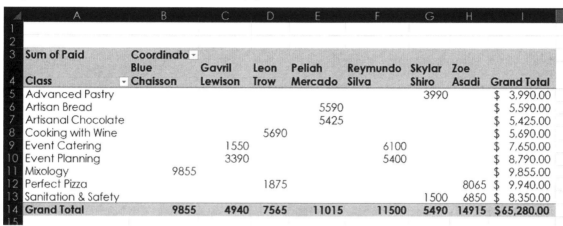

Sum of Paid	Coordinato ▾							
Class ▾	Blue Chaisson	Gavril Lewison	Leon Trow	Peliah Mercado	Reymundo Silva	Skylar Shiro	Zoe Asadi	Grand Total
Advanced Pastry						3990		$ 3,990.00
Artisan Bread				5590				$ 5,590.00
Artisanal Chocolate				5425				$ 5,425.00
Cooking with Wine			5690					$ 5,690.00
Event Catering		1550			6100			$ 7,650.00
Event Planning		3390			5400			$ 8,790.00
Mixology	9855							$ 9,855.00
Perfect Pizza			1875				8065	$ 9,940.00
Sanitation & Safety						1500	6850	$ 8,350.00
Grand Total	9855	4940	7565	11015	11500	5490	14915	$65,280.00

Instantly, the Pivot Table tells you certain things about the data:

- Leon Trow is the coordinator of Cooking with Wine, and it's generated $5690.
- Event Planning has had two coordinators: Gavril Lewison and Reymundo Silva.
- Peliah Mercado is coordinator of Artisan Bread and Artisanal Chocolate and has generated $11,015.

Example 2: Counting Values with a Pivot Table

As shown here, a Pivot Table can help you count values.

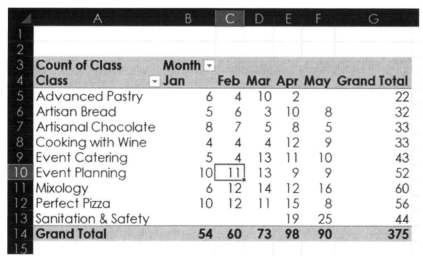

Count of Class	Month ▾					
Class ▾	Jan	Feb	Mar	Apr	May	Grand Total
Advanced Pastry	6	4	10	2		22
Artisan Bread	5	6	3	10	8	32
Artisanal Chocolate	8	7	5	8	5	33
Cooking with Wine	4	4	4	12	9	33
Event Catering	5	4	13	11	10	43
Event Planning	10	11	13	9	9	52
Mixology	6	12	14	12	16	60
Perfect Pizza	10	12	11	15	8	56
Sanitation & Safety				19	25	44
Grand Total	54	60	73	98	90	375

What are some details the data is telling you?

- Sanitation & Safety may be a new course and wasn't available for registration before April.
- Mixology had the greatest total number of registrations (60) and the second highest number of registrations in May.
- Artisanal Chocolate has never had more than 10 registrations.

Note: The original data includes specific dates. In order to get monthly summaries, you use the Group feature for Pivot Tables. You'll learn about this feature later, on page 66.

Example 3: Filtering with a Pivot Table

As shown here, a Pivot Table can help you filter data.

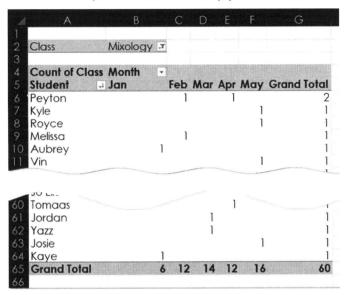

Notice in cell B2 that Mixology is the class. A4:G65 in the Pivot Table show which students took Mixology, by month. You can see that Peyton took the course twice.

Getting to Know the Pivot Table Interface

So far you've seen that if you have the source data set up properly, a Pivot Table can help you get the details you need. Without Pivot Tables, it would undoubtedly take hours or days to write the formulas and rearrange the data to get meaningful insights.

The previous examples show common uses of Pivot Tables, but there's far more available. This book doesn't cover everything, but in the next section we'll go a little deeper, and I will point out even more areas that are worth exploring on your own.

Going back to the raw data on the Registration sheet from the examples above, with the cursor in any cell in the data region, select Insert | Pivot Table.

The Pivot Table wizard launches.

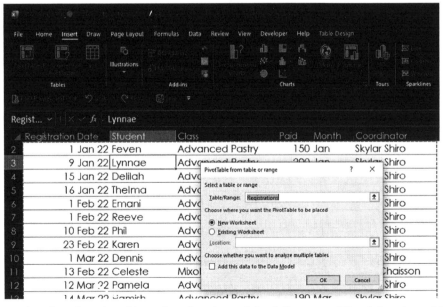

Notice that the wizard has already selected the full range of the dataset, and the Table/Range field accurately shows the range of the data. The wizard also defaults to placing the new Pivot Table on a new worksheet. Click OK. The interface shown below appears.

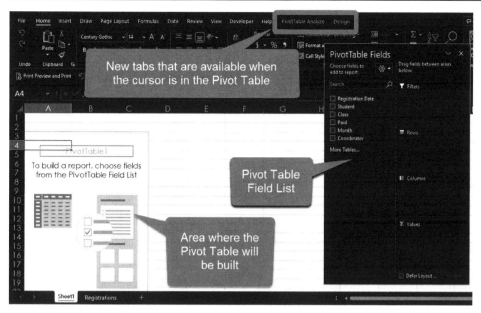

Notice a few things about the Pivot Table interface shown above:

- A new worksheet, Sheet1, was created.
- There's a preset area where the Pivot Table will be built and modified.
- The big PivotTable Fields pane, also called the field list, is where you make most of your changes to a Pivot Table. It pops up any time your cursor is in the Pivot Table area, and it goes away when the cursor is outside the Pivot Table area.
- Two new tabs in the ribbon (PivotTable Analyze and Design) are visible only when the cursor is in the Pivot Table range. Notice in the image above that the cursor is in A4. If you move it over to, say, E1, the tabs and the field list go away.
- You can use the cog wheel in the field list to rearrange the fields and the drop zones vertically or side-by-side.

Now you're ready to build a Pivot Table!

Building a Pivot Table to Sum and Count Values

To sum what's been paid, by coordinator and by month:

1. Click on Coordinator in the field list and drag it to the Rows drop zone.
2. Drag Month into Columns.
3. Drag Paid into Values.

There it is! You have a Pivot Table:

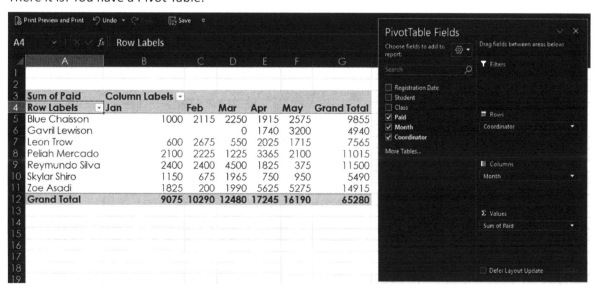

Notice that when you dropped Paid into Values, it defaulted to Sum of Paid. All of the 375 values in the Paid column have been added together and split in such a way that it's easy to see Zoe Asadi's course(s) generated $14,915.

How about a count of payments?

1. Click the arrow next to Sum of Paid.

2. Select Value Field Settings. The Value Field Settings dialog opens, giving you various options.

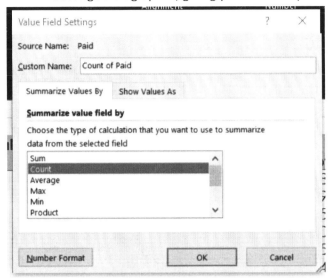

3. Select Count and click OK.

There ya go! The count of payments, by month and by coordinator:

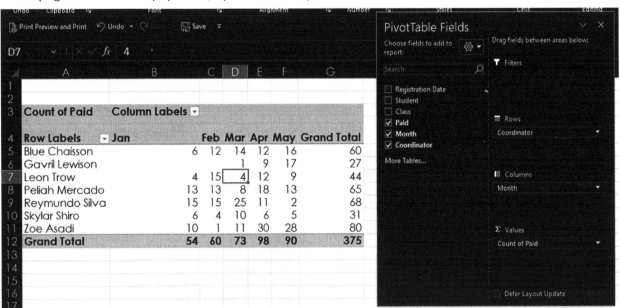

Count of Paid	Jan	Feb	Mar	Apr	May	Grand Total
Blue Chaisson	6	12	14	12	16	60
Gavril Lewison			1	9	17	27
Leon Trow	4	15	4	12	9	44
Peliah Mercado	13	13	8	18	13	65
Reymundo Silva	15	15	25	11	2	68
Skylar Shiro	6	4	10	6	5	31
Zoe Asadi	10	1	11	30	28	80
Grand Total	54	60	73	98	90	375

Notice that in a previous image (see page 63), Gavril Lewison shows a 0 in March instead of a blank. In the image above, there's a 1 for Gavril in March. The Pivot Table is making a distinction between nothing and a calculation of 0. Here, there was one person who paid $0.00, as opposed to there having not been any registrations.

Note: Imagine what you would have had to do to manually create this summary. You can see why people running a business could spend an entire weekend creating this type of summary if they didn't know how to use Pivot Tables.

Summing and Counting Side-by-Side ... and a Filter

You might be asking: "But, Oz! What if I want to see the sum and count together?"

I reply: "Let's do it ... and take it a step further and filter to only look at February and March."

1. Drag Paid into the Values drop zone. (Yes! Drag the same field twice.)

2. Click the arrow by the Column Labels and tick only February and March.

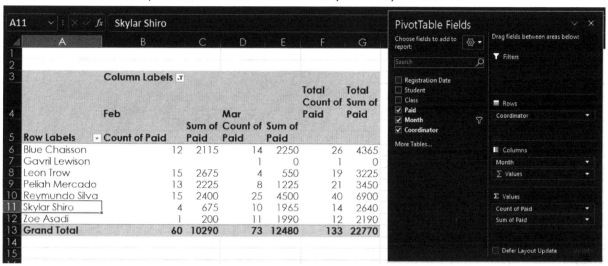

The count for March is in column D, and the sum is next to it, in column E.

> **Note:** The Summarize Value Field By list in the Value Field Settings dialog offers many options that are worth exploring: Sum, Count, Average, Max, Min, Product, Count Numbers, StdDev, StdDevp, Var, and Varp.

Filtering with the Pivot Table

- Let's say you're only interested in the Mixology and Cooking with Wine courses, and you want to see the months beneath each Coordinator:

1. Drag Class into the Filters drop zone.

2. In cell B2 click the filter icon.

3. Click Select Multiple Items.

4. Tick the boxes for Cooking with Wine and Mixology.

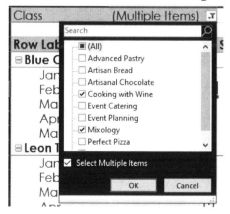

5. Click OK.

6. Drag Coordinator and then Month to the Rows drop zone.

7. Drag Student and then Paid to the Values drop zone.

Here is the resulting Pivot Table:

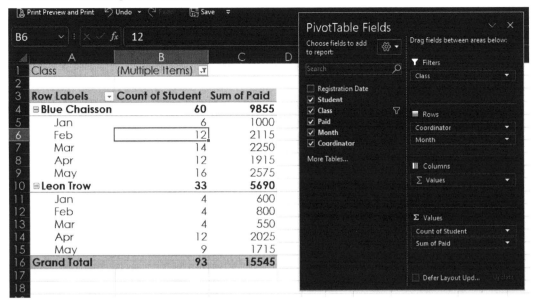

- This layout requires you to remember that there are two courses selected. To see which courses, the filter in B2 has to be expanded.

Grouping Dates in the Pivot Table

Want to look at the registrations by quarter? That's a little tricky because the source data has every one of the 375 transactions listed by date, and when you drag Registration Date into the Rows zone, the Pivot Table makes a row for each date.

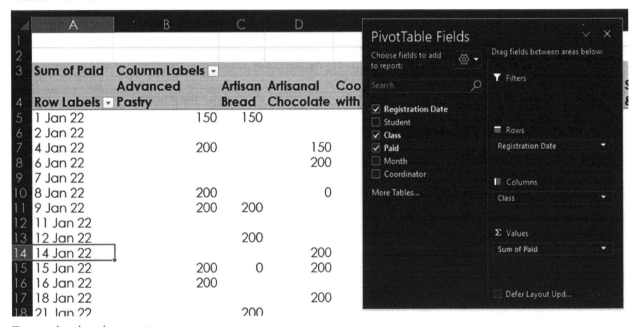

To see the data by quarter:

1. Select any date in column A.

2. Right-click and select Group. The Grouping dialog opens.

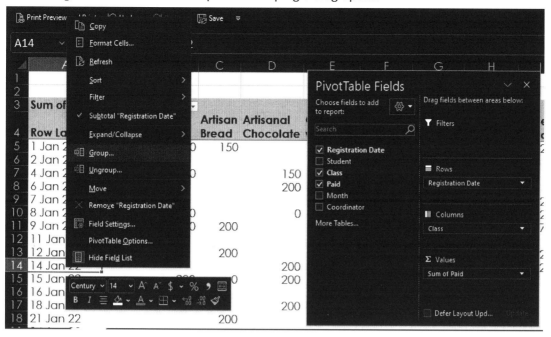

3. Select Quarters.

4. Click OK.

And there it is!

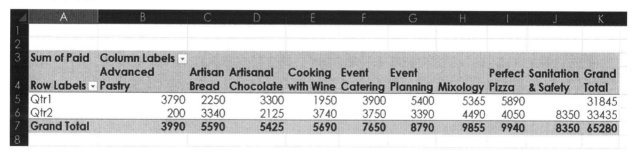

Sum of Paid	Column Labels									
Row Labels	Advanced Pastry	Artisan Bread	Artisanal Chocolate	Cooking with Wine	Event Catering	Event Planning	Mixology	Perfect Pizza	Sanitation & Safety	Grand Total
Qtr1	3790	2250	3300	1950	3900	5400	5365	5890		31845
Qtr2	200	3340	2125	3740	3750	3390	4490	4050	8350	33435
Grand Total	3990	5590	5425	5690	7650	8790	9855	9940	8350	65280

Caution: If you group by month or quarter, you have to be careful. If your source data covers more than one year and you group by month, the Pivot Table will *only* group by month. Thus, July 2013, July 2014, and July 2015 will all be grouped under July. You have to select Month and Year if you want to see July 2013, July 2014, and July 2015 separately.

Using the Pivot Table to Get the Percentage of the Total

What if you want to see your data in percentages? A Pivot Table can do that for you:

1. Start with the Pivot Table configured as shown below.

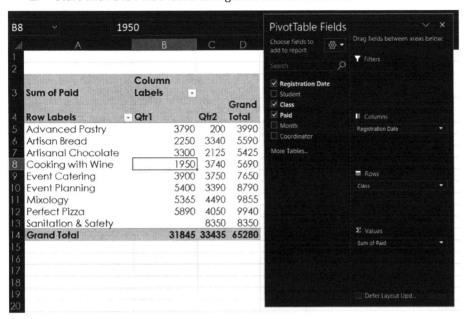

2. Click on the arrow next to Sum of Paid.
3. Select Value Field Settings. The Value Field Settings dialog appears.

4. Choose the Show Values As tab.
5. Under Show Values As, hit the dropdown arrow and select % of Grand Total.
6. Click OK.

GOT IT! 🔥🔥🔥

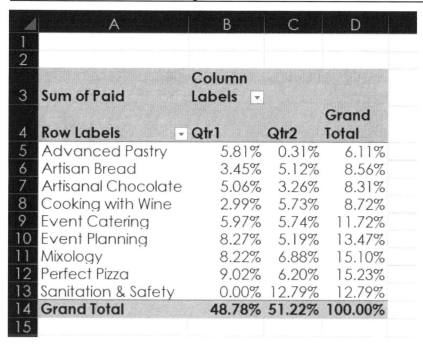

Sum of Paid	Column Labels ▾		
Row Labels ▾	Qtr1	Qtr2	Grand Total
Advanced Pastry	5.81%	0.31%	6.11%
Artisan Bread	3.45%	5.12%	8.56%
Artisanal Chocolate	5.06%	3.26%	8.31%
Cooking with Wine	2.99%	5.73%	8.72%
Event Catering	5.97%	5.74%	11.72%
Event Planning	8.27%	5.19%	13.47%
Mixology	8.22%	6.88%	15.10%
Perfect Pizza	9.02%	6.20%	15.23%
Sanitation & Safety	0.00%	12.79%	12.79%
Grand Total	48.78%	51.22%	100.00%

Notice:

- Qtr1 accounted for 48.78% of the total.
- Perfect Pizza's two quarters combined for 15.23% of the grand total.

Tip: Take some time to explore the options in the Value Field Settings dialog. Sometimes you want totals as a % of Row Total or % of Column Total. Maybe you want the Avg, Max, or Min. They're all there for your use.

Pivot Table Percentages Without Totals

In the example below, the exam score of each student is listed (there's a total of 24 entries in the dataset, only the first eight are showing).

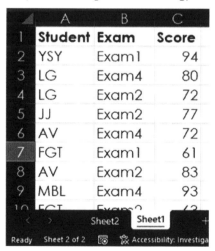

	Student	Exam	Score
1	Student	Exam	Score
2	YSY	Exam1	94
3	LG	Exam4	80
4	LG	Exam2	72
5	JJ	Exam2	77
6	AV	Exam4	72
7	FGT	Exam1	61
8	AV	Exam2	83
9	MBL	Exam4	93
10	FGT	Exam2	63

Using this data as a source, a raw, default pivot table will provide totals for the rows and columns. However, if the goal is to get each individual's average and there's no reason for the group's total average or the average for each exam, you can get the Pivot Table to only show row totals and disregard column totals.

Average of Score	Column Labels				
Row Labels	Exam1	Exam2	Exam3	Exam4	Grand Total
AV	85	83	76	72	79
FGT	61	63	0	61	46.25
JJ	80	77	65	81	75.75
LG	73	72	78	80	75.75
MBL	82	76	77	93	82
YSY	94	100	89	88	92.75
Grand Total	79.16666667	78.5	64.16666667	79.16666667	75.25

On the Design tab, open the Grand Totals dropdown menu and choose On for Rows Only. This removes the grand total at the bottom of each column, also known as the "grand total row."

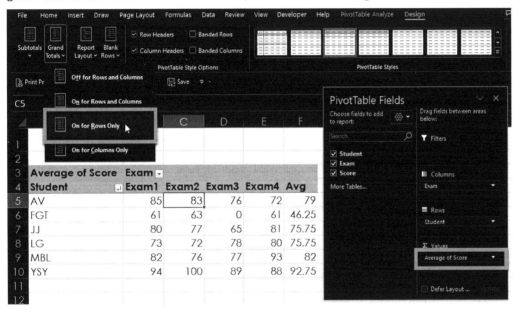

Using the Pivot Table to Drill Down for Isolated Details

Now say that you want specific details about the $2125 for Artisanal Chocolate in Qtr2, as shown here:

Sum of Paid	Column Labels		
Row Labels	Qtr1	Qtr2	Grand Total
Advanced Pastry	3790	200	3990
Artisan Bread	2250	3340	5590
Artisanal Chocolate	3300	2125	5425
Cooking with Wine	1950	3740	5690
Event Catering	3900	3750	7650
Event Planning	5400	3390	8790
Mixology	5365	4490	9855
Perfect Pizza	5890	4050	9940
Sanitation & Safety		8350	8350
Grand Total	31845	33435	65280

Double-click that value, and Excel creates a new page showing only the data that makes up the $2125:

	A	B	C	D	E	F
1	Registration Date	Student	Class	Paid	Month	Coordinator
2	11 May 2022	Hadley	Artisanal Chocolate	200	May	Peliah Mercado
3	9 May 2022	Imran	Artisanal Chocolate	100	May	Peliah Mercado
4	2 May 2022	Hamish	Artisanal Chocolate	200	May	Peliah Mercado
5	1 May 2022	Tomaas	Artisanal Chocolate	200	May	Peliah Mercado
6	1 May 2022	Orland	Artisanal Chocolate	0	May	Peliah Mercado
7	28 Apr 2022	Zayn	Artisanal Chocolate	200	Apr	Peliah Mercado
8	24 Apr 2022	Luke	Artisanal Chocolate	200	Apr	Peliah Mercado
9	18 Apr 2022	Leilani	Artisanal Chocolate	100	Apr	Peliah Mercado
10	16 Apr 2022	Grover	Artisanal Chocolate	175	Apr	Peliah Mercado
11	14 Apr 2022	Vonnie	Artisanal Chocolate	150	Apr	Peliah Mercado
12	5 Apr 2022	LeeAnne	Artisanal Chocolate	200	Apr	Peliah Mercado
13	5 Apr 2022	Clinton	Artisanal Chocolate	200	Apr	Peliah Mercado
14	4 Apr 2022	Gray	Artisanal Chocolate	200	Apr	Peliah Mercado

Deleting a Pivot Table

It's not possible to delete a row or column in a Pivot Table. If you try to do it, you'll get an error. But you can completely get rid of a Pivot Table, using three different methods:

- **Option 1:** Highlight all the columns of the Pivot Table and press Delete.
- **Option 2:** Highlight all the rows of the Pivot Table and press Delete.
- **Option 3:** Delete the entire worksheet.

Caution: When you delete an entire worksheet, you cannot reverse the action by using Undo. Excel warns you of this when you try to delete a worksheet.

Saving Your Favorite Pivot Table Settings Using Pivot Table Defaults

As you create more Pivot Tables, you might find that you are frequently making the same tweaks to every Pivot Table.

For example, consider this Pivot Table, with two row fields (Sector and Customer) and one column field (Product).

	A	B	C	D	E
3	Sum of Revenue	Column Labels			
4	Row Labels	ABC	DEF	XYZ	Grand Total
5	Communications		344019	290342	634361
6	AT&T		271339	227598	498937
7	Lucent			62744	62744
8	SBC Communications		72680		72680
9	Energy	294138	185286	259299	738723
10	Exxon	294138	185286	224935	704359
11	Texaco			34364	34364
12	Financial	643245	281958	205758	1130961
13	BankUnited	406326			406326

Ever since Excel 2007, Microsoft has mixed and mingled all of the text from the row fields in the first column of the Pivot Table. That means that rows 5, 9, and 12 contain sectors, while rows 6–8, 10, 11, and 13 contain customers. How are you supposed to tell these apart? Yes, Excel indents the customers, but there is no formula in the world that is ever going to be able to detect that this row contains a customer based on the indentation level.

To many people, the layout shown above, known as Compact Form, is an abomination. Every time I create a Pivot Table, I immediately head to the Design tab, open the Report Layout dropdown menu, and change from the default Compact Form by choosing Show in Tabular Form.

In Tabular Form, each row field in the Pivot Table is given its own column. Sectors are in column A, and customers are in column B. The meaningless headings Row Labels and Column Labels are replaced with actual labels such as Sector, Customer, and Product.

	A	B	C	D	E	F
3	Sum of Revenue		Product ▾			
4	Sector ▾	Customer ▾	ABC	DEF	XYZ	Grand Total
5	⊟Communications	AT&T		271339	227598	498937
6		Lucent			62744	62744
7		SBC Communications		72680		72680
8	Communications Total			344019	290342	634361
9	⊟Energy	Exxon	294138	185286	224935	704359
10		Texaco			34364	34364
11	Energy Total		294138	185286	259299	738723
12	⊟Financial	BankUnited	406326			406326
13		CitiGroup	203522	204234	205758	613514
14		CUNA Insurance		51240		51240
15		State Farm	33397	26484		59881
16	Financial Total		643245	281958	205758	1130961

There are still problems with this layout. Humans will recognize that because A5 says Communications and A6 and A7 are blank, the blank cells mean that these rows are also for Communications. However, once you get to the Values area of the Pivot Table, all of those blank cells mean that there were no sales at all.

1. To fill the blank cells in column A, use Design | Layout | Repeat All Item Labels.

2. To fill the blank cells in the Values area, right-click the Pivot Table and choose PivotTable Options.

3. On the Layout & Format tab in the PivotTable Options dialog, there is a checkbox that says For Empty Cells Show. You can either leave this ticked and type a 0 in the box or untick the checkbox. Either will replace the empty cells with zeros.

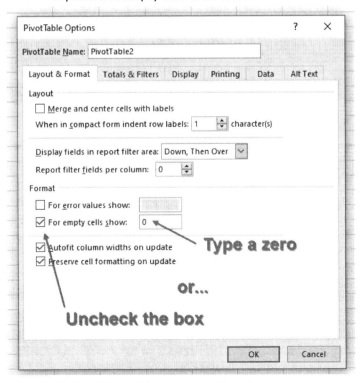

Here is the final Pivot Table after making these changes:

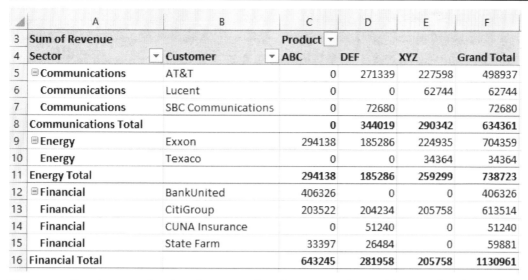

Sum of Revenue	Product			
Sector	Customer	ABC	DEF	XYZ	Grand Total
⊟Communications	AT&T	0	271339	227598	498937
Communications	Lucent	0	0	62744	62744
Communications	SBC Communications	0	72680	0	72680
Communications Total		0	344019	290342	634361
⊟Energy	Exxon	294138	185286	224935	704359
Energy	Texaco	0	0	34364	34364
Energy Total		294138	185286	259299	738723
⊟Financial	BankUnited	406326	0	0	406326
Financial	CitiGroup	203522	204234	205758	613514
Financial	CUNA Insurance	0	51240	0	51240
Financial	State Farm	33397	26484	0	59881
Financial Total		643245	281958	205758	1130961

These are the changes that I make every time I create a Pivot Table. It only takes 6 clicks to create a Pivot Table, but these formatting changes require another 10 clicks:

- Design | Report Layout | Show in Tabular | Design | Report Layout | Repeat All Item Labels (6 clicks)
- Right-click, Options, type a 0, OK (4 clicks)

I began lobbying the Excel team for a way to say that all future Pivot Tables should start in Tabular Form instead of Compact Form. After garnering hundreds of votes at Excel.UserVoice.Com, the feature was finally added to Excel in April 2017.

Here is how to use it:

1. Go to File | Options.

2. Look at the categories along the left side. If you have Data as the third category, then you will have the ability to set Pivot Table defaults. This new category was created in 2017 to hold the Edit Default Layout button. All of the other settings in this category were relocated here from other tabs.

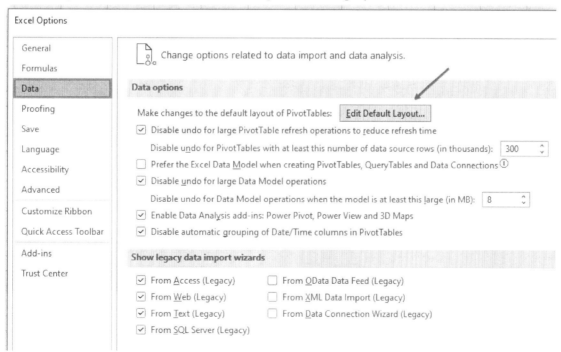

3. Click the Edit Default Layout button. The Edit Default Layout dialog box appears.

4. In the Edit Default Layout dialog box:
   - Set Subtotals to Show All Subtotals at Bottom of Group.
   - Set Report Layout to Show in Tabular Form.

- Tick Repeat All Item Labels.
- Tick Included Filtered Items in Totals.
- Click PivotTable Options to open the PivotTable Options dialog.
- Type a 0 in the box after For Empty Cells Show.

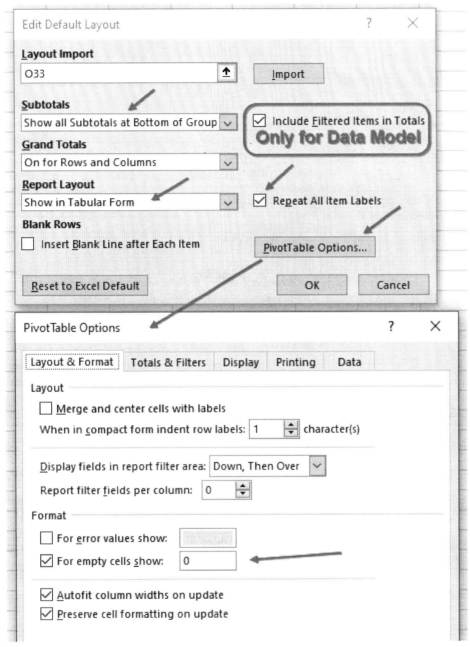

After making these changes, all future Pivot Tables will start in Tabular Form and have far fewer blank cells than usual.

Sadly, the Pivot Table defaults do not let you specify a specific number format that will be the default. Every new Pivot Table will start in General format. You will have to right-click a cell in the Values area, choose Number Format, and then select your favorite setting for number formats.

Tip: Rearrange the field list: The gear wheel dropdown menu near the top of the field list allows you to show the pane in one of five configurations. The Excel project manager in charge of Pivot Tables, Howie Dickerman, suggested that Microsoft should have long ago adopted Fields Section and Areas Section Side by Side as the default. This keeps the drop zone boxes the same size but provides far more vertical space to accommodate a long list of fields. The next time you have a Pivot Table, change the setting, and it will be remembered for all future Pivot Tables.

Creating a Year-over-Year Report in a Pivot Table

Say that you have a dataset that includes two years of sales. It is very easy to create a year-over-year report by using the Date grouping feature.

The image below shows the top and bottom rows with data stretching from January 2024 to the end of 2025.

	A	B	C	D	E	F	G	H	I
1	Region	Product	Date	Sector	Customer	Quantity	Revenue	COGS	Profit
2	Central	ABC	1/1/2024	Transport:	Southwest	100	2257	984	1273
3	East	ABC	1/1/2024	Healthcare	Merck	800	18552	7872	10680
563	East	ABC	12/24/2025	Financial	BankUnite	700	15225	7154	8071
564	Central	ABC	12/25/2025	Manufactu	General M	900	15363	7623	7740

Create a Pivot Table with dates along the Rows area:

1. Select any date in the Pivot Table and select Group Field, as shown here.

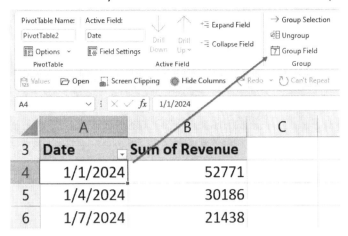

2. In the Grouping dialog, choose both Months and Years.

3. Click OK.

In March 2022, Microsoft began rolling out a change that impacts what happens next. If you have the new version, you will notice:

- The original Date field stays and still shows daily dates.
- A new virtual field called Years (Date) has been added to the Pivot Cache.
- A new virtual field called Months (Date) has been added to the Pivot Cache.
- The Years and Months fields replace the Date field in the Pivot Table layout.

This new logic is an improvement over the old logic. Most readers will still have the old logic through calendar 2022 and for part of 2023. Using the old logic, you would notice several things:

- The Date field, which formerly contained daily dates, now includes months.
- A new virtual field called Years has been added to the Pivot Cache.
- The new Years virtual field has been added to the same area as the Date field.

Note that there are other ways to group. What if you chose Days, Months, Quarters, and Years? Then you would have a Pivot Table that looks like the one below. In this case, the Date field continues to contain daily dates. Three new virtual fields called Months, Quarter, and Years are added to the Pivot Cache and to the Pivot Table.

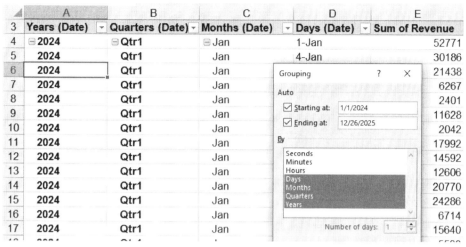

	A	B	C	D	E
3	Years (Date)	Quarters (Date)	Months (Date)	Days (Date)	Sum of Revenue
4	2024	Qtr1	Jan	1-Jan	52771
5	2024	Qtr1	Jan	4-Jan	30186
6	2024	Qtr1	Jan		21438
7	2024	Qtr1	Jan		6267
8	2024	Qtr1	Jan		2401
9	2024	Qtr1	Jan		11628
10	2024	Qtr1	Jan		2042
11	2024	Qtr1	Jan		17992
12	2024	Qtr1	Jan		14592
13	2024	Qtr1	Jan		12606
14	2024	Qtr1	Jan		20770
15	2024	Qtr1	Jan		24286
16	2024	Qtr1	Jan		6714
17	2024	Qtr1	Jan		15640

What if you want to group by year and week? That is not allowed—at least not using the Grouping dialog. If you choose just Days and set Number of Days to 7, it will work. But selecting Years will gray out the Number of Days setting.

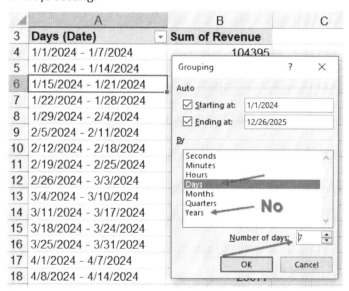

	A	B	C
3	Days (Date)	Sum of Revenue	
4	1/1/2024 – 1/7/2024	104395	
5	1/8/2024 – 1/14/2024		
6	1/15/2024 – 1/21/2024		
7	1/22/2024 – 1/28/2024		
8	1/29/2024 – 2/4/2024		
9	2/5/2024 – 2/11/2024		
10	2/12/2024 – 2/18/2024		
11	2/19/2024 – 2/25/2024		
12	2/26/2024 – 3/3/2024		
13	3/4/2024 – 3/10/2024		
14	3/11/2024 – 3/17/2024		
15	3/18/2024 – 3/24/2024		
16	3/25/2024 – 3/31/2024		
17	4/1/2024 – 4/7/2024		
18	4/8/2024 – 4/14/2024		

Those were interesting alternatives, but this section is supposed to be about creating a year-over-year report, so go back to grouping by month and year:

1. Drag the Years field from the Rows area to the Columns area. You now have an almost-beautiful report showing last year vs. this year for each month.

	A	B	C	D
3	Sum of Revenue	Years (Date)		
4	Months (Date)	2024	2025	Grand Total
5	Jan	262,025	278,136	540,161
6	Feb	292,721	268,169	560,890
7	Mar	266,654	240,949	507,603
8	Apr	246,573	314,848	561,421
9	May	297,138	339,895	637,033

2. To remove the grand total in column D, right-click on D4 and choose Remove Grand Total.

3. Unselect Date and choose Sector.

You now have a report showing this year and last year for each sector. This is a very powerful report that can answer many questions.

Sum of Revenue	Years (Date)	
Sector	2024	2025
Communications	368,159	266,202
Energy	322,481	416,242
Financial	583,186	547,775
Healthcare	22,104	20,212
Manufacturing	1,257,788	1,476,387
Retail	517,027	519,271
Transportation	181,618	209,360
Grand Total	3,252,363	3,455,449

You can do this all day. Take sector out and put customer in. Take customer out and put product in. There are many possibilities.

Adding a Percentage Change Column

While the reports above are beautiful, you know that your manager is going to ask you to add a calculation in column D to show percentage change. If the number this year is larger, how much did the company grow?

That is an easy calculation. The formula in D5 should be =C5/B5-1. But there is a trap that is going to get you, and it has been around since 2002. I call it the GetPivotData bug (although Microsoft will tell you it is not a bug, it is a feature).

Say that you add the heading % Change in D4. Then you click D5 and type an equals sign. You click C5. Without looking, you type a slash, then use the left arrow key to point to B5. Type minus one. Press Enter. That formula will appear to work!

You can even grab a calculator and do the math. A 27.7% decrease is correct. But if you look in the formula bar, you will notice a ticking time bomb that is about to explode. Where the formula should be =C5/B5-1, you instead have an insanely long formula that starts with =GETPIVOTDATA.

	A	B	C	D	E
3	Sum of Revenue	Years (Date)			
4	Sector	2024	2025	% Change	
5	Communications	368,159	266,202	-27.7%	
6	Energy	322,481	416,242		
7	Financial	583,186	547,775		
8	Healthcare	22,104	20,212		
9	Manufacturing	1,257,788	1,476,387		
10	Retail	517,027	519,271		
11	Transportation	181,618	209,360		
12	Grand Total		3,252,363	3,455,449	
13					

The GETPIVOTDATA function was invented in Excel 2002. In an effort to get people to discover it, Microsoft turned on the option Use GetPivotData Function for Pivot Table References. This is an obscure setting found under File | Options | Formulas | Working with Formulas.

Note: I actually understand the motivation behind turning this feature on. A small group of engineers probably spent hundreds of hours coding GETPIVOTDATA. If they waited for people to actually discover File | Options | Formula, then 1 out of 100,000 Excellers would ever discover this function. By lobbying to turn the feature on, they made sure many more people discover the feature (and their annoyance with the feature). They then have to discover the setting in order to turn it off.

One problem with the GETPIVOTDATA formulas automatically created by Excel: The field values such as Communications are hard-coded into the formula, instead of using cell references such as $A5. This means that as you copy the automatic GETPIVOTDATA function, it keeps giving you the answer for the first sector. In this case, the -27.7% is the answer for Communications, but it appears for every sector.

	A	B	C	D
3	**Sum of Revenue**	**Years (Date)** ▾		
4	**Sector** ▾	2024	2025	% Change
5	Communications	368,159	266,202	-27.7%
6	Energy	322,481	416,242	-27.7%
7	Financial	583,186	547,775	-27.7%
8	Healthcare	22,104	20,212	-27.7%
9	Manufacturing	1,257,788	1,476,387	-27.7%
10	Retail	517,027	519,271	-27.7%
11	Transportation	181,618	209,360	-27.7%
12	**Grand Total**	**3,252,363**	**3,455,449**	-27.7%

There are several ways to prevent GETPIVOTDATA from happening:

- Instead of pointing to cells in the Pivot Table using the mouse or arrow keys, you could simply type the entire formula: =C5/B5-1. Type that formula, and it will copy perfectly.
- Go to File | Options | Formulas and untick Use GetPivotData Functions for PivotTable References.
- Select a cell in a Pivot Table. On the PivotTable Analyze tab, the bottom-left icon is the Options icon. Don't click on it. Just to the right of the Options icon is a dropdown arrow. Open that dropdown menu and unselect Generate GetPivotData.

Caution: There are other reasons why having formulas outside of Pivot Tables might not be a good idea. If you switch from Sector to Customer, you will need to copy the formulas down further. If you switch from Sector to Product, you will have more formulas than you need that suddenly start returning #DIV/0 errors because there is no denominator in those rows that no longer have data.

	A	B	C	D
3	**Sum of Revenue**	**Years (Date)** ▾		
4	**Product** ▾	2024	2025	% Change
5	ABC	1,261,860	1,028,128	-18.5%
6	DEF	1,120,351	1,251,176	11.7%
7	XYZ	870,152	1,176,145	35.2%
8	**Grand Total**	**3,252,363**	**3,455,449**	6.2%
9				#DIV/0!
10				#DIV/0!
11				#DIV/0!
12				#DIV/0!

The hard-core will eliminate the #DIV/0 by wrapping the formula in column D in the IFERROR function, as described earlier.

🐉 The Best Way for the % Change Column

About a page ago, I wrote a very casual sentence that implied you could remove Sector and add Customer or Product to the Pivot Table.

You really have to be careful to remove the field before you add a new field. As you can see above, the actual Pivot Table is in A3:C8. If you remove Product first, the Pivot Table will be in A3:B5. Then you add Sector. The Pivot Table will expand back to A3:C12, and all of the formulas in column D keep working.

Many who are not Excel masters might think that you could add Sector and then remove Product. Oh, brother! All you are doing is unticking Product and checking Sector. Why would it matter if you do those in the opposite order?

It matters big time. If you add Sector before you remove Product, then the Pivot Table will very temporarily grow to have an extra column. For just an instant, you will have Product in column A and Sector in column B. The Pivot Table growing will wipe out your formulas in column D. There is a warning that appears. But since most people click the default button in any message before reading the message, it will be too late.

Note: Read that paragraph again and listen very closely. You can hear the ghost of a former Excel project manager cackling, "It wouldn't have been a problem if you would have stuck with Compact Layout!"

So, look … if you are really going to be needing % Growth in 1000 Pivot Tables per year, there is a more elegant way to solve this. I rarely go to this extent, but it might be something you would adopt.

Here are the steps:

1. Create a Pivot Table with daily dates. Group those dates up to years and months. Put Years in the Columns area.
2. Add Revenue to the Values area
3. Put any field or fields in the Rows area.
4. Drag Revenue to the Values area a second time. This gives you a Sum of Revenue2 field in the Pivot Table.
5. Double-click the Sum of Revenue2 field in the Pivot Table. This opens the Value Field Settings dialog.
6. Click the Show Values As tab in the Value Field Settings dialog.
7. In the Show Values As dropdown, choose % Difference From.
8. For Base Field, choose Years.
9. For Base Item, choose (previous). Seriously. The top item is called (previous). Yes. With the parentheses.
10. In the Custom Name field, type % Change.
11. Click OK.

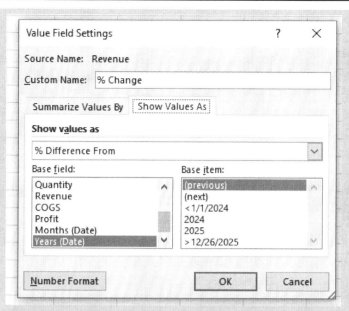

Who comes up with this? I learned it in Dallas, from Tobias Ljung, who had flown from Sweden to Dallas to attend the three-day Excelapalooza conference.

Look at the awesome column F below. Even with multiple row fields, it continues to show the percentage change inside the Pivot Table.

	A	B	C	D	E
3		Years (Date) ▼	Values		Perfect!
4		2024	2024	2025	2025
5	Sector ▼	Sum of Revenue	% Change	Sum of Revenue	% Change
6	Communications	368,159	no data	266,202	-27.69%
7	Energy	322,481		416,242	29.07%
8	Financial	583,186	here since	547,775	-6.07%
9	Healthcare	22,104		20,212	-8.56%
10	Manufacturing	1,257,788	there is no	1,476,387	17.38%
11	Retail	517,027	(previous)	519,271	0.43%
12	Transportation	181,618		209,360	15.27%
13	Grand Total	3,252,363		3,455,449	6.24%
14					

It is beautiful ... until you notice column D. The Values area is blank. This is because there is no 2023 data in the dataset. So for the 2024 calculation, there is no (previous) to use in the calculation.

You could hide column D. Or maybe set the column width to 0.01. But if you add/remove fields to the Rows area, you will have to change the column that is hidden.

	A	B	C	E	F
3			Years (Date) ▼		
4			2024	2025	2025
5	Sector ▼	Product ▼	Revenue	Revenue	% Change
6	⊟Communications	DEF	223,813	120,206	-46.29%
7	Communications	XYZ	144,346	145,996	1.14%
8	Communications Total		368,159	266,202	-27.69%
9	⊟Energy	ABC	166,456	127,682	-23.29%
10	Energy	DEF	77,048	108,238	40.48%

For this skirmish, you've seen two solutions. Both have problems. I am tempted to call it a draw. But I am biased since I actually use the first solution all the time. By calling this skirmish a draw, I am actually admitting that Thomas's method is superior.

Counting Distinct Values in a Pivot Table

Say that you want to know how many customers you have in each industry sector. In the Pivot Table below, you can mentally count that the Communications sector has three customers: AT&T, Lucent, and SBC. Energy has two, Financial has four. How can you get the numbers 3, 2, and 4 to appear in the Pivot Table?

In the image below, you can try dragging the Customer field to the Values area. Excel says it is showing you Count of Customer. But in this case, "Count of Customer" means that there is some text in the Customer column 40 times where the customer is AT&T. It is good to know that there were 40 invoices to AT&T. But your manager isn't asking how many invoices. Your manager wants to know how many distinct customers there are.

	A	B	C
3	Sector ▼	Customer ▼	Count of Customer
4	⊟Communications	AT&T	40
5	Communications	Lucent	4
6	Communications	SBC Communications	4
7	Communications Total		48
8	⊟Energy	Exxon	66
9	Energy	Texaco	4
10	Energy Total		70
11	⊟Financial	BankUnited	28
12	Financial	CitiGroup	48
13	Financial	CUNA Insurance	4
14	Financial	State Farm	4
15	Financial Total		84

There is a very easy solution to this. But it is hard to find.

When you initially create the Pivot Table, tick Add This Data to the Data Model.

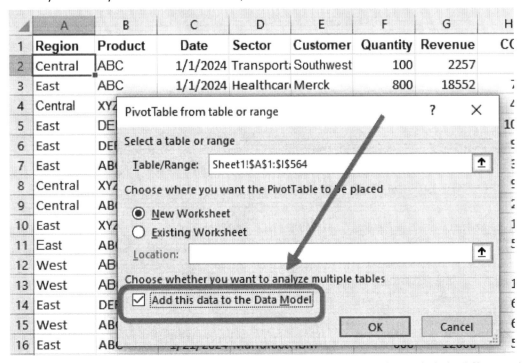

For whatever reason, the calculations available in the Data Model are slightly different than in Pivot Tables based on the Pivot Cache. After you drag Customer to the Values area, double-click the Count of Customer heading. Scroll all the way to the bottom of the list and choose Distinct Count. Your calculations will become correct.

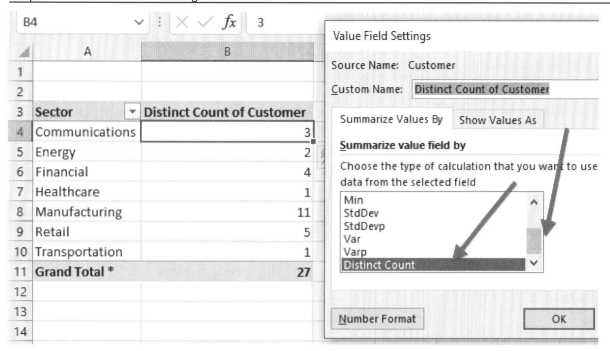

Pivot Table Conclusions

Explore Pivot Tables! This chapter has only scratched the surface of this tool, which can do some amazing things for you.

I've noticed that Excel users who develop savvy with Pivot Tables also structure their spreadsheets well. Pivot Tables work best when you keep a dataset as one solid range. It's intuitive to break data into sets on multiple worksheets, as in this example of expense data:

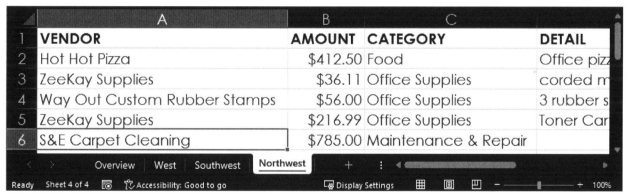

It's difficult to create a summary of data spread across three different areas. But if you create a column for the data you'd otherwise split into worksheets, you can use Pivot Tables and data models, which both help you minimize the number of formulas you have to write. Structuring a worksheet this way makes for data that can be an impenetrable block for the human eye, but it's much easier for Excel to handle:

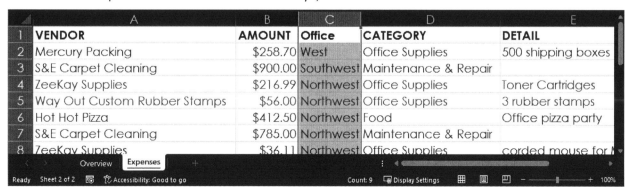

🐉 Flattening a File: Preparing to Use a Pivot Table

Flattening a file is the process of converting a report into a wall of rows and columns that can be sorted, filtered, and otherwise easier to work with in Excel.

Consider …

Here's a report that's sent out every month for managers to review. It's easy to see that Loren ran the report, and the Q1 total for May was $6388.93.

			January	February	March	Q1		April	May	June		Q2
Store 377		Computers	441.25	447.05	429.61	$ 1,317.91		834.73	1054.75	754.56		$ 2,644.04
		Electronics	858.31	984.01	527.15	$ 2,369.47		1710.11	1808.61	1682.15		$ 5,200.87
		Automotive	819.22	574.35	510.53	$ 1,904.10		1046.25	1478.53	1631.98		$ 4,156.76
		Food	983.35	836.24	712.48	$ 2,532.07		877.2	1639.29	353.76		$ 2,870.25
		Garden	923.85	711.3	905.56	$ 2,540.71		1494.11	407.75	922.5		$ 2,824.36
	TOTAL		4025.98	3552.95	3085.33	$10,664.26		5962.4	6388.93	5344.95		$17,696.28
Store 810		Computers	992.89	773.05	901.09	$ 2,667.03		758.75	1784.1	1972.73		$ 4,515.58
		Electronics	848.18	1213.68	968.3	$ 3,030.16		1421.37	1379.6	1227.86		$ 4,028.83
		Food	313.35	1270.81	1584.5	$ 3,168.66		794.12	1681.55	377.65		$ 2,853.32
		Garden	590.5	1954.7	500.04	$ 3,045.24		1429.64	718.04	347.77		$ 2,495.45
	TOTAL		2744.92	5212.24	3953.93	$11,911.09		4403.88	5563.29	3926.01	0	$13,893.18
Report												
	9 Jul 23		Q1	$22,575.35								
By: Loren			Q2	$31,589.46								
			Q3									
			Q4									

Sheet1   Table1   Sheet2   +

But you need it for a different purpose.

Let's say you need the overall data—regardless of the store—to compare these values against another report that has the monthly and quarterly goals, and you need to isolate values that fell short of the goals.

You can wait a week for the database admin to get you that report, but the data you need is all here.

If you have a subscription service, they might want a fee to get you your desired report … in a week.

Or, you can flatten this data and not only satisfy your immediate need but anything else you might want from this data.

In this example, flattening the file includes:

- Getting rid of the date and the name of the person who ran the report in B14:B16. If you need this data, it can be manually added after the flattening.
- Getting rid of the subtotals. When the data is flattened, you can easily get any totals you want by using a Pivot Table, Power Query, or formulas.
- Deleting any empty rows or columns (e.g., columns G and I). This will make the data a solid contiguous range that can be loaded into a Pivot Table or into Power Query.
- Closing the gaps in B4:B7 and B10:B12. Thus, if you ever need it, you'll be able to distinguish between Electronics from Store 377 vs. Electronics from Store 810.
- Deleting the data in D15:E18. Again, this is data that you can easily calculate if you ever need it.

Here is what the flattened file can look like:

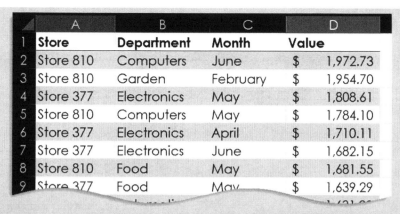

	A	B	C	D
1	Store	Department	Month	Value
2	Store 810	Computers	June	$ 1,972.73
3	Store 810	Garden	February	$ 1,954.70
4	Store 377	Electronics	May	$ 1,808.61
5	Store 810	Computers	May	$ 1,784.10
6	Store 377	Electronics	April	$ 1,710.11
7	Store 377	Electronics	June	$ 1,682.15
8	Store 810	Food	May	$ 1,681.55
9	Store 377	Food	May	$ 1,639.29

A raw wall of filterable rows and columns. If you have to write any formulas against this dataset, it's much easier than writing formulas against the report form of the data. Using this as a source, you can create multiple Pivot Tables and Power Query queries.

Think about this:

When you have a report, it's an easily digestible view of your data for a specific purpose. When you flatten a file, it's not designed for reading; it's used as a source to get any view of your data that you want.

In this example, you could satisfy someone who calls and requests a report of:

- All values that are <$1000; February thru April; separated by store; for Electronics and Food.
- Same as the above but for values ≥$1000.

This is why Power Query is next! Power Query is the gift the Universe gave human beings to import, compare, merge, parse, clean, and flatten data. A deep arsenal in the fight for clean, useful data.

Chapter 7: Power Query

You have got to know about Power Query! If you work with data that's not immediately ready for use ... POWER QUERY!

If you have to split columns of data, import and merge files from multiple sources, stack data that's on several worksheets, clear blank rows ... POWER QUERY! Anything involving the import, cleansing, or restructuring of data ... POWER QUERY!

The challenge I face in writing this chapter is: What can I show without the book becoming 50% Power Query?

There is so much in Power Query that's useful, whether you're a beginner or a longtime professional. Sadly, one thing I've noticed as I've met seasoned Excel users is many of them don't know that Power Query exists, even though it's been around at least 7 years. However, it doesn't help that Power Query has gone through several names. It arrived on the scene as Data Explorer. And then it was presented as an add-in named Power Query for Excel 2010.

Today, Power Query is a feature inside Excel, but it's on the Data tab, under the name Get & Transform Data.

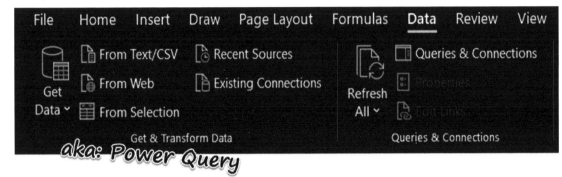

Note: Power Query isn't fully available on Excel for Mac or Excel Online. However, progress is being made. Until recently, someone on a Mac couldn't even open a file that included Power Query queries. Today, yes, a Mac user can open such files.

Power Query is the term commonly used out in the wild. So, that's what I'll use in this book.

For a complete dive into Power Query—beyond what we can cover here—there are a lot of resources, including:

* My YouTube channel, <u>Excel on Fire</u>, where a significant amount of my content is on Power Query
* My 52-page ebook that you can find at MrExcel.com: *Cleaning Excel Data with Power Query: Straight to the Point*
* The recently published *Master Your Data with Power Query in Excel and Power BI*, written by Ken Puls and Miguel Escobar

Power Query: A Little Background

Power Query was developed for Excel by Microsoft's SQL team. It was a response to what's going on in the real world:

* A lot of Excel users have to clean data:
  * Comparing, merging, and parsing datasets
  * Splitting columns (e.g., when a name and an email address are in the same field and need to be separated)
  * Stacking data from multiple worksheets or Excel files
  * Converting a report into data that can be sorted and filtered
* Excel is often used like a database:
* Storing lots of data in Excel on multiple sheets
* Using exotic formulas to bring the data together in various forms for a multitude of needs

Yes, these uses can cause problems, especially when these files are emailed or collaborated on, and version control issues crop up, making a strong case for getting data out of Excel files and into a centralized database. But what's the reality that keeps people in Excel and not databases?

- Databases can be hell to configure and maintain.
- Any place that does have a database typically has at least one dedicated professional who can run it.
- Not many small businesses have the resources for configuring and maintaining a database and hiring a dedicated professional. But they do have Excel.

Does Power Query replace the need for databases? No. I wouldn't suggest running a global enterprise on Excel. But a global enterprise will have teams of dedicated people to run their databases.

I appreciate that Power Query is now part of Excel because it empowers us to get what we need from our data—with some database-like functionality—based on the reality of the contexts we work in. As someone who did work in a global enterprise, one problem I consistently faced was how slow and painful it was to get data and get it in the desired format. It could be days, and it included asking a database admin, who'd roll his eyes and grudgingly agree, "I'll get it to you tomorrow morning, after I finish the reports for the director of marketing."

Eventually, I learned how to write basic queries in the company database to extract data dumps (raw rows and columns of data that were full of duplicates, incomplete and inconsistent entries, and random mess). Then, I would use my crude Excel skills to clean and convert a data dump into what I needed to support customers or support my director of customer service.

Oh, how I wish Power Query had been available to simplify the cleansing and transformation of my data! For one of my monthly tasks, I had a three-day manual process that likely could have been reduced to a half-day and partially automated with Power Query.

I share this story because that was a situation where we did have a database and support teams. But my context was: one guy in customer service, trying to solve very narrow ad hoc problems while navigating gatekeepers, eyerolls, and indignant sighs and having to wait days for something that was often not what I'd asked for. There was even the statement that a DBA made to me: "Your 5000 customers are too small for me to make a priority when I'm supporting the president of the company and this whole enterprise."

OUCH! ☹ That hurt, but it was true.

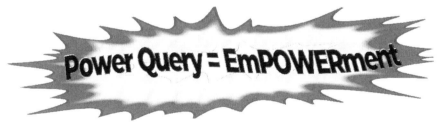

Important details about using Power Query:

- Power Query forces you to think about entire columns or an entire dataset. It's not so easy to operate at the cell level. This means you have to know your data and consider addressing granular issues before you bring data into Power Query.
- Changes have to be made in your source data.
- Steps are recorded to help you automate your tasks.
- Everything needs to be done via queries. If you need to combine three datasets, you'll need to create three queries before the datasets can be combined.
- Nulls, blank cells, and 0 are three different things in Power Query.

Next, let's look at some Power Query features that can be immediately useful to you when you need to get crap data to straighten up, start cooperating, and give you what you need.

Filling Down and Splitting Columns by Delimiter

Here is inventory data from two warehouses. What if you want to sort by the count or get a sum of the counts by color and size?

	A	B
1	Location	Color, Size, Count
2	Warehouse1	Gold, 10 ounce, 5
3		Orange, 10 ounce, 6
4		Orange, Dark, 10 ounce, 2
5		Purple, 10 ounce, 5
6		Red, 10 ounce, 7
7		Red, 3 ounce, 12
8		Yellow, Pale, 3 ounce, 3
9	Warehouse2	Gold, 10 ounce, 1
10		Gold, 3 ounce, 11
11		Orange, Bright, 3 ounce, 10
12		Purple, 3 ounce, 9
13		Yellow, Pale, 3 ounce, 5
14		Yellow, Neon, 3 ounce, 8

Stop and look at the data. Notice:

- The color, size, and count data for each entry are all in the same cell.
- Separating the colors, sizes, and counts is tricky because of a few colors:
  - **Row 3 is easy:** Orange, 10 ounce, 3. Just split by the commas.
  - **Row 4 creates a problem:** The full name of the color is Orange, Dark. Here's an example of the desired result:

Location	Color	Size (oz.)	Count
Warehouse1	Orange	10	6
Warehouse1	Orange, Dark	10	2
Warehouse2	Yellow, Neon	3	8
Warehouse2	Gold	3	11

- Column A has gaps that need to be filled in so that, for example, if you sort by the count, you can still see that "Purple, 3 ounce, 9" is in Warehouse2.

Now! Time to transform this data so that it can be sorted.

Place your cursor in the dataset | right-click | Get Data from Table/Range.

> **Note:** The icon that says Table/Range was previously known as From Selection and From Sheet. Depending on your version of Excel, it could have any of those names, or it could have a fourth name that we cannot predict as this book goes to press.

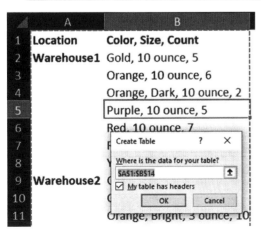

The marching ants automatically surround the range that will be imported into Power Query. In the Create Table dialog box, notice that the selected range is showing, and the box is ticked to say that yes, the table does have headers. Click OK. The image below shows that you are now in the Power Query editor. Here are a few things to notice:

- On the far right, under Properties, you can name the query. In this case, the name has defaulted to Table1.

- Everything you do in the query is recorded under Applied Steps. This allows you to make updates to the data without having to redo the steps.

- The Changed Type step is a default step where Power Query guesses what data types are in your data. The ABC in the column headers says that both of those columns are text data.

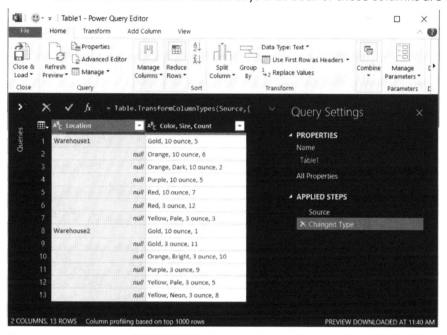

To make this data useful, highlight the Location column, right-click | Fill | Down.

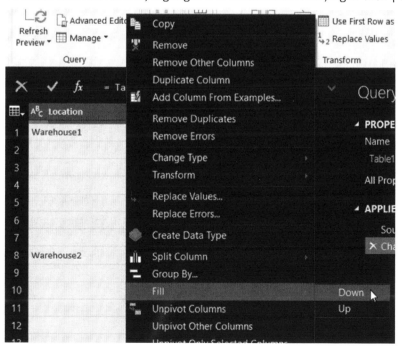

That closes the holes in the Location column.

Next, to split the Color, Size, Count column, Home | Transform | Split Column | By Delimiter.

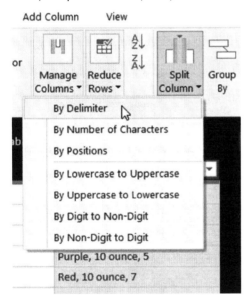

Here is where you tell Power Query where and how you want the column split:

- **Select or Enter Delimiter:** I've selected Custom, and in that second field I've entered **comma-space, not just a comma.** When the split happens, both the comma and the space after it will be deleted. Thus, you won't have trailing spaces to clean out later.

- **Split At:** Now this is sexy. Power Query gives you options. If you choose Each Occurrence of the Delimiter, the split will happen at every comma-space—and that means Orange, Dark will be separated into Orange and Dark in two different cells. You don't want that. You can select Right-most Delimiter, and only the count will be split.

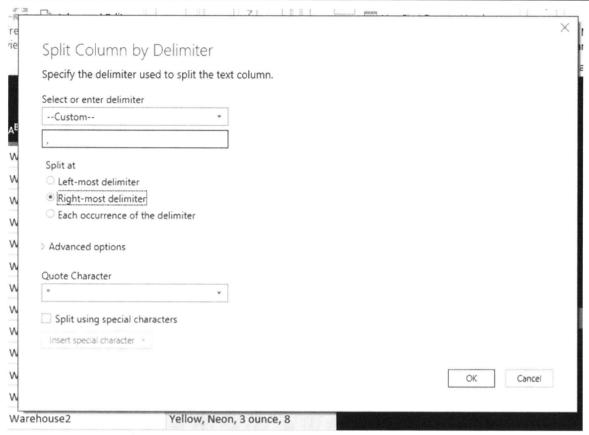

Warehouse2   Yellow, Neon, 3 ounce, 8

Click OK. And boom! ✳

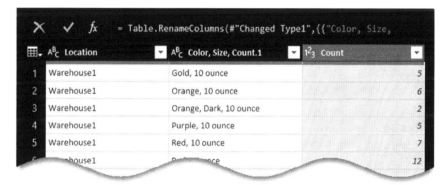

The image above shows that the count has been split, and I've renamed the column Count. Also notice the 123 next to the Count header. Power Query is guessing that the values in the column are integers.

Next, repeat the previous steps to separate the sizes and rename the column.

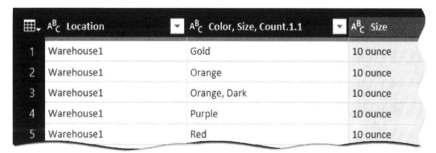

See! Sexy! The sizes are separated, and the colors are intact. Dark Orange remains.

Next, get rid of *ounce* in the Size column: Highlight the column | right-click near the header | Replace Values. This opens the Replace Values dialog box.

Once again, think about the space in front of *ounce* so that it doesn't have to be cleaned out later. Therefore, for Value to Find, enter ounce preceded by a space and leave Replace With blank since *ounce* is just being deleted and not being replaced with anything. Click OK.

Rename the second column Color.

And here is the data ... USEFUL data! Ready to be sorted, filtered, merged, appended ... whatever you need.

	Location	Color	Size	Count
1	Warehouse1	Gold	10	5
2	Warehouse1	Orange	10	6
3	Warehouse1	Orange, Dark	10	2
4	Warehouse1	Purple	10	5
5	Warehouse1	Red	10	7
6	Warehouse1	Red	3	12
7	Warehouse1	Yellow, Pale	3	3
8	Warehouse2	Gold	10	1
9	Warehouse2	Gold	3	11
10	Warehouse2	Orange, Bright	3	10
11	Warehouse2	Purple	3	9
12	Warehouse2	Yellow, Pale	3	5
13	Warehouse2	Yellow, Neon	3	8

Tip: Explore the other options for splitting columns so that you know they're there when you need them.

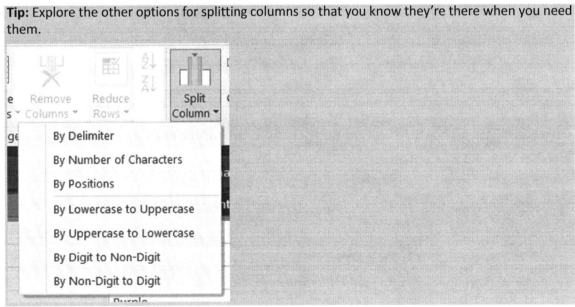

In this final example of splitting columns by delimiter, this softball team's player data is all in a single cell. To get it separated into columns for the player names, jersey numbers, and positions, the first move would be to split non-digit to digit. Hopefully you can split the rest. 👆

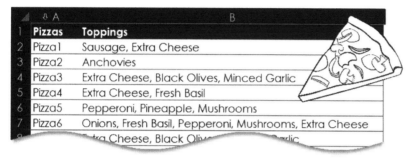

Player, Number, Position
A. Helen Shirai 33 Third Base
Alanna Pacifico 51 Pitcher
Ayodeji Okochoa 19 First Base
Che Chiyun 4 Left Field
Daphne Kay Arnone 28 First Base
Hannah Yesterday 9 Catcher
Lilo K. Taneja 1 Second Base
Luther McCoy 40 Pitcher
Marcel H. Smith 7 Shortstop
Mouse 22 Shortstop
Pippa Kristoff 26 Right Field
Preston Shaw 13 Center Field

Splitting Column into Rows, Grouping By, and Duplicating a Query

In this example, 30 pizzas were sold. Now it'd be nice to know how many times each topping was ordered.

	A	B
1	**Pizzas**	**Toppings**
2	Pizza1	Sausage, Extra Cheese
3	Pizza2	Anchovies
4	Pizza3	Extra Cheese, Black Olives, Minced Garlic
5	Pizza4	Extra Cheese, Fresh Basil
6	Pizza5	Pepperoni, Pineapple, Mushrooms
7	Pizza6	Onions, Fresh Basil, Pepperoni, Mushrooms, Extra Cheese

You could eyeball the Toppings column and count mushrooms, and then count extra cheese, and so on and so on … but that's a hassle and likely to be inaccurate.

Power Query is going to handle this for you.

Splitting Column into Rows

Inside the Power Query editor, with the Toppings column highlighted:

1. Right-click | Split Column by Delimiter.

2. In the Split Column by Delimiter dialog:
    *   The column is being split by comma-space at each occurrence.
    *   Advanced Options has been expanded.
    *   Split into rows.

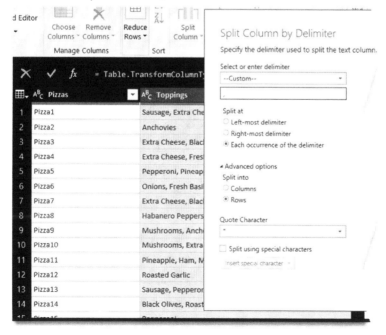

3. Click OK.

Check that out! Ain't that spectacular?! 😵

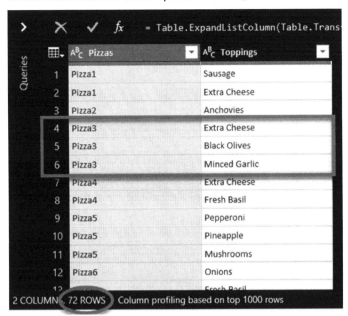

The circle in the image above shows that there are 72 rows of data with each topping on its own row—expanded from the 35 original rows. You can also see that, for example, Pizza3 is on three rows representing each of the three toppings: Extra Cheese, Black Olives, Minced Garlic.

Using Group By to Get a Count of Each Row

Next, use Group By to count how many times each topping is represented:

1. Home | Transform | Group By.

2. In the Group By dialog:

    - Toppings is the column to group by.

    - The new column name: Topping Count.

    - The operation: Count Rows.

3. Click OK.

Looky looky looky! Here's the result:

13 distinct toppings, and mushrooms is the winner, requested on 11 of the 30 pizzas.

Take this a step further and get a count of how many toppings were requested on each pizza.

Duplicating a Query

In the Queries & Connections pane, double-click the Pizzas query to go back into the Power Query editor.

In the Queries section on the left of the Power Query editor, right-click on the Pizzas query | Duplicate.

Rename the new query from the default Pizzas(1) to TCount.

These steps will let you keep all of the work you've already done, and you won't have to re-import the data and split the Toppings column again.

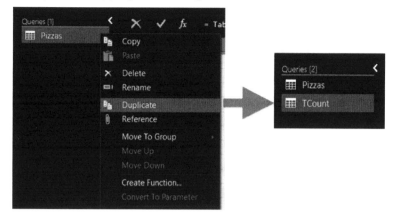

Next, in Query Settings, click the gear next to the step Grouped Rows so that the data can be grouped a different way.

The Group By dialog opens. This time group by Pizzas.

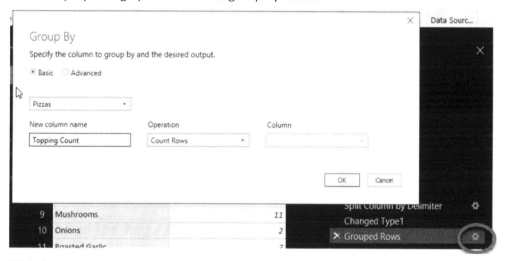

Click OK.

Sort the Topping Count column descending.

This query shows that 1 pizza had 5 toppings, and 12 of the 30 pizzas had 3 toppings.

If you add more data to the Pizzas table on Sheet1, all you have to do is refresh, and both queries will update!

See! Power Query = Empowerment.

Don't you feel yourself getting stronger, with a new swagger surging in your body? When crap data or messy or ornery data shows up, you can bang your fist on the table and say, "These sinister shenanigans are over! You're about to get unpivoted, split into rows, grouped-by, sorted, and filtered."

Data Types and Power Query

Power Query is very strict about the data types in your columns.

When you're working with data on a worksheet, Excel will allow you to do something strange like add a date and dollar amount and divide by a check number.

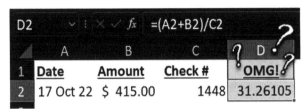

Power Query has restrictions that prevent you from being able to mix data types, thus minimizing the possibility of mistakenly adding a date to a dollar amount or an integer. But you have to be vigilant. Power Query adds a Changed Type step and guesses your data type.

Take this gift card data into Power Query and see what happens.

Gift Card	Value	Purchased At	Purchased	Balance
22045922	$25.00	Website	12 Jul 22	$25.00
24348971	$200.00	A&J Shoppe	26 May 22	$200.00
25802015	$100.00	Red & Otter's	29 Apr 22	$11.00
27387827	$100.00	Website	8 Jul 22	$0.00
29963540	$100.00	1730	29 Apr 22	$9.88
34187141	$200.00	A&J Shoppe	23 Jul 22	$64.20
34655659	$150.00	Website	26 Jul 22	$0.38
36874785	$75.00	1730	16 Jul 22	$75.00

Place your cursor in the dataset | right-click | Get Data from Selection.

Here's the data inside Power Query:

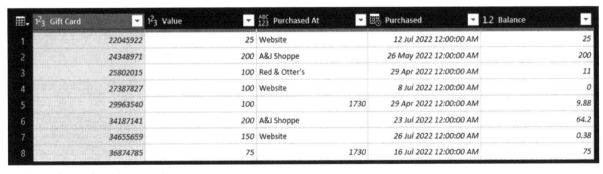

In the column headers notice:

* The Gift Card and Value columns show 123 in the header because Power Query sees the data as whole numbers.

* Purchased At shows ABC123 because there's a mix of numbers and text in the column, but you and I know that 1730 is the name of a store.

* Purchased has the calendar and clock icon because Power Query has converted the dates into date and time values.

* Balance shows 1.2, representing a decimal data type.

Remember, when the data is brought in, Changed Type is automatically added to the Applied Steps list. If you click the X to delete it, all of the column headers revert to ABC123, as shown here:

You can leave the Changed Type step, and when you change a data type, you'll get a popup asking if you want to replace the Changed Type step that's already there. Click Replace Current.

Now. Time to clean these up.

The first move would be to convert the Purchased column into dates by clicking on the ABC123 and using the menu to change the data type to Date.

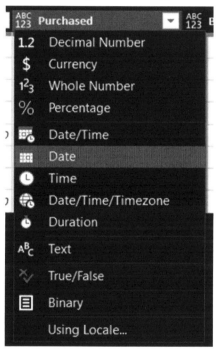

The image below shows the changes that I've made:

- Changed Gift Card to text (ABC) because it's not likely to have any math applied to it. You might use that field for making matches (e.g., to compare two datasets to match gift cards and purchases), but you won't need to use this value for sums or division.
- Changed Value and Balance to currency data type ($).
- Changed Purchased At to text, and notice that 1730 is now aligned left because it's text.

Why is this important? Native Excel will allow you to make errors like adding a date and a dollar amount. Power Query will not. If you try, you'll get an error, as shown here after I added Purchased and Balance:

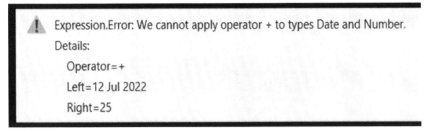

> ⚠ Expression.Error: We cannot apply operator + to types Date and Number.
>
> Details:
>
>   Operator=+
>   Left=12 Jul 2022
>   Right=25

The error is stating explicitly that you cannot apply addition to the data types date and number. However, you can subtract Balance from Value to see what's been spent because they are both the currency data type.

Adding Custom Columns and Writing Formulas in Power Query

You might be thinking, "But Oz, what if I need to add a number to a date to calculate deadlines?"

Answer: You'll need to write a formula using Date.AddDays.

To illustrate that, let's take a brief detour from the gift card data and use a simpler dataset. Starting with this data:

	Project	Start	Days to Complete
1	Purple	5 May 2022	90
2	Silver	26 Aug 2022	15
3	Violet	3 Sep 2022	21

Add Column | Custom Column.

This dialog box pops up:

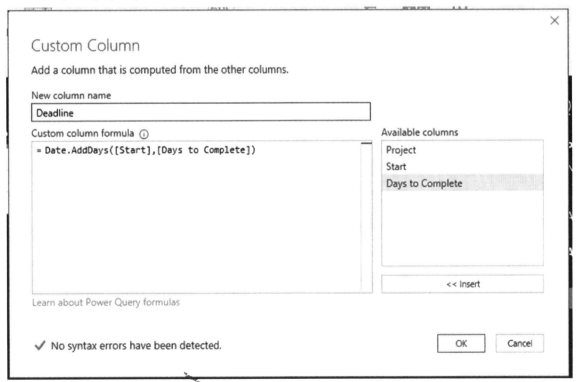

Set New Column Name to Deadline.

Specify the syntax Date.AddDays(*the date you want to add, the value you want to add*).

Click OK.

And here's the result (after I changed the data type from ABC123 to a date):

Data types also impact the options for filtering. In this example, maybe you want to filter for donations ≥100. With text and numbers in the Donations column, the options for filtering are Equals or Does Not Equal.

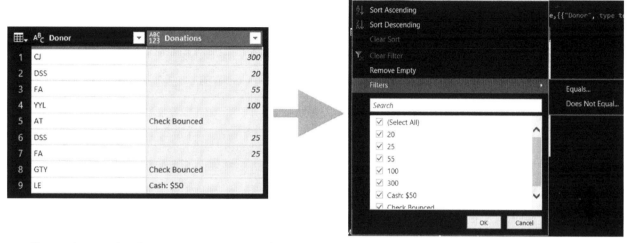

But if you change the data type to currency, the text values will error out, and your filter options will show as number filters, letting you filter by Equals, Does not Equal, Greater Than, Between, etc.

Sorting in Power Query

Sorting in Power Query doesn't include an interface like you get in native Excel. Instead, you have to know this:

If you want to sort by multiple levels, you must do it in the order that you want the sorting to happen.

In this example, you're going to sort by count, then by color, and then by size. Start by highlighting the Count column, then: Home | Sort | Z to A to sort descending.

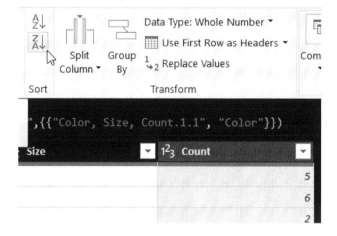

And then sort the Color column, ascending, and the Size column, ascending. Notice the result in the image below.

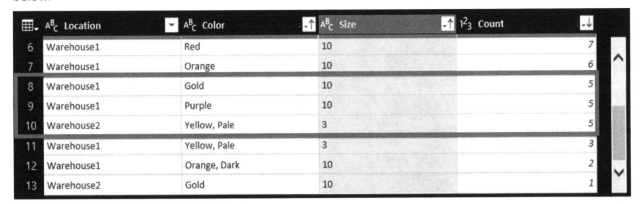

	ABC Location	ABC Color	ABC Size	123 Count
6	Warehouse1	Red	10	7
7	Warehouse1	Orange	10	6
8	Warehouse1	Gold	10	5
9	Warehouse1	Purple	10	5
10	Warehouse2	Yellow, Pale	3	5
11	Warehouse1	Yellow, Pale	3	3
12	Warehouse1	Orange, Dark	10	2
13	Warehouse2	Gold	10	1

In rows 8, 9, and 10, the count is 5, and the colors are sorted as requested. Also notice the arrows in the Color, Size, and Count columns. These show that the columns are sorted. There's no arrow in the Location column because it's not sorted.

The Query Settings Pane

As you work in Power Query, the steps are being recorded. Here are all of the steps that were used in the previous example where colors, sizes, and counts were split, and then the data was sorted:

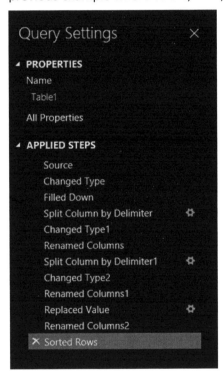

If you want to review an intermediate step, click on it. In the image below, the Filled Down step is selected, and that's the step shown in the editor.

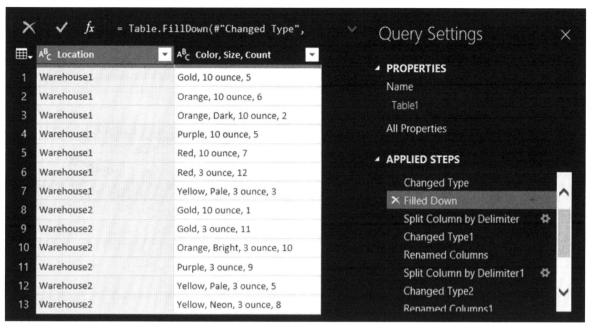

Something else that's sexy about Power Query is the code that's generated in the background. You can see some of it in the formula bar above the data. Use View | Formula Bar to display the formula bar.

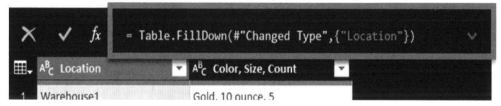

To see all of the code: View | Advanced Editor.

The Advanced Editor opens, and you can see it all. You've got to admit that this is some hot stuff! You didn't have to write that code manually, but it automates the work when your data changes. You just have to refresh. Also, at advanced levels, you can write your own code.

Now, click Cancel to get out of here.

To load the data back into native Excel: File | Close & Load.

The data is on an Excel worksheet, ready for whatever you need. Notice that the Queries & Connections pane is showing any queries that are in the workbook. I've renamed the query Inventory. To do that, hover over the query name (which defaulted to Table1 because Table1 is the name of the table on the worksheet) | right-click | Rename.

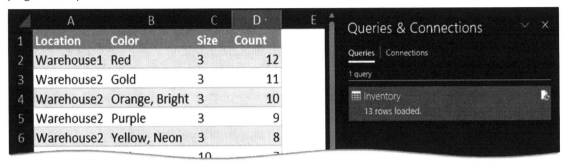

Adding More Source Data

Back on Sheet1, notice that the original data is now in a table. Power Query automatically puts the data in a table if it wasn't already in one.

In rows 18:21, there's more data that needs to be added. Highlight it and drag it into the table, making sure the new data is absorbed into the table.

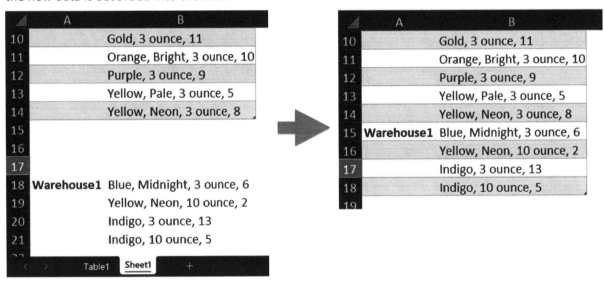

It's said that "the proof is in the pudding." Actually, the proof is in the tasting. Previously, I've said that Power Query automates tasks. Are you ready for a taste? Grab a spoon ...

Go back to the Table1 sheet. Then: Data | Queries & Connections | Refresh All.

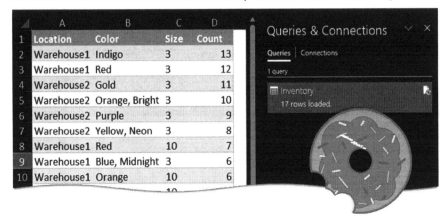

Doesn't that taste delicious?

- The new data has been split and sorted.
- The column headers were renamed.
- Indigo was part of the data that was just added. It's the first entry because of the way the data was sorted in Power Query.
- In the Queries & Connections pane, the Inventory query shows that 17 rows of data were loaded onto the worksheet. Before the new data was added, there were only 13 rows.

Unpivoting and Filtering

Unpivot is the first feature that I ever used in Power Query. A client sent me some data that looked like a Pivot Table—similar to the image below:

	Instructor	Quarter	Meals	Hotel	General Expenses
1	Instructor	Quarter	Meals	Hotel	General Expenses
2	Mike	Q1	$293.93	$455.60	$87.12
3	Siobhan	Q1	$217.78	$401.71	$0.00
4	Addie	Q2	$251.03	$267.33	$81.81
5	Elias	Q2	$206.16	$243.06	$0.00
6	Mike	Q2	$218.15	$532.69	$50.00
7	Siobhan	Q2	$180.66	$486.92	$102.68
8	Siobhan	Q2	$139.85	$209.66	$333.22
9	Addie	Q3	$227.28	$257.66	$24.99
10	Brook	Q3	$105.56	$409.67	$64.24
11	Elias	Q3	$190.59	$262.17	$0.00
12	Elias	Q3	$88.10	$190.96	$37.20
13	Siobhan	Q3	$143.06	$606.31	$0.00
14	Addie	Q4	$98.51	$183.14	$0.00
15	Elias	Q4	$104.23	$361.55	$161.12
16	Siobhan	Q4	$122.90	$511.33	$9.85

Column headers across the top, row headers along the side, and values in B2:E16. What if the goal is to isolate all values that are ≥$300, regardless of whether they're under meals, hotel, or general expenses?

I thought I was going to have to look up MrExcel's video on unwinding a Pivot Table to get columns C, D, and E into a single column and then sort and filter for the desired values.

And then I remembered a video I had seen on unpivoting data. The unpivot feature that I'm about to show you saved me at least 20 minutes.

Time to flatten this data and do some unpivoting.

Your mission: Isolate all values in columns C:E that are ≥$300.

The information is all here, but gee whiz! This report was designed for someone who wanted to see, for example, that Siobhan submitted two different expense reports for Q2, and one of them included $139.85 for meals.

This would be easier if the Meals, Hotel, and General Expenses headers were in a single column, and the dollar amounts were in their own column, as shown below:

	Instructor	Quarter	Category	Exp Amt
1	Instructor	Quarter	Category	Exp Amt
2	Siobhan	Q3	Hotel	606.31
3	Mike	Q2	Hotel	532.69
4	Siobhan	Q4	Hotel	511.33

In this format, you could sort descending and remove any values that are less than 300. Or, you could filter out all values that are less than 300. Let's unpivot!

Place the cursor anywhere inside the dataset. Then: Data | Get & Transform | From Sheet.

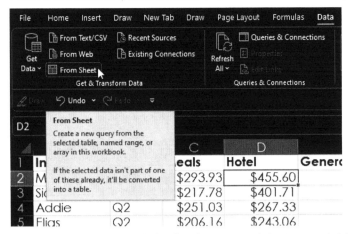

The marching ants highlight the dataset, and the Create Table dialog box asks if the data has headers. Click OK.

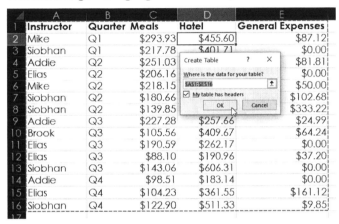

And here's the data inside the Power Query editor:

Note: The image above shows the Instructor and Quarter columns highlighted. Initially, the Instructor column was highlighted, by default. I held down the Ctrl key and then selected the Quarter column. Why? **Because of the way the data is set up, it's important to keep the quarters and instructor names on the same row with the data after its unpivoted**.

Hover the mouse over either the Instructor or Quarter column | right-click | Unpivot Other Columns.

BLAM! ☀ Unpivoted!

Notice in the lower left, Power Query says there are now 45 rows, not just the 15 in the source data.

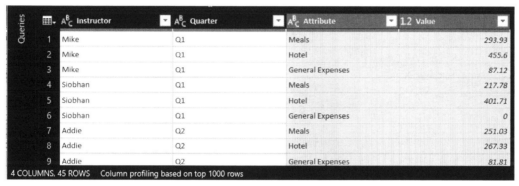

The next image shows that I renamed the Attribute and Value columns Category and Exp Amt, respectively. I sorted the Exp Amt column by highlighting the Exp Amt column | Home | Sort Descending.

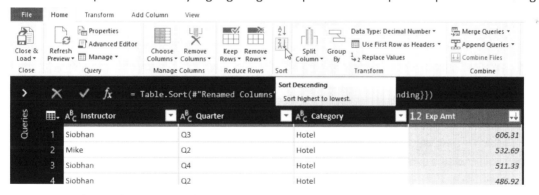

Next step: Filter to keep values that are ≥300.

Right-click the Exp Amt column header | Greater Than Or Equal To.

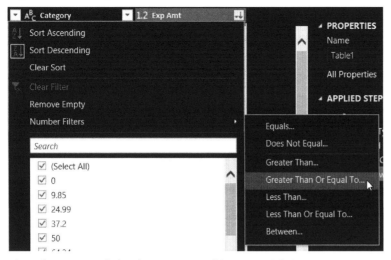

The Filter Rows dialog box appears | input 300 | OK.

And there it is! The nine rows that are of interest.

The next step is to get the data back onto an Excel worksheet: Home | Close & Load. Then you can click the upper portion of the Close & Load icon to automatically send the results to a brand new worksheet or click the lower portion and expand the options and choose Close & Load. The Close & Load To option will be used later in this chapter.

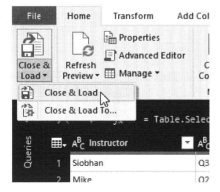

The data is on a new worksheet, ready for anything you need to do with the data. On the right side, you see the Queries & Connections pane showing nine rows were loaded.

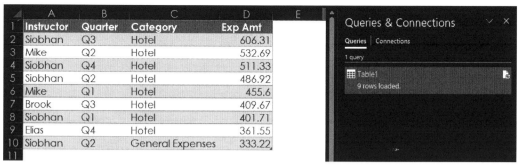

Blanks, Nulls, and Zeros: They Aren't the Same in Power Query

In the dataset shown below, we have instructors and the number of students they taught in two classes. The goal is to use Power Query to add the Class1 and Class2 columns for a total for each instructor.

For Dustin, both classes have empty cells. Maybe the data hasn't come in yet, or these are supposed to be 0s. Nora taught 22 students in Class1, and there's a blank for Class2.

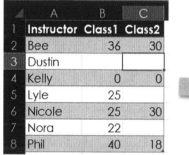 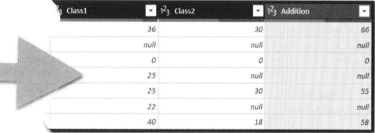

In Power Query, I added the columns together. Here's how: Highlight the Class1 column then hold down the Ctrl key and highlight the Class2 column. Then: Add Column | From Number | Standard | Add.

The result is what you see on the right in the Addition column. Notice:

- In the Class1 and Class2 columns, cells that were originally empty have been filled in with *null*.
- Bee's numbers totaled 66.
- Dustin's nulls resulted in a null.
- Where a null was added to a number (Lyle and Nora), the result is a null.

In these situations, you have to know your data. If the nulls are actually 0s, use Replace Values to change the nulls to 0s. If the nulls represent "data hasn't been submitted yet," you can leave everything as is and update as the data comes in; or, separate completed entries from incomplete entries and work with the data that's complete.

Joins and Merges in Power Query

Inner join, left anti-join … inside of what? Anti what? What do they mean, and what do they do?

Thanks to my friend and fellow Excel MVP Ken Puls for his blog post that helped me understand Power Query's six merges/joins. They can be tough to understand, but once you understand them, they are invaluable.

Why would you want to know about these joins? If you have to compare datasets or combine them or even segment datasets, you'll need to use a join.

Let's say you have an apartment building and two sets of data. In the image below, columns A:C have data about the owners of each unit. Columns F:H contain resident data.

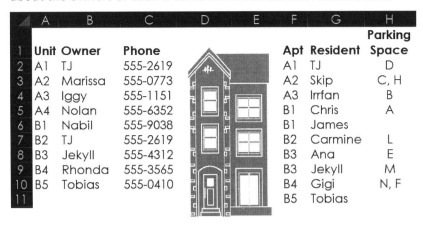

	Unit	Owner	Phone		Apt	Resident	Parking Space
1							
2	A1	TJ	555-2619		A1	TJ	D
3	A2	Marissa	555-0773		A2	Skip	C, H
4	A3	Iggy	555-1151		A3	Irrfan	B
5	A4	Nolan	555-6352		B1	Chris	A
6	B1	Nabil	555-9038		B1	James	
7	B2	TJ	555-2619		B2	Carmine	L
8	B3	Jekyll	555-4312		B3	Ana	E
9	B4	Rhonda	555-3565		B3	Jekyll	M
10	B5	Tobias	555-0410		B4	Gigi	N, F
11					B5	Tobias	

Some things to observe about the data:

- TJ owns two units (A1, B2) and lives in A1.
- Marissa owns A2, but Skip is the resident.
- Unit B3 lists two residents: Ana and Jekyll.
- Nolan owns A4, but no one lives there.
- The Unit and Apt columns are the same thing, just different header names.

To help understand the joins and why use them, here are some details that could be found using joins:

- For all of the residents, retrieve and match the phone numbers from the owner dataset.
- List **only** the people who are both an owner and a resident.
- Create a single list of **all** residents **and** owners and make matches where there are matches to be made.
- Match the owners and the parking spaces assigned to the units.

Overview of the Six Joins

There are six joins/merges in Power Query:

- Left outer join
- Right outer join
- Inner join
- Full outer join
- Left anti join
- Right anti join

I've simplified the data in the previous example in order to focus on each type of join. In these two lists, Owners and Residents, you can see that some people are on both lists, and some are on one but not the other.

OWNERS
Iggy
Jekyll
Marissa
Nabil
TJ
Tobias

RESIDENTS
Chris
Irrfan
Jekyll
Skip
TJ
Tobias

In this Venn diagram, it's easier to see who fits in which category. **Notice that there's a left side and a right side.**

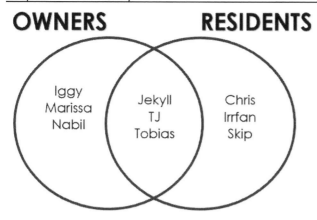

Let's walk through the six joins, what they do, and possible scenarios.

Left Outer Join

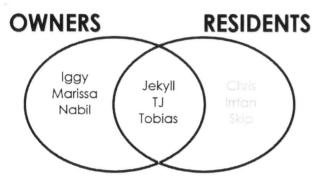

Returns everyone on the left side—all of the owners—whether there is a match on the right side or not.

Possible case: You need to contact all of the owners about purchasing a new elevator.

Right Outer Join

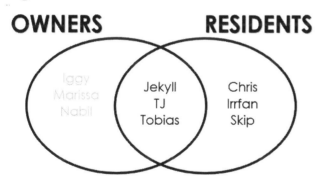

Returns everyone on the right side—the residents—whether there's a match on the left side or not.

Possible case: You need to contact all residents about moving their cars next week so the parking lot can be cleaned.

Inner Join

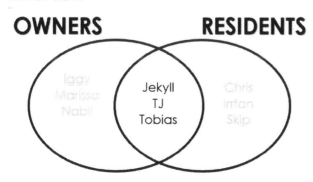

Returns only the people who are in both datasets.

Possible case: You need to notify people who own and reside in the building of special benefits (e.g., free storage unit, free parking).

Left Anti Join

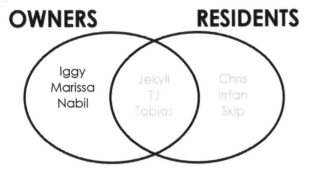

Returns the people who are only on the left side—owners who are not also residents.

Possible case: You need to notify these owners about changes to the property that they aren't aware of because they aren't around to see the changes.

Right Anti Join

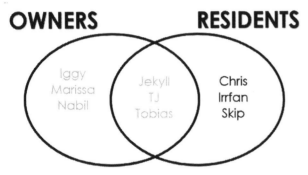

Returns people who are only on the right side: the residents who are not also owners.

Possible case: You need to notify renters of changes in the rental agreement.

Full Outer Join

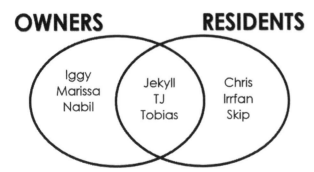

Returns everyone, and where there are matches, those matches will be made.

Possible case: The Owners dataset has detailed information about the units, and the Residents dataset has contact information. You want to create one big list and have Power Query make matches where there are matches.

Understanding the Merge Interface: Top/Bottom Not Left/Right

Here's the part that makes the joins especially hard to understand. In the Merge interface, **there is no left or right; there's a top and a bottom**. The top is the left side, and the bottom is the right side. Turn the Venn diagram clockwise 90°, and then you can think of, say, a left anti join as a "top anti join."

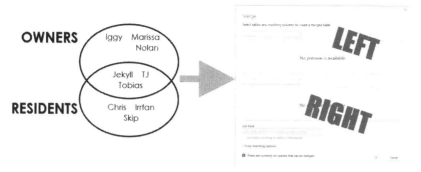

IMPORTANT! You choose which of your data to assign to the left and right sides. In the image below, on the worksheets, the owners are on the left, and the residents are on the right. In the Merge interface, the residents are on the top—i.e., the left side of the join. The join kind is left outer. Can you see what the result will be?

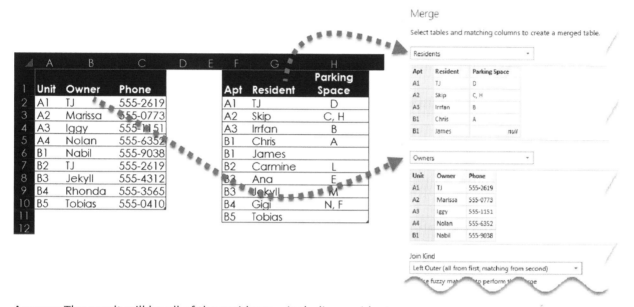

Answer: The result will be all of the residents—including resident-owners.

Let's Join!

The image below shows the Residents dataset, and in the Query Settings pane, you can see the query has been named Residents. On the far left you can see the queries that have been created: Owners and Residents.

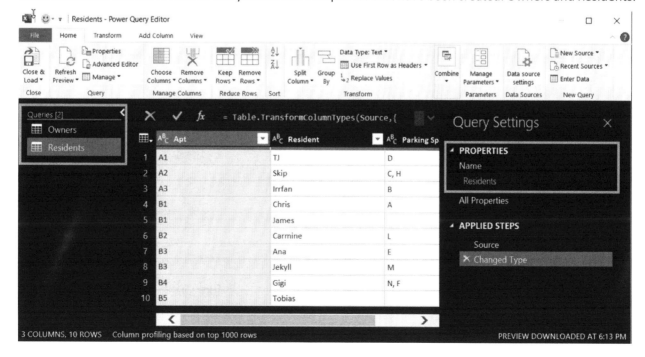

In the image below, on the Queries & Connections pane, the queries are listed as *Connection only*. This basically reduces clutter in the workbook. In this situation, the queries are intermediate steps that are needed in order to complete a merge. Thus, loading the queries onto a worksheet would just take up space.

Now that the queries are created, let's generate a list of the owners who are also residents.

To start the merge: Data | Get Data | Combine Queries | Merge.

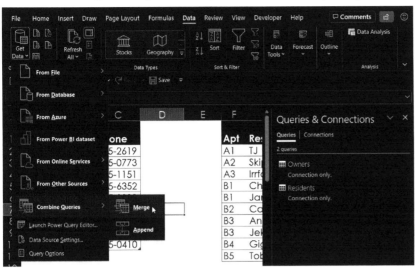

The Merge dialog appears. I've selected the Owners query to be the left side of the query (the top) and the Residents query for the right side (the bottom).

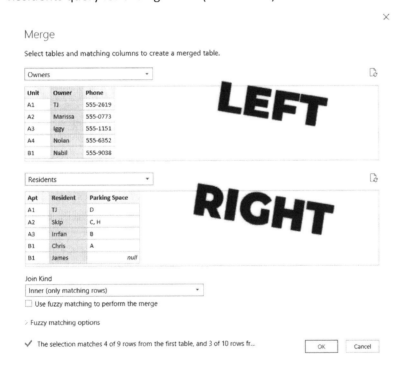

The Owner and Residents columns are highlighted because that's what we want to match.

> **Note:** For joins, the headers don't need to be identical because the interface requires the user to be explicit about what to match. This is why Owner and Residents can be used to create the merge. This is different from the Append feature (as you'll see later), which does require headers to be identical.

The join kind is inner since the objective to list the people who are in both datasets. Click OK.

Inside the Power Query editor, **the left side of the merge (the Owners query) is expanded**, showing the Unit, Owner, and Phone columns. **The right side is the collapsed query named Residents** (as signified by the diverging arrows).

To expand the right side, click on the arrows in the Residents column. The dialog box shown below will appear. This is helpful because sometimes there are columns that aren't needed in the result. In the current scenario, you could untick Resident since the inner join only shows people who are on both lists; i.e., the Owner and Resident columns will be the same. However, to prove that this works, I'm leaving Resident ticked.

The result:

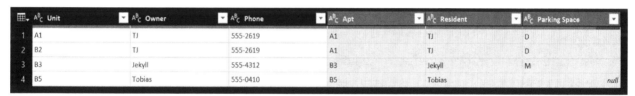

Check it out!

- TJ, Jekyll, and Tobias are the residents who also own.
- Tobias lives in and owns unit B5 and doesn't have a parking space.
- Rows 1 and 2 are interesting. The inner join matched both of the units that TJ owns and duplicated the resident side of the data.

Next steps:

1. Hover your mouse over the Resident header | right-click | Remove.

2. Close & Load.

And here's the data on a new worksheet:

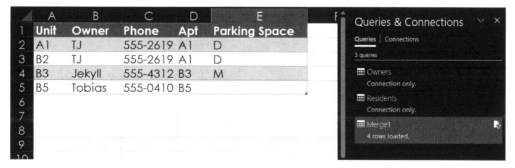

Notice that the Merge1 query (the one that was just created) is in the Queries & Connections pane, showing four rows loaded. If you want to rename the query to something useful like Resident-Owners: Hover over the Merge1 query | right-click | Rename | rename it to whatever you want.

Outer Join vs. XLOOKUP (or VLOOKUP)

An outer join can be thought of as an XLOOKUP or VLOOKUP because these functions retrieve matching data from one set to another. What XLOOKUP or VLOOKUP won't do is return multiple results. A Power Query join will match data no matter how many results there are.

In this dataset, units B1 and B3 have more than one resident. After completing the outer join, both Chris and James have been matched with unit B1, and Jekyll and Ana have been matched with unit B3.

	Unit	Owner	Resident	Parking Space
1	A1	TJ	TJ	D
2	A2	Marissa	Skip	C, H
3	A3	Iggy	Irrfan	B
4	A4	Nolan	null	null	null
5	B1	Nabil	Chris	A
6	B1	Nabil	James	null
7	B2	TJ	Carmine	L
8	B3	Jekyll	Ana	E
9	B3	Jekyll	Jekyll	M
10	B4	Rhonda	Gigi	N, F
11	B5	Tobias	Tobias	null

🐉 Know Your Data

Skirmish

You have just gotten a look at another reason why an intimate understanding of your data is vital. If you know that your data has 1:1 matches, an XLOOKUP or VLOOKUP would be fine. But if you know there's a possibility for multiple matches, you need to execute a join in Power Query.

Also notice that the joins bring together the entire datasets. If you need to retrieve the data from multiple columns, you'll need multiple XLOOKUPs if you don't use Power Query.

Anti Joins

One way to think about anti joins: What's over here that's **not** over there?

In one of my workshops, someone mentioned that he regularly uses anti joins to find out which checks have been sent out and still haven't been cashed. Let's use that as an example for an anti join.

In this data, notice in the Merge interface that ChecksCashed is on the left side (the top) of the join, and ChecksSent is on the right (bottom).

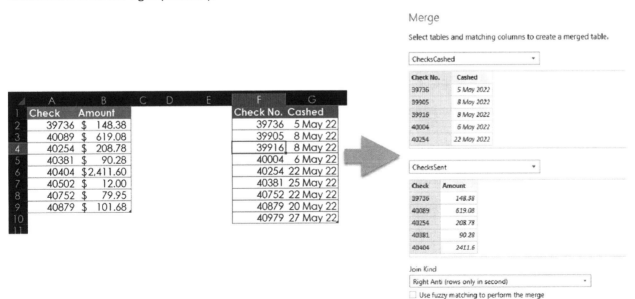

Inside the Power Query editor, the left side is expanded, and the right side is collapsed. Why does it make sense that the right side shows *null*?

Answer: The anti join is isolating the checks that have been sent but **not** cashed.

Before expanding the right side, you can get rid of the Check No. and Cashed columns: Highlight the ChecksSent column | right-click | Remove Other Columns.

Then, expand by clicking the outward-facing arrows and unselect Use Original Column Name as Prefix. Click OK.

Here are the three checks that still haven't been cashed, and their amounts.

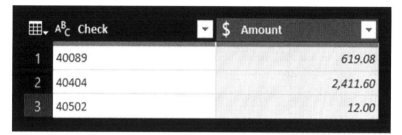

Notice that I've changed the Check column's data type to text (ABC) and the Amount column's data type to currency ($).

> **Note:** I'm not going to go through all six types of joins in this chapter. I invite you to play with them in the exercise files. Also, make up your own datasets and think about why you'd use a specific join and what you expect the results to be.

Merging with Multiple Criteria

What happens if you need to merge by multiple criteria? Let's check that out.

The image below shows two datasets from two different stores. For this purpose, the merge needs to consider three criteria to ensure that, for example, salmon-colored pants from Too Fancy are matched only with salmon-colored pants from Too Fancy—not matched with salmon-colored pants from Dandies.

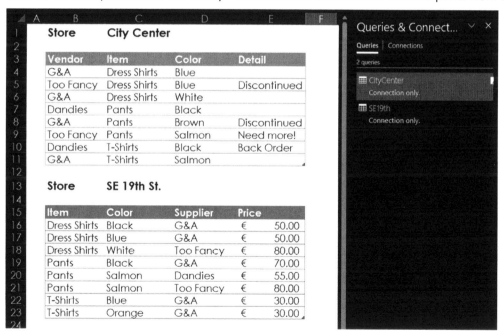

Here's how it's done.

The CityCenter and SE19th queries have already been created. To merge them: Data | Get Data | Combine Queries | Merge.

When the Merge interface appears, select your first criteria: Vendor and Supplier. Hold down the Ctrl key and select the next criteria: Item and Item. While still holding Ctrl, select the final criteria: Color and Color.

Note: The columns are not in the same order for the two queries (e.g., Item is the second column for City Center, but it's the first column for SE 19th St.). That's fine. The column orders are not important.

Important! Notice the small numbers in the headers that are being matched. Vendor and Supplier both have a 1 next to them, showing that they are being matched, Item and Item both have a 2, and Color and Color have a 3. The number order doesn't matter; these numbers just help you see what's being matched with what.

Select Full Outer as the join kind and click OK.

After expanding the SE19th table in the Power Query editor, here's the result:

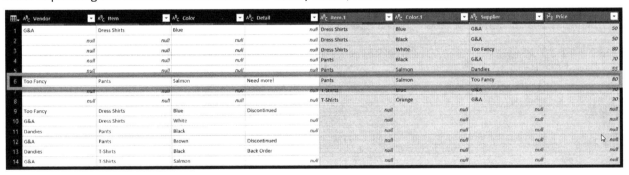

Where there's a match, a match was made. For example, in row 6, salmon-colored pants from Too Fancy are showing as Need more! and they cost €80.

Appending (aka Stacking Stuff Up)

The joins in Power Query are great for matches and mismatches. But how about just plain getting datasets stacked up in one place? Sometimes that's all you need—nothing fancy.

No. Not fancy, but without Power Query, this is task is messy if the stacking involves cutting and pasting or writing wild formulas.

The image below shows three different datasets on three different worksheets, each representing a different apartment building:

- On the left, the circles show the Marquette sheet, and the dataset is in a table named MarquettePark.
- In the center are the Vargas worksheet and a table named VargasPlace.
- On the right are the Bucktown sheet and the Bucktown table.

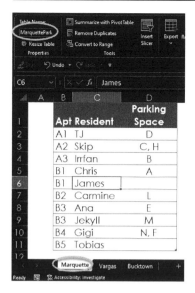
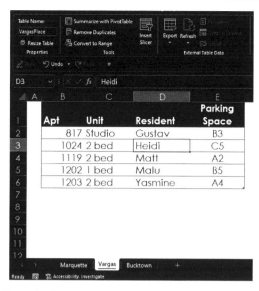
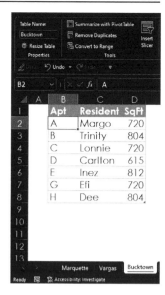

It would be nice to get the data all stacked in one dataset.

What's the first step?

Answer: Stop and examine the data. That's always the first step. Remember: **Don't just dive in.**

Observations:

- All the tables have columns for Apt and Resident, but that's all they have in common.
    - VargasPlace and MarquettePark have a Parking Space column.
    - Bucktown has a column for square footage (SqFt).
    - VargasPlace has a Unit column.
- VargasPlace has a Unit column between the Apt and Resident columns. The other datasets have Apt and Resident next to each other.

Here again, it's necessary to slow down because appending is a finicky process. Time for some Q&A

What if column headers don't have the same names? Does that matter?

YES! That does matter. Unlike with joins, with appends, the user doesn't manually set what gets matched with what. The Append feature needs everything to be exact. Even in the image at right, Apt and Apt. will not be appended because one has a period.

Name	Apt
Kat	1501
Ty	628

Name	Apt.
Moe	1512

What if the columns aren't in the same order?

That depends. As long as the columns are named the same thing, the Append feature will line the columns up. The image below represents column headers from four different datasets. Append will match them all up because they're consistent. The order doesn't matter.

Name	Apt	Lease Length	Move-in Date
Apt	Name	Move-in Date	Lease Length
Name	Apt	Move-in Date	Lease Length
Apt	Lease Length	Name	Move-in Date

As you'll see later, the column order matters only if you have a preferred order. Let's say the third option above is preferred. Then that's the query that needs to be on top when the Append action kicks off.

How about a dataset that has a column that the other datasets don't have—e.g., five datasets all have City, Country, and Population, but one of the five has a column for Official Language(s)?

Power Query will make an entire column for the oddball column. You'll soon see a similar example.

Okay! Time for some Append action!

The image below shows that the three queries MarquettePark, VargasPlace, and Bucktown are created and loaded as connection-only queries. To start stacking stuff up: Data | Get Data | Combine Queries | Append.

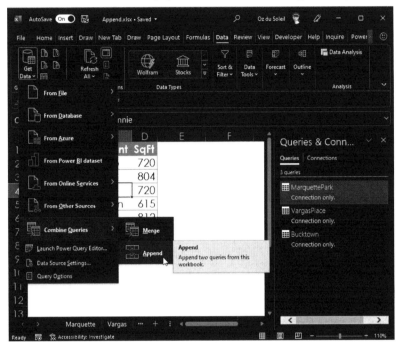

And here is the Append interface.

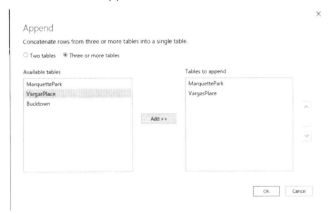

I selected Three or More Tables, then I highlighted MarquettePark and clicked Add, then highlighted VargasPlace and clicked Add.

Now, a decision needs to be made. Based on the headers on the three datasets, is there a preferred order?

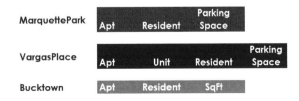

Let's pick the VargasPlace order.

Add Bucktown to the *Tables to Append* window.

Highlight VargasPlace and click the up arrow until VargasPlace is at the top.

Click OK. Now, what are we looking at in the image below?

- All three datasets are stacked up! *BRAVO!* 🔥🔥🔥
- The Apt and Resident columns are lined up.
- Bucktown is the only dataset with a SqFt column, and Power Query made an entire column for it. Similarly, there's a Unit column because it's in the Bucktown dataset.

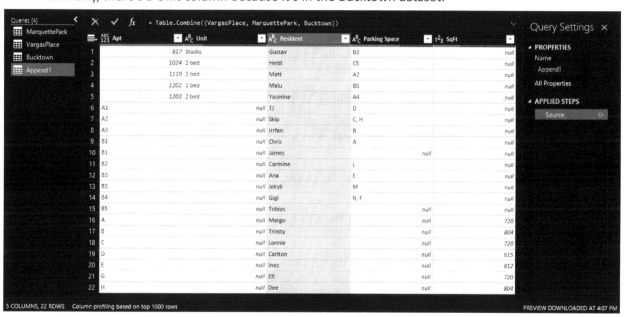

Importing from a File or from a Folder

The import features in Power Query are mind-blowing because they ended one of the most terrifying fights in the battle for useful data: bringing data into Excel and compiling it in one place.

Imagine having a workbook named Counties.xlsx with 25 sheets that you'd like stacked in one place.

Power Query makes this as simple as opening a new Excel file, navigating to import Counties.xlsx, and making a few clicks. Then all 25 pages will be right there!

Importing from a File

You must **pay close attention** as I go through this because there are some quirky details along the way. However, those quirks are miniscule compared to the olden days of copying and pasting or writing wild formulas to get data consolidated.

Let's have a look.

In the image below, there are four worksheets representing data for Thillium County, Boot County, Yasmine County, and Trentti County.

It'd be so great if this data were on a single sheet.

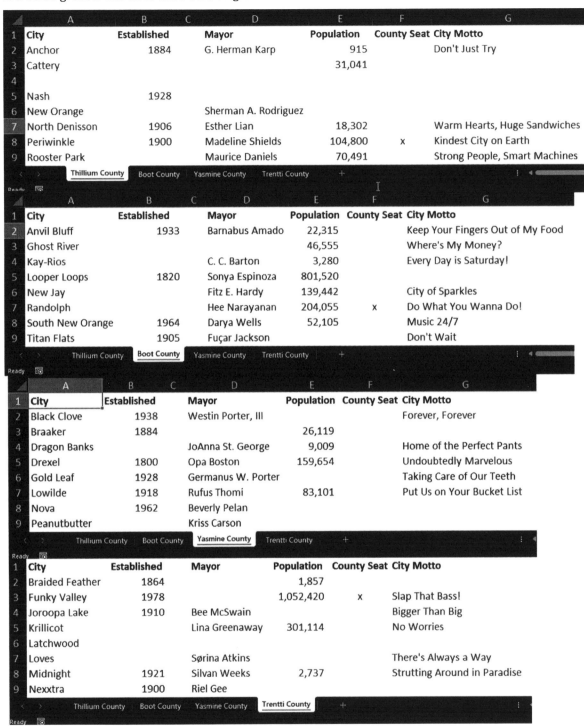

Notes about this data:

- Row 4 on the Thillium County sheet is blank.
- Columns A:G are the same for all four counties and in the same order.
- Column C is blank in all of the sheets.

Important!

- Unlike Append, Import from Workbook imports the repeated headers. You'll have to clean those out after the import.

- Unlike the Append feature, Import from Workbook does not honor column headers. Therefore, if the columns aren't in the same order, you have several options:
  - Arrange the columns in the individual source files.
  - Anticipate rearranging them in Power Query.
  - Import the files that are identical in separate steps, get them cleaned up, and then append. For example, if Boot, Yasmine, and Thillium are the same but Trentti has Established and Mayor reversed, import the first three counties; then import Trentti; then append the two queries.

Let's get this county data imported!

In a new workbook: Data | Get Data | From File | From Workbook.

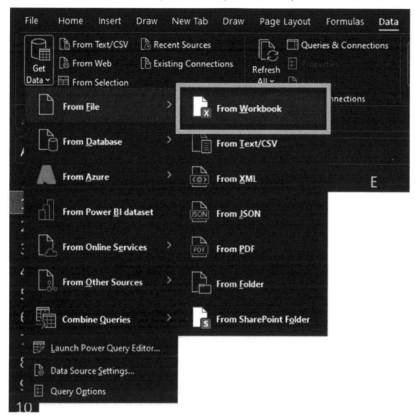

Navigate to the file.

The next image shows the Navigator. Here, I've selected the Counties folder so that all of the sheets in Counties.xlsx will be imported. In other situations, you could select just one sheet or use the Select Multiple Items option if you only need to import two or three sheets.

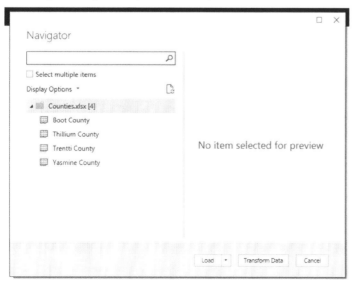

From here: Transform Data | OK.

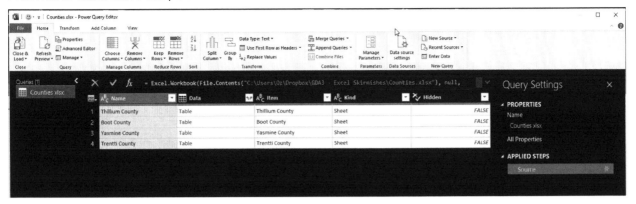

Notice:

- The sheets are in the order in which they appear in the Counties workbook.
- Under Applied Steps, Source is highlighted. While that's highlighted, in the formula bar you can see the file path to the Counties.xlsx file.
- The Name column lists the names of the worksheets.
- The Data column is collapsed—as denoted by the outward-facing arrows. This is where the sheet contents are. It's good that the data is collapsed because it gives you a chance to see if all of the sheets have been imported, and you can filter out any that you don't want.
- The columns Item and Kind go together. In row 1, Power Query is telling you that there's a sheet named Thillium County.
- There is nothing hidden.

With the Name column highlighted, hold down the Ctrl key and select the Data column | right-click | Remove Other Columns.

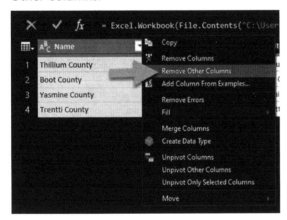

> **Note:** For this exercise, keep the Name column so that you always know what city is connected to what sheet/county. Even if you don't care about the county—maybe you just need the city data—it's helpful to know which sheet to refer to if you need to investigate something peculiar or make a change.

You'll be left with the Name and Data columns, and this is the exciting part. You're about to unfurl the splendor!

Click the outward-facing arrows in the Data column. The dropdown list will appear. Untick the box Use Original Column Name as Prefix.

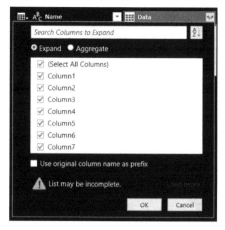

Click OK.

HOLY MOLY! There's the data! ☺

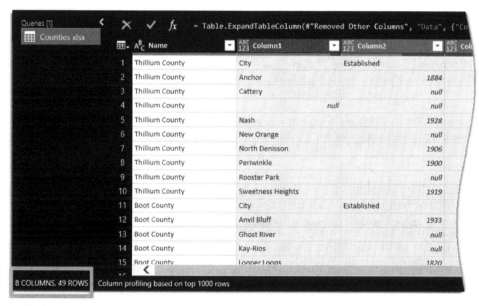

In the lower left of the image, you see that 8 columns and 49 rows have been imported. Everything is here!

CELEBRATION TIME!

If this were 25 worksheets—instead of 4—that needed to be appended, you'd have already saved a lot of time and avoided anguish. But things are about to get tricky as we go through and clean this data. **Pay very close attention to what I'm about to describe about the column headers.**

As I mentioned earlier, Power Query did import the repeated headers. You can see that in rows 1 and 11. City and Established are in Column1 and Column2, respectively. And that's the same for the other columns: Mayor, Population, County Seat, and City Motto.

💣💣 If you're following along with the file open, **DO NOT** perform this next step. 💣💣

To get rid of the Column1 through Column7 headers and replace them with the City through City Motto headers, one move is to use the feature Use First Row as Headers.

One major frustration with Power Query, however, is that it hard codes values in its recorded steps.

Don't worry about the code in this next image. I just want you to see that Thillium County, City, Established, etc. are hard coded.

```
let
    Source = Excel.Workbook(File.Contents("C:\Users\Oz\Dropbox\GDA3 - Excel
        Skirmishes\Counties.xlsx"), null, true),
    #"Removed Other Columns" = Table.SelectColumns(Source,{"Name", "Data"}),
    #"Expanded Data" = Table.ExpandTableColumn(#"Removed Other Columns", "Data", {"Column1",
        "Column2", "Column3", "Column4", "Column5", "Column6", "Column7"}, {"Column1", "Column2",
        "Column3", "Column4", "Column5", "Column6", "Column7"}),

    #"Changed Type" = Table.TransformColumnTypes(#"Promoted Headers",{{"Thillium County", type
        text}, {"City", type text}, {"Established", type any}, {"Column4", type any}, {"Mayor",
                                                                                   xt}
    })
in
    #"Changed Type"
```

This isn't a problem for the columns that will always be the same or if this is a one-time task. However, if the Thillium County sheet is later removed or renamed or another sheet is added, there will be problems!

In this image, Antelope County has been added in front of Thillium County.

When you refresh the query, you'll get an error message saying that Thillium County could not be found.

Here is a solution: Add a custom column so that File Name is always in row 1, column 1.

Adding a Conditional Column

To add the custom column: Add Column | Conditional Column.

Configure the Add Conditional Column dialog as shown below.

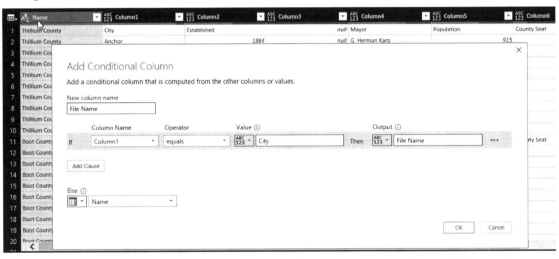

The image is configured so that whenever City is in Column1, your new column will show File Name. Otherwise, the new column will duplicate the value in the Name column.

Click OK.

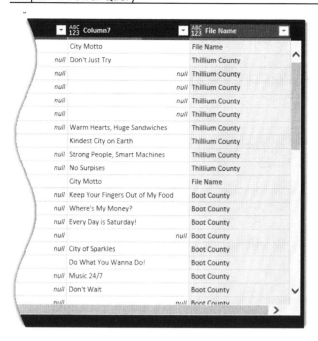

The image above shows the File Name column has been added after the last column in the dataset. Move it back to the beginning this way: Right-click the File Name column | Move | To Beginning.

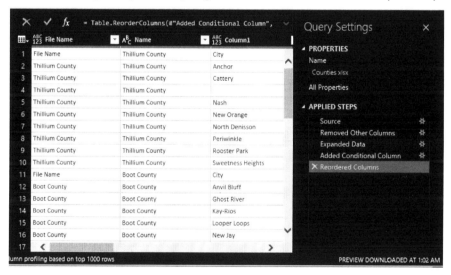

The File Name and Name columns are side-by-side.

Now the clean-up can begin!

Select the Name column | right-click the Name header | Remove.

Next, column3 reflects that blank column that all of the original worksheets have. Hover your mouse over it and select Remove.

Next, get the proper headers into position: Home | Use First Row as Headers.

Looking good so far!

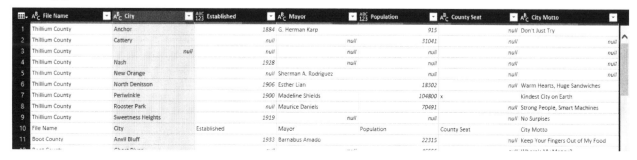

Now, get rid of the repeated headers. You can use any of the columns for this next step. I'll open the dropdown in the County Seat header and untick County Seat.

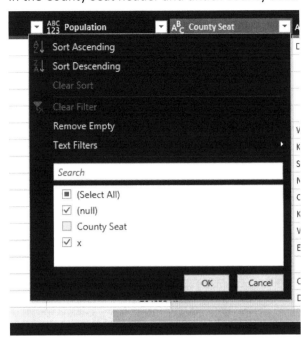

Click OK.

One more problem: Some of the worksheets had blank rows. To clear them, you have to be very careful.

Where there is no data, Power Query shows a *null* value. Therefore, you have to know your data and think about how you can be precise in the rows that get deleted. In this situation, you will always have a city name even if you don't have any other details. So ...

Open the dropdown next to City and untick null.

Click OK.

The data is all in one place. It's all cleaned up. It's ready to load onto a worksheet in Excel. But first, sort the City column, ascending: Select the City column | Home | Sort | Sort A to Z.

Finally: Home | Close & Load.

There is the data! Shout "Amen!"

All of the data is here! The Queries & Connections pane shows that 40 rows have been loaded.

SUCCESS!

Now the data can be used for Pivot Tables. You can get a tally of how much data is missing. Most importantly:

- The data from all four sheets is in one place.
- If any data is added, removed, or updated in Counties.xlsx, all you have to do is save the changes in that file. Then, in this file: Data | Refresh All.

A Note About Changing File Paths and Names

A final warning: If you anticipate changes being made to the source data (Counties.xlsx), the source file and the file that you imported the data into need to stay where they are and keep their original names because of the file path that's been recorded in the query. The files **do not** need to be in the same folder. You can have the source file on your C: drive inside a folder named City Analysis and have the import file on your Desktop. But once that file path has been established, try not to move them.

If you have to move one or both of the files or rename a file or folder in the file path:

1. Go into the query.
2. Under Applied Steps, click the gear next to Source.
3. In the Excel Workbook dialog, click Browse.
4. Navigate to the source file.
5. Click OK.

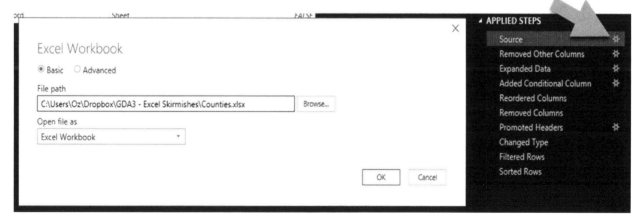

Alternatively, once the Excel Workbook dialog is open, you can type in the changes and skip the navigation. That will establish a new file path, and the rest of the steps in the query will be fine.

Importing from a Folder

In this example, the county data has arrived in separate files. You can set up a dedicated folder, as shown in the image below. All of the files are in a folder named County Data.

Also notice that there's a picture of a monorail in the folder.

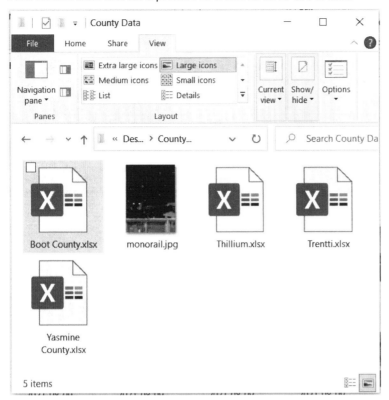

To import the files into Power Query: Data | Get & Transform | Get Data | From Folder.

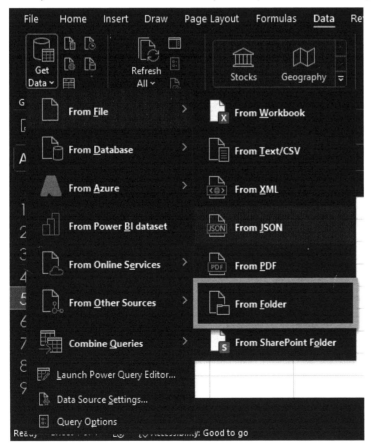

Navigate to the folder and click on the folder. DO NOT double-click the folder because it's the contents of the folder that you want.

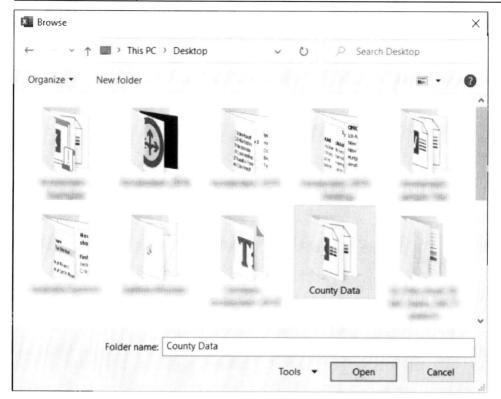

Click Open.

You'll get the dialog box shown below, which lists the files in the folder.

Click Transform Data.

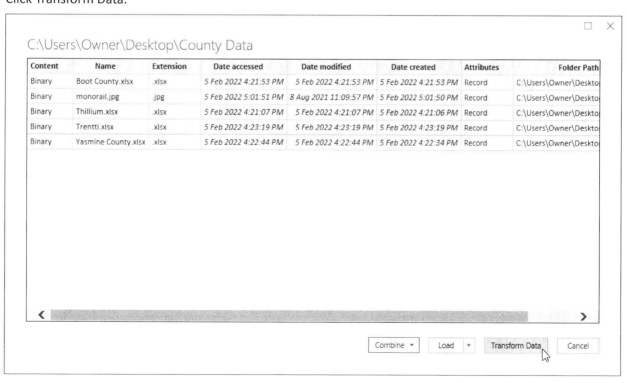

And here are the files!

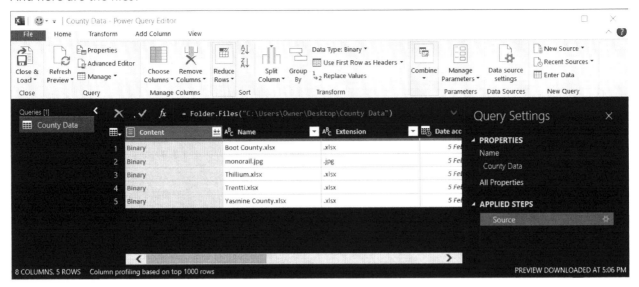

The available columns are:

Content	Name	Extension	Date Accessed	Date Modified	Date Created	Attributes	Folder Path

The data is collapsed in the Content column. Sometimes the other columns will be important to you. Maybe you want to show the Date Modified column in your final report.

In this case, the Extension column is important for filtering out the .jpg file. Click the arrow next to the Extension header and untick the .jpg entry.

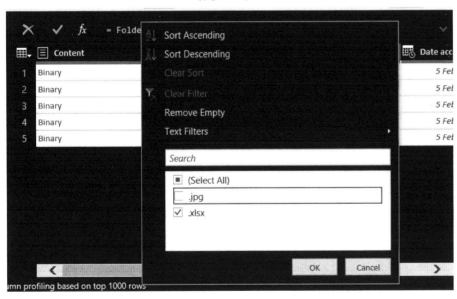

Click OK.

In this case, you don't want the Name or other columns because you just want the city data appended in one place. Therefore: Select the Content column | right-click | Remove Other Columns.

Click the down-pointing double arrows in the column header, and you'll get the Combine Files dialog.

Select the folder named Parameter1 [1] | OK.

Inside the Power Query editor, you'll see data in the Queries pane on the left and an extra step in the Applied Steps section on the right. These are automated actions that Power Query added to combine the files.

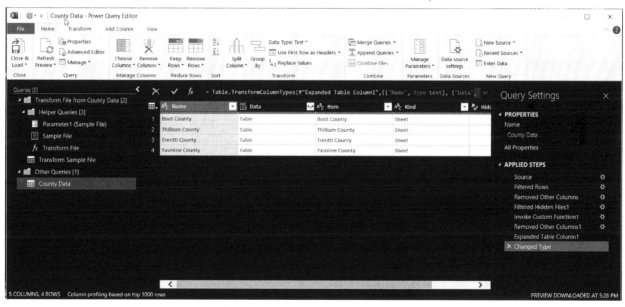

Next, highlight the Name column | right-click | Remove Other Columns.

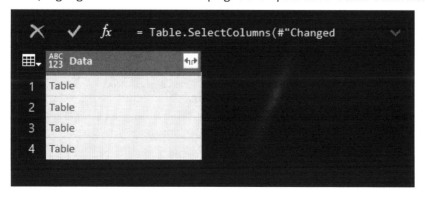

Click the outward-facing arrows in the Data column header.

Untick Use Original Column Name as Prefix | OK.

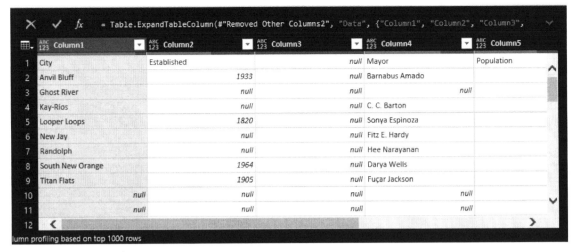

There's the data ... but ...

HOLD ON!

The file from Caster County just came in. Close and load the data in Power Query so that you can check to ensure that Caster.xlsx has the same format as the other files.

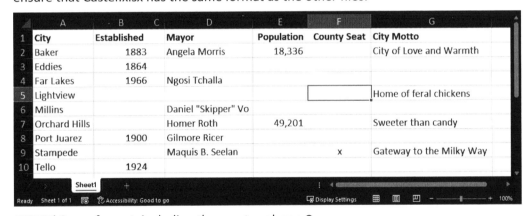

GREAT! Same format, including the empty column C.

Save Caster.xlsx in the dedicated folder County Data.

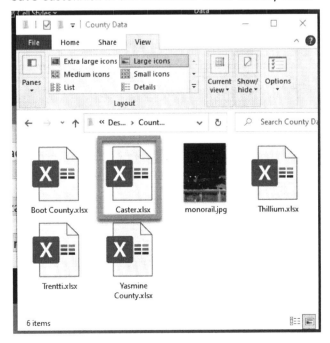

In the file into which the data was imported: Data | Queries & Connections | Refresh.

Note: You can also refresh from inside Power Query: Home | Query | Refresh Preview.

After refreshing, check to ensure the new cities were imported, as shown in this image:

Eddies and Far Lakes appear in the Column1 dropdown list, and if you scroll through, you'll see the other cities from Caster County. GREAT!

From here, you can go through and clean this data as described in the earlier section "Importing from a File."

Transformation Tables

A Power Query transformation table eliminates a certain type of data cleansing where you want to do a merge but first realize that there are inconsistencies in the data. Recall that merges require exact matches. Consider *New York City*. It can be listed many ways, including:

- New York
- New York City
- NY, NY
- Manhattan
- Brooklyn
- NYC
- N. Y.

Note from Bill: I was surprised when Oz showed me this transformation table feature. I was expecting him to simulate a VLOOKUP with a couple of joins, but this feature is even better and easier.

In this example, you need a merge to retrieve the rep and address and match them with the Name and Assigned columns. Lloyd can easily be matched with his rep, Darren, because New York matches with New York.

There are problems, though. For example, UK and LHR should be London. But, this doesn't have to be cleaned up in the source data. Instead, you can create a transformation table, like the one in this image in the range F7:G12.

Also notice that there are three queries: Reps, Names, Bridge. The transformation query is the one named Bridge.

Time to make the merge: Data | Get & Transform Data.

The image below shows that a left outer join is being used, and the Assigned and Location fields are what you want to match.

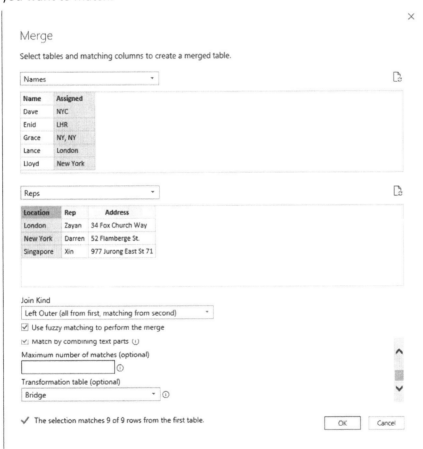

To use the transformation table, tick the box Use Fuzzy Matching to Perform the Merge. This will enable the options where you'll scroll down to Transformation Table, select the query that you've set up to be the transformation table, and click OK.

As shown below, everything is now all properly matched.

If a record is added later, and it's got an alternative that doesn't already exist (e.g., Manhattan instead of New York), just add it to the transformation table and refresh.

The image below has new entries for Will and Garson. There's also a new location: Los Angeles. The transformation table is set up to accept LA and convert it to Los Angeles and accept Manhattan and convert it to New York.

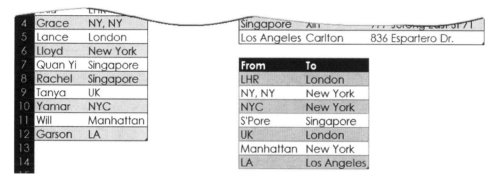

Notes: The transformation table does not need to include entries that are proper matches. Thus, London, New York, Singapore, and Los Angeles are omitted.

A transformation table requires the headers From and To.

A transformation table requires the From and To columns to be text data types.

Fuzzy Matching

Fuzzy matching is the official name of a task that can be really harsh because the data you need to match has inconsistencies: misspellings, typos, legitimate alternatives, etc.

Say that you've got a lot of data that needs to be matched or compared, but entries are inconsistent or just plain wrong. Imagine trying to get the entries in the table below matched up.

Example	Match1	Match2
1	00006531	6531
2	NE	NorthEast
3	California	Calffornia
4	Mr. Jean-Pierre	Jean P. Marius
5	212-555-1862	212.5551862
6	Rita Kay Roe	Rowe, Rita

Example 1 could be bank account numbers. The official data from the bank includes the leading zeros, and that dataset needs to be matched with a dataset that's clipped off the leading zeros.

Example 3 shows that you need to match U.S. state names, including matching California with a misspelling.

Example 5 is a phone number with inconsistent formatting.

In small datasets, you can manually go through and fix what needs to be fixed to get exact matches. But if you have a lot of data, cleaning one entry at a time … *OUCH!* This is where hardcore guerrilla data analysis is required because Power Query's fuzzy matching feature can help you whoop this type of crap data—**but you have to be very wary and implement a strategy.**

In the example below, the goal is to match each person in column A with their project lead in column F. The Project ID and Project fields are what you need to get everything matched.

Notice in the Queries & Connections pane that the Leads and Assignments queries have been created.

Here you're going to use a left outer join to make the matches, but first look at the data based on the assumption that the Project column has the correct formal format for each value. The Project ID column has data that may have been pasted in from several emails, or perhaps several people collaborated to manually type in their details.

Observations:

- Cell B2 says L-2609-X, but in the Project column in E8, there is L-2609X.
- In B14 there's a typo, and the code starts with a colon instead of the L that's shown in E9.
- Cell B7 contains J44406, which should probably be matched with JC-4406E in E6.

Ready for some fuzzy matching? Here we go!

Data | Get & Transform Data | Get Data | Combine | Merge.

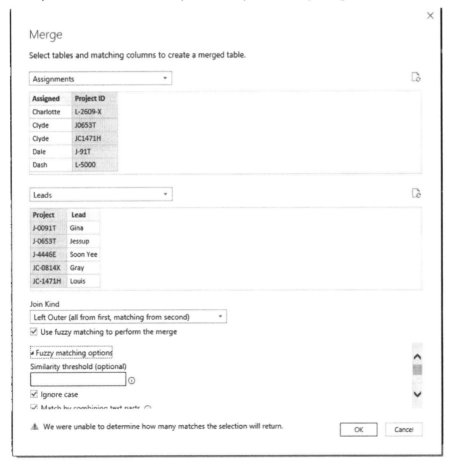

In the Merge dialog box, you can see that:

- Assignments are on the left/top.
- Leads are on the right/bottom.
- The Project ID and Project fields are being matched.

Tick the box Use Fuzzy Matching to Perform the Merge.

Note: For Similarity Threshold, acceptable values are 0 to 1. If you leave the field blank, the default is 0.8, which means matches will be made if there is at least 80% similarity.

For this example, leave the Similarity Threshold field empty to accept the 80% threshold. Click OK.

Here is the result in the Power Query editor:

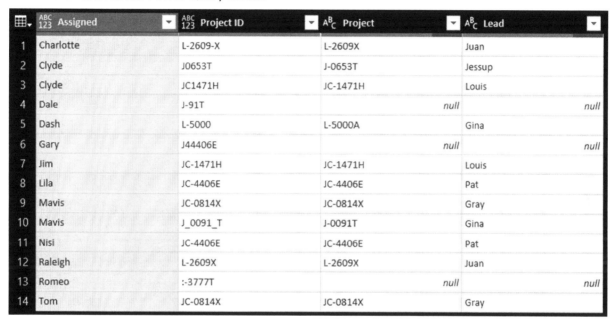

	Assigned	Project ID	Project	Lead
1	Charlotte	L-2609-X	L-2609X	Juan
2	Clyde	J0653T	J-0653T	Jessup
3	Clyde	JC1471H	JC-1471H	Louis
4	Dale	J-91T	null	null
5	Dash	L-5000	L-5000A	Gina
6	Gary	J44406E	null	null
7	Jim	JC-1471H	JC-1471H	Louis
8	Lila	JC-4406E	JC-4406E	Pat
9	Mavis	JC-0814X	JC-0814X	Gray
10	Mavis	J_0091_T	J-0091T	Gina
11	Nisi	JC-4406E	JC-4406E	Pat
12	Raleigh	L-2609X	L-2609X	Juan
13	Romeo	:-3777T	null	null
14	Tom	JC-0814X	JC-0814X	Gray

The fuzzy matching went fairly well.

Observations:

- Rows 4, 6, and 13 don't have matches. Everything else is good. On row 10, J_0091_T was properly matched with J-0091T.
- In row 13, even though the only difference is the colon instead of an L, no match was made.

The image below shows three fuzzy matches with different thresholds. On the left: 95%, center: 55%, right: 30%.

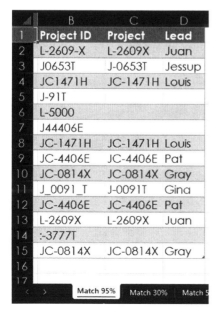

- With the 95% match, four rows don't have a match compared to three non-matches at 80%. The pair that are no longer matched: L-5000 and L-5000A.
- The 55% and 30% matches have three extra rows. Why? On both of those results, J44406E was matched with **both** J-4446E and JC-4406E in rows 7, 8, 14, and 15.
- 55% and 30% properly matched :-3777T with L-3777T.
- In none of the examples did J-91T get matched with J-0091T.

What happens at 22%?

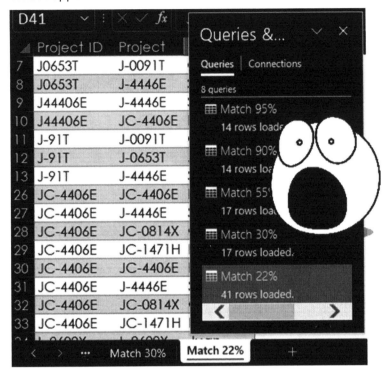

- 41 rows of data loaded. The original dataset has 14 rows.
- J-91T has three matches. In the previous examples, it had zero. In row 11 there's a proper match. The other two matches are what you and I would consider wrong, but they meet the 22% threshold.
- JC-4406E has eight matches.

Note: Fuzzy matching only works on text data types. Therefore, if you need to match data that looks like numbers (e.g., credit card numbers) or dates, you'll first have to convert them to text to perform the match.

Final Word on Fuzzy Matching

Use of fuzzy matching needs to happen inside a strategy. This is not like doing an unpivot, then raising your arms in victory.

Maybe you start with a 0.9 or 0.8 threshold, check the accuracy of the matches, and if they're good, set them aside. Then try a lower threshold on the remaining non-matches. Do this until everything is matched or you're left with entries that need to be manually cleaned and matched.

It's possible that the higher threshold makes enough matches that the remaining non-matches can be handled manually. Conversely, it's also possible that the 0.9 threshold makes no matches or makes a lot of wrong matches.

You have to know your data and your tools.

Chapter 8: Conditional Formatting

Being able to quickly see interesting details in your data helps you plan, make decisions, and develop strategies. Conditional formatting makes this possible by allowing you to create rules and alerts in your spreadsheets that will automatically highlight specific details.

One of my earliest uses of conditional formatting was to set alerts that warned me about upcoming deadlines because I often worried that I'd forget about a deadline until it was too late. With conditional formatting, however, I found it easy to plan the upcoming week based on the alerts I would see each Monday when I opened the document. I used red cells to warn of deadlines that were 3 days away and yellow cells to warn of deadlines 10 days away. Thus, lots of red meant a hectic week was ahead. I didn't have to eyeball each date and mentally calculate the levels of urgency.

Let's look at some of the many ways that conditional formatting can help you.

Using Conditional Formatting to Find Duplicates

In the group of names shown in the next figure, everyone should be listed only one time. You can scan through the range and identify a few duplicates (e.g., Kate Prentiss in cells B8 and C5). But you don't really want to rely on your eyes for this task—and you *really* don't want to do that when you have a massive dataset to evaluate.

To get more accurate results than you can get with your eyeballs, use conditional formatting to expose all duplicates. Here are the steps:

1. In the worksheet shown in the next figure, highlight the entire range A2:C13 and then: Home | Styles | Conditional Formatting | Highlight Cell Rules | Duplicate Values. The Duplicate Values dialog appears.

2. As shown, the data range has Light Red Fill with Dark Red Text already being applied.

3. Click OK and notice what happens: Ruben Capp and Justin Wilks are revealed as additional duplicates.

4. Delete Justin Wilks in B7, and the highlight in B6 goes away.

5. Decide which groups Kate Prentiss and Ruben Capp belong in and delete the entries where they don't belong.

Note: If you are reading the printed book, you won't be able to see the colors we're talking about here and in the next section. Just trust us!

Using Icons with Conditional Formatting

Icon sets are easy to apply, but there are several secret settings for customizing them.

The icon sets are found in Home | Conditional Formatting | Icon Sets.

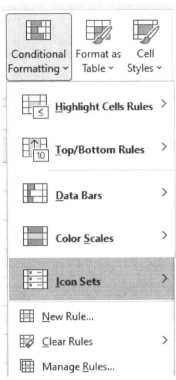

Of the 20 icons sets, some have three, four, or five icons. Try to choose icons that rely on both different shapes and different colors. Some of the people using your worksheets will have difficulty seeing the difference between green and red, making the first set under Shapes impossible to interpret. If you choose the second item under Indicators instead, it is easier to differentiate them.

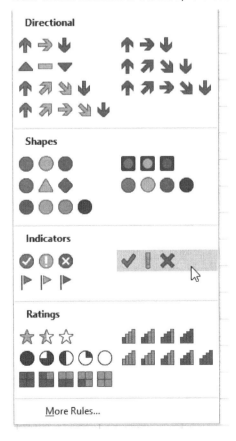

To apply an icon set, select a range that contains numbers and then choose the icon set you want.

You probably store numbers using right alignment. The icons added to cells are always left-aligned. I like to use a rarely used setting called Increase Indent to keep the right edge of the numbers aligned but move the numbers closer to the icons.

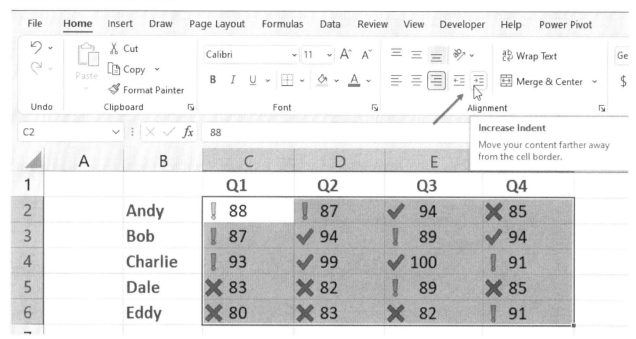

Look at the numbers in the figure above. The smallest number is 80. The largest number is 100. There are three different icons available. With 21 possible discrete integers, Excel will use the red X icon for 80 through 86, the yellow ! icon for 87 to 93, and the green checkmark for 94 to 100. In this case, using the default icon settings works just fine.

However, the defaults won't always work out "just fine." What happens if next year, Eddy only scores 30 in Q1? Doing the same calculation as above, you have 71 discrete values between 30 and 100. This means 30 through 52 get the red X icon, 53 to 76 get the yellow ! icon, and 77 and up get the green checkmark. One outlier causes everyone else to get green checkmarks. "Last year, your 82 sucked, but because one person did really badly this year, it is awesome" is not a sentence that you would expect to hear.

	Q1	Q2	Q3	Q4
Andy	✔ 88	✔ 87	✔ 94	✔ 85
Bob	✔ 87	✔ 94	✔ 89	✔ 94
Charlie	✔ 93	✔ 99	✔ 100	✔ 91
Dale	✔ 83	✔ 82	✔ 89	✔ 85
Eddy	✖ 30	✔ 83	✔ 82	✔ 91

To prevent this, you can override the default settings used for icon sets: Home | Conditional Formatting | Manage Rules. Select the Icon Set rule and click Edit Rule.

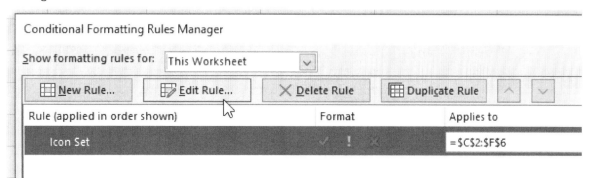

There are many settings you can change for an icon set.

- Click Reverse Icon Order to have the "worst" icon appear for high numbers.
- Click Show Icon Only to display just the icon, not the value. This is useful in dashboards. Note that when using this setting, you can use the Left/Center/Right Align buttons to move the icon from the left edge of the cell.
- It is very subtle, but you can choose > or >= for each icon. Using >90 means that the highest icon would be used for 91 to 100. Using >=90 would include 90 in the top group.
- You can change the symbol used for each icon, allowing you to mix and match icons from different sets. If you want to mix a left arrow, red diamond, and downward-pointing triangle, you can do that. You can also specify no cell icon for any group.
- There are four choices available in the Type dropdown, as discussed next.

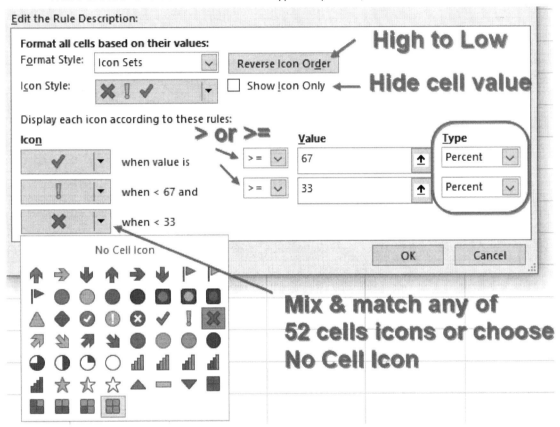

The Type dropdown menu offers four options for setting the limits for each group: Number, Percent, Formula, or Percentile.

The Number option is the easiest. Choose > or >= and type a number (e.g., >90, >=80).

Formula is the most complex option. You could write a formula to make sure everything that is one standard deviation above the mean gets a gold star.

Percent and Percentile are the most confusing options. If your numbers are equally distributed, then Percent and Percentile will give you the result shown in columns A:E below. The datasets in H:L and O:S are heavily skewed toward small low numbers. The values are mostly 1 to 20, with a few outliers going up to 100. If you leave Type at the default Percent, then Excel does the calculation (Max – Min) / Number of Icons to create ranges that are equal sized. This results in most cells falling into the lower red diamond group. If you switch from Percent to Percentile, then you will end up with roughly one-third of the cells being assigned to each group.

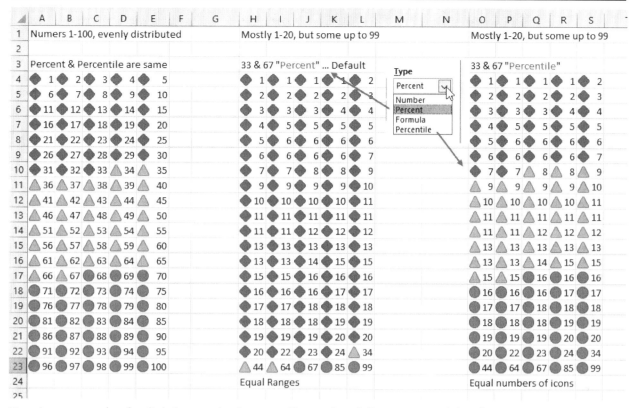

Here is an example of a slightly complex icon set. If your data follows a normal distribution, you will have 68% of the people in the middle … within one standard deviation below and above the mean.

	A	B	C	D	E	F	G	H
1			Q1	Q2	Q3	Q4		
2		Andy	✔ 76	36	39	✖ 25		
3		Bob	✔ 75	53	62	✖ 31		
4		Charlie	✖ 31	46	✔ 71	63		
5		Dale	43	58	52	56		
6		Eddy	54	56	65	✖ 26		
7			Numbers generated with =INT(NORM.INV(RAND(),50,15))					
8			It should be roughly a mean of 50 and a standard deviation of 15					
9		Mean	50.9					
10		St Dev	15.384733					
11								
12		Green checkmarks for >=(Mean + St Dev)						
13		Red X for (Mean - St Dev)						

Icon			Value			Type	
✔	▼	when value is	>= ▽	=$C$9+$C$10	↑	Formula ▽	
No Cell Icon ▼		when < Formula and	>= ▽	=$C$9-$C$10	↑	Formula ▽	
✖	▼	when < Formula					

Helper formulas in C9 and C10 calculate the mean and standard deviation. The settings for the conditional formatting use Mean + Standard Deviation as the upper limit and Mean − Standard Deviation for the lower limit. This means that 68% of the people in the middle won't get an icon. It is just the people more than one standard deviation beyond the mean who are highlighted.

🐉 Using the Up, Flat, and Down Icon Set

Seventeen of the icon sets were released in Excel 2007. Three years later, Microsoft gave us three more, including the one with the inaccurate name 3 Triangles. Anyone who is an alumni of Sesame Street would call this 2 Triangles and a Rectangle, but I digress.

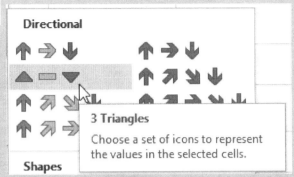

It was a good addition in Excel 2010, but it is the one icon set that cannot be simply applied to a range of numbers. As an example, let's get some stock history.

Getting Stock History

In the old days, if I needed a year's history of a stock price, I was heading out to Finance.Yahoo.com and downloading a CSV file. Today, this is easy to generate by using a single formula and the new STOCKHISTORY function.

In the image below, I retrieved a year of Microsoft stock closing prices using a single formula. Here are the arguments and how to use them:

- **stock**: Use a stock symbol such as MSFT or a cell containing a stock data type.
- **start_date:** You can hard-code a date or generate something from a year ago by using TODAY()-365. If you specify a start date before the company was publicly traded, you will get all of the history for the company. So, you could simply type 1 here to get all history.
- **end_date**: Use TODAY() or TODAY()-1. The closing price for today won't be available until a few hours after the market closes.
- **interval**: 0 for daily, 1 for weekly, or 2 for monthly. Do you want a quarterly interval? Tough luck. That is not an option.
- **headers**: 0 for none, 1 for a single row, or 2 for stock name on row 1, headers on row 2, and data starting in row 3.
- **properties1** through **properties99**: Seriously, Excel allows 99 columns to be returned. Currently, there are only six things you can return. Use 0 for date, 1 for close, 2 for open, 3 for high, 4 for low, or 5 for volume. In the image below, I used 0,1 to get date and close. You can specify the fields in any order. To get volume, high, low, date, you would use 5,3,4,0.

◢	A	B	C	D	E	F
1	MSFT Closing Prices					
2	=stockhistory(stock,start_date,end_date,interval,headers,properties1,...)					
3	=STOCKHISTORY("MSFT",TODAY()-365,TODAY()-1,0,1,0,1)					
4						
5	Date	Close	Up or Down?			
6	1/25/2021	$ 229.53				
7	1/26/2021	$ 232.33				
8	1/27/2021	$ 232.90				
9	1/28/2021	$ 238.93				

Showing Up, Flat, and Down Icons

To show the up, flat, and down symbols, use a helper column. In cell C7 in the image below, you want to know if today's close is higher or lower than yesterday's. The formula =B7-B6 in cell C7 will show that the price is up by $2.80 today. You don't particularly care how much it is up or down. You just want to know if it is up or down. The SIGN function is great for this. Any positive numbers becomes 1. Any negative number becomes -1. Zero stays as 0.

Wrap the formula in the SIGN function, =SIGN(B7-B6), and copy down.

Apply the 3 Triangles icon set.

	A	B	C	D	E	
5	Date	Close	Up or Down?			
6	1/25/2021	$229.53				
7	1/26/2021	$232.33	▲	=SIGN(B7-B6)		
8	1/27/2021	$232.90	▲			
9	1/28/2021	$238.93	▲			
10	1/29/2021	$231.96	▼			
11	2/1/2021	$239.65	▲			
12	2/2/2021	$239.51	▼			
13	2/2/2021	$239.51	▬	*Faked for Groundhog Day*		
14	2/3/2021	$243.00	▲			
15	2/4/2021	$242.01	▼			

Note that I added a fake row in there … with Groundhog Day (February 2) repeating so you can see the yellow rectangle that appears for zero.

To hide the 1, 0, -1 values, go into the Conditional Formatting Rules Manager, edit the rule, and tick Show Icon Only.

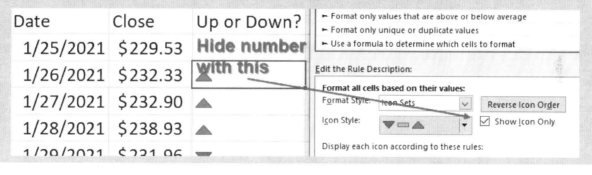

Chapter 9: De-duping in Excel

De-duping is a highly strategic task. You have to know your data and possibly apply several different methods to iterate through and de-dupe a large, complex dataset.

Excel offers a number of ways to de-duplicate a list.

De-duping with Advanced Filter

Our good friend and fellow MVP Roger Govier will point out that using Advanced Filter is an easy, non-destructive way to get a unique list of values.

Columns A through D below contain a small dataset. Let's say you want the unique list of sales rep names.

Follow these steps:

1. Go to a blank section of the worksheet. Type the heading Rep because this is the field where you would like to remove duplicates.

2. Select one cell in the original dataset.

3. From the Data tab, find the Filter group. Click Advanced.

4. In the Advanced Filter dialog, shown below, choose Copy to Another Location. The List range should be correct. Click in the Copy To box and then touch cell F1 with the mouse. Tick the Unique Records Only box.

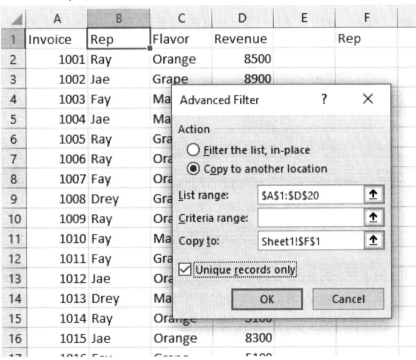

5. Click OK, and you get a unique list of sales reps starting in F2.

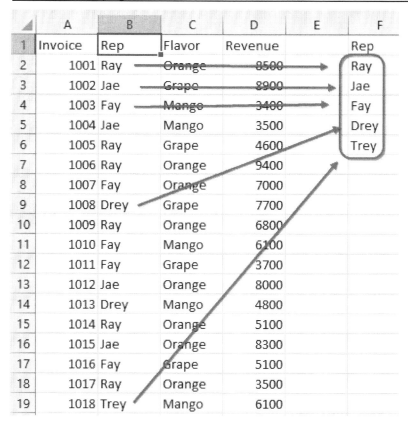

	A	B	C	D	E	F
1	Invoice	Rep	Flavor	Revenue		Rep
2	1001	Ray	Orange	8500		Ray
3	1002	Jae	Grape	8900		Jae
4	1003	Fay	Mango	3400		Fay
5	1004	Jae	Mango	3500		Drey
6	1005	Ray	Grape	4600		Trey
7	1006	Ray	Orange	9400		
8	1007	Fay	Orange	7000		
9	1008	Drey	Grape	7700		
10	1009	Ray	Orange	6800		
11	1010	Fay	Mango	6100		
12	1011	Fay	Grape	3700		
13	1012	Jae	Orange	8000		
14	1013	Drey	Mango	4800		
15	1014	Ray	Orange	5100		
16	1015	Jae	Orange	8300		
17	1016	Fay	Grape	5100		
18	1017	Ray	Orange	3500		
19	1018	Trey	Mango	6100		

Note: The unique list is not sorted alphabetically. The items in the list match the sequence in the original data.

As shown below, you can specify a combination of multiple fields, and you can even reorder the fields, reversing Flavor and Rep.

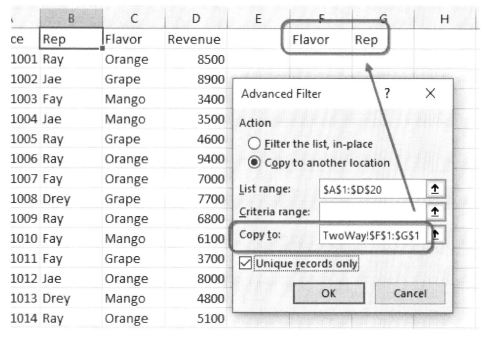

	B	C	D	E	F	G	H
ce	Rep	Flavor	Revenue		Flavor	Rep	
1001	Ray	Orange	8500				
1002	Jae	Grape	8900				
1003	Fay	Mango	3400				
1004	Jae	Mango	3500				
1005	Ray	Grape	4600				
1006	Ray	Orange	9400				
1007	Fay	Orange	7000				
1008	Drey	Grape	7700				
1009	Ray	Orange	6800				
1010	Fay	Mango	6100				
1011	Fay	Grape	3700				
1012	Jae	Orange	8000				
1013	Drey	Mango	4800				
1014	Ray	Orange	5100				

Advanced Filter dialog:

Action
- ○ Filter the list, in-place
- ● Copy to another location

List range: $A$1:$D$20

Criteria range:

Copy to: TwoWay!$F$1:$G$1

☑ Unique records only

[OK] [Cancel]

This use of Advanced Filter will provide every combination of sales rep and flavor. It is easy to control the output by simply changing the field headings in the Copy To range.

The result:

E	F	G
	Flavor	Rep
	Orange	Ray
	Grape	Jae
	Mango	Fay
	Mango	Jae
	Grape	Ray
	Orange	Fay
	Grape	Drey
	Grape	Fay
	Orange	Jae
	Mango	Drey
	Mango	Trey

There are other ways to remove duplicates. The Remove Duplicates command will remove duplicates, but it is destructive. You always want to use it on a copy of the data.

Later, you will read about the UNIQUE function, which provides another way to remove duplicates.

De-duping Gets Ugly!

This section addresses one of the very earliest problems I faced in Excel. People had multiple profiles, and their data was spread across those profiles. In this image, I don't want Excel's de-duping tool to decide which Jerry Crane to delete.

First Name	Last Name	Birthday	Start Date	Office
Kate	Cordale	31-Dec-85	01-Jun-17	7E
Jerry	Crane	29-Oct-78	10-May-20	
Jerry	Crane		10-May-20	
Jerry	Crane			7G
Jerry	Crane	29-Oct-78	09-May-20	
Michael	Crane		15-May-21	5B

He's got two different start dates; his office number is on his third record; his birthday is on the first and fourth records. It's critical to know that there are four entries for Jerry Crane, and they need to be reviewed and modified before you keep one and delete the other three. (Of course, this example assumes that this is just one Jerry Crane and not two, three, or four different people.)

Using IF to "LOOK"

In this example, there is de-duping that needs to be done. Consider Gina Sanford.

Gina Sanford's ID is in row 14, and her age is in row 13. In this case, a formula was used in column F to flag duplicates so that someone can go in and check which of the duplicate records can be removed. Here's the formula:

```
=IF(AND(C2=C1,D2=D1),"LOOK","")
```

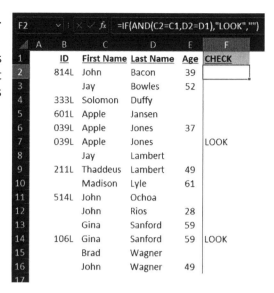

De-duping with an Assembled ID

Often, real data doesn't have exact matches. So, here's a strategy that can get you closer to victoriously de-duping a dataset.

In this revised example there are:

- Apple Kerry Jones
- Apple K. Jones
- Apple Jones
- Gina Renee Sanford
- Gina R. Sanford

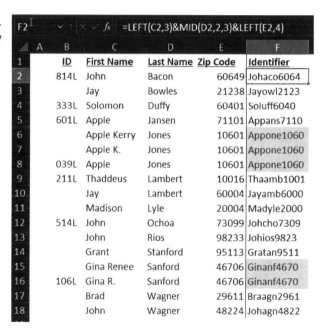

The formula in F2 builds an identifier for each record:

```
=LEFT(C2,3)&MID(D2,2,3)&LEFT(E2,4)
```

It's taking the first three characters of the first name; three characters from the last name, starting on the second character; and then the first four characters of the zip code. And then conditional formatting is applied to the Identifier column to highlight which values are matching.

Chapter 10: Dynamic Arrays

Released in September 2019, the new dynamic arrays required a complete rewrite of the Excel calculation engine. They were released along with SORT, SORTBY, FILTER, UNIQUE, SEQUENCE, and RANDARRAY. Today, there are many more functions that can use dynamic arrays, including XLOOKUP.

In short, a dynamic array allows one formula to return many results. The formula exists in the top-left cell, but the results can spill to adjacent rows and columns.

Here is very simple example using SEQUENCE. In this formula, you want to generate five rows by four columns. Start at the number 10 and increment by 12. The formula is entered in B2. The results of the formula appear in B2:E6.

	A	B	C	D	E	F
1						
2		10	22	34	46	
3		58	70	82	94	
4		106	118	130	142	
5		154	166	178	190	
6		202	214	226	238	
7						

B2: =SEQUENCE(5,4,10,12)

If you select any other cell in the results range, the formula appears in the formula bar but is grayed out.

If you use a formula such as =SUM(B2), you get 10 because that is the value in B2. However, if you add a hash (#) after B2, you are asking Excel to give you all of the results returned by the array in B2.

A1: =SUM(B2#)

	A	B	C	D	E	F
1	2480					
2		10	22	34	46	
3		58	70	82	94	
4		106	118	130	142	
5		154	166	178	190	
6		202	214	226	238	
7						

Tip: The # symbol has many names. I grew up calling it the number sign or pound sign. But in the UK, they look at me like I am crazy calling it a pound sign. This symbol was always on touch-tone telephones, and the people at Bell Labs called it an octothorpe. Today, it is often used to make hashtags, such as #Excel, and many people refer to the symbol as a hash. This seems to be the favored name today. Feel free to call it number, pound, or even octothorpe if that suits your fancy.

SORT

I love to think about when I used to build a dashboard for my manager's manager. This guy was a VP level. Great guy. Great sense of humor. But he was never a guy that I could train to sort data. I wanted to be able to say to him, "Hey, John, I need you to open this workbook. Click one of these cells in column D. Go to the tab that says Data and then click the button that says ZA." But saying such a thing to my VP of Sales would never have worked.

By using the SORT function, I could always make sure that the sales data was sorted high to low on any dashboard that I built for my manager's manager.

One oddity with the SORT function is that you don't include the headings as part of the formula.

In the image below, the raw data is in M1:O12. Copy the headings from M1:O1 over to A1. Then, in A2, a single formula brings all the rows of data and sorts them:

```
=SORT(M2:O12,3,-1)
```

In this formula, M2:O13 is the data to sort. 3 is the column to sort by. The third argument is either 1 for ascending or -1 for descending. Using -1 there ensures that the customers are sorted high to low.

A2				✓ fx	=SORT(M2:O12,3,-1)			
	A	B	C	D	M	N	O	
1	Customer	Region	Forecast		Customer	Region	Forecast	
2	More4Apps	West	768558		Fintega Financial Modelling	East	460,530	
3	JEVS Human Services	East	704143		Frontline Systems	Central	605,185	
4	Harlem Globetrotters	West	650183		Harlem Globetrotters	West	650,183	
5	Serving Brevard Realty	East	609148		JEVS Human Services	East	704,143	
6	Frontline Systems	Central	605185		MAU Workforce Solutions	Central	504,417	
7	www.ExcelTricks.de	West	572226		More4Apps	West	768,558	
8	WM Squared Inc.	Central	524323		Serving Brevard Realty	East	609,148	
9	MAU Workforce Solutions	Central	504417		Tennessee Moon	Central	476,235	
10	Tennessee Moon	Central	476235		Wilde XL Solutions Ltd.	East	396,030	
11	Fintega Financial Modelling	East	460530		WM Squared Inc.	Central	524,323	
12	Wilde XL Solutions Ltd.	East	396030		www.ExcelTricks.de	West	572,226	
13								

Next, a few variations.

Two-Level Sort

For a two-level sort, you have to pass an array constant for the second and third arguments. Say that you want to sort by region ascending. Within each region, you want the forecast descending.

The second argument specifies the column to sort by. You want to sort first by column 2 and then by column 3. So you use {2,3}. The third argument is the sort direction. You want the Regions column sorted ascending and the Forecast column descending, so the third argument is {1,-1}.

A2				✓ fx	=SORT(M2:O12,{2,3},{1,-1})			
	A	B	C	D	M	N	O	
1	Customer	Region	Forecast		Customer	Region	Forecast	
2	Frontline Systems	Central	605185		Fintega Financial Modelling	East	460,530	
3	WM Squared Inc.	Central	524323		Frontline Systems	Central	605,185	
4	MAU Workforce Solutions	Central	504417		Harlem Globetrotters	West	650,183	
5	Tennessee Moon	Central	476235		JEVS Human Services	East	704,143	
6	JEVS Human Services	East	704143		MAU Workforce Solutions	Central	504,417	
7	Serving Brevard Realty	East	609148		More4Apps	West	768,558	
8	Fintega Financial Modelling	East	460530		Serving Brevard Realty	East	609,148	
9	Wilde XL Solutions Ltd.	East	396030		Tennessee Moon	Central	476,235	
10	More4Apps	West	768558		Wilde XL Solutions Ltd.	East	396,030	
11	Harlem Globetrotters	West	650183		WM Squared Inc.	Central	524,323	
12	www.ExcelTricks.de	West	572226		www.ExcelTricks.de	West	572,226	
13								

Caution: In the Sort dialog box, there is a way to use a custom list for the sort order. This is not supported in the SORT function.

Left-to-Right Sort

It is possible to use the Sort dialog to sort left to right. The Excel SORT function also supports left-to-right sorting. In this example, the fourth argument in the SORT function says you want to sort by column. The 6 for the *sort_by* argument tells Excel to sort by the totals in the 6th row of the sort range.

B3			fx	=SORT(B12:G17,6,-1,TRUE)			

◢	A	B	C	D	E	F	G
1	Sort data left to right with most sales first					**Sort by Column**	
2							
3	Quarter	Flo	Andy	Ed	Chris	Barb	Diane
4	Q1	40,332	18,006	11,130	22,431	11,753	11,671
5	Q2	43,071	25,088	30,513	22,579	25,939	18,288
6	Q3	34,967	22,991	17,617	16,408	16,945	12,023
7	Q4	34,519	22,492	28,519	19,782	21,343	23,199
8	Total	152,889	88,577	87,779	81,200	75,980	65,181
9							
10	Original data, unsorted						
11							
12	Quarter	Andy	Barb	Chris	Diane	Ed	Flo
13	Q1	18006	11753	22431	11671	11130	40332
14	Q2	25088	25939	22579	18288	30513	43071
15	Q3	22991	16945	16408	12023	17617	34967
16	Q4	22492	21343	19782	23199	28519	34519
17	Total	88577	75980	81200	65181	87779	152889
10							

SORTBY for Something That Won't Be Returned

SORTBY is a close cousin to SORT. With SORTBY, you can specify that you want to sort by something that won't necessarily be returned by the SORTBY function. What if you want to show the list of top prospects from the earlier example, but you don't need to show the forecasted revenue?

The formula below says that you want to sort the customer names in column K by the forecast in column M. The -1 means to sort descending.

A4			fx	=SORTBY(K4:K14,$M$4:$M$14,-1)		

◢	A	B	K	L	M
1	Sort by Forecast, but don't show the Forecast				
2					
3	Customer		Customer	Region	Forecast
4	More4Apps		Fintega Financial Modelling	East	460,530
5	JEVS Human Services		Frontline Systems	Central	605,185
6	Harlem Globetrotters		Harlem Globetrotters	West	650,183
7	Serving Brevard Realty		JEVS Human Services	East	704,143
8	Frontline Systems		MAU Workforce Solutions	Central	504,417
9	www.ExcelTricks.de		More4Apps	West	768,558
10	WM Squared Inc.		Serving Brevard Realty	East	609,148
11	MAU Workforce Solutions		Tennessee Moon	Central	476,235
12	Tennessee Moon		Wilde XL Solutions Ltd.	East	396,030
13	Fintega Financial Modelling		WM Squared Inc.	Central	524,323
14	Wilde XL Solutions Ltd.		www.ExcelTricks.de	West	572,226
15					

FILTER

The FILTER function lets you apply a filter with a formula. In the image below, someone would select a region from the validation dropdown in B1. The formula in A4 would return the records from M4:O14 where the region matches the selected region.

| A4 | | ⌵ | ⋮ | ✕ ✓ | *fx* | =FILTER(M4:O14,N4:N14=B1) | | |

◢	A	B	C	D	‖	M	N	O
1	Choose a Region	East						
2								
3	Customer	Region	Forecast			Customer	Region	Forecast
4	Fintega Financial Modelling	East	460530			Fintega Financial Modelling	East	460,530
5	JEVS Human Services	East	704143			Frontline Systems	Central	605,185
6	Serving Brevard Realty	East	609148			Harlem Globetrotters	West	650,183
7	Wilde XL Solutions Ltd.	East	396030			JEVS Human Services	East	704,143
8						MAU Workforce Solutions	Central	504,417
9						More4Apps	West	768,558
10						Serving Brevard Realty	East	609,148
11						Tennessee Moon	Central	476,235
12						Wilde XL Solutions Ltd.	East	396,030
13						WM Squared Inc.	Central	524,323
14						www.ExcelTricks.de	West	572,226
15								

RANDARRAY

RANDARRAY is just fantastic! As an instructor, I have to create a lot of fake data: sales data, website visits, birthdays, expirations dates, etc. RANDARRAY has made it so easy to create fake data. You'll see some fake data creation in this section.

Fake data isn't used just for making examples. Often it's used for testing when you're developing a model before you have real data.

There is another key use for fake data that I wish more people knew about: **anonymizing actual data**.

If you need help or are offering to help someone who has actual zip codes or IDs or Social Security numbers, you can anonymize it with fake zip codes, etc.

> **Caution:** RANDARRAY is volatile. Having a lot of volatile functions or features in a workbook can slow down calculations in the workbook.

RANDARRAY's syntax:

```
=RANDARRAY([rows],[columns],[min],[max],[whole_number])
```

Creating Random Orders for Interviews

In this example, 11 candidates are being randomly assigned the order for their interviews using the RANDARRAY formula in C3:

```
=RANDARRAY(11,1,1,25)
```

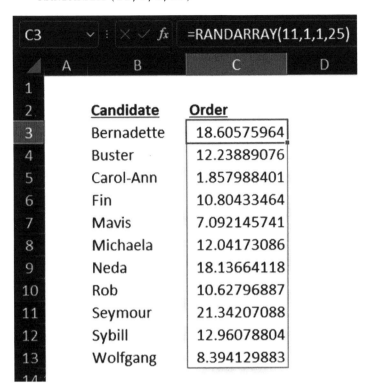

Note: If you're following along, your numbers won't look like mine because these values are truly random.

The formula is telling Excel I want 11 rows and 1 column of data, values ranging from 1 to 25. (I chose 1 to 25 for no particular reason. I could have used 1 to 11.)

> **Caution:** Be very careful because of RANDARRAY's volatility! Once you have the order you want to keep, you have to immediately copy it and paste as values. If you make any other changes in Excel or even a change in another open workbook, the values will recalculate. You can also recalculate by hitting F9.

After copying and pasting as values, then sorting the Order column ascending, here's the order of the interviews:

Candidate	Order
Carol-Ann	1.857988401
Mavis	7.092145741
Wolfgang	8.394129883
Rob	10.62796887
Fin	10.80433464
Michaela	12.04173086
Buster	12.23889076
Sybill	12.96078804
Neda	18.13664118
Bernadette	18.60575964
Seymour	21.34207088

Generating 60 Random Start Dates

Say that you need 60 fake random start dates, as shown below.

19 Nov 20	6 Dec 21	13 Sep 20	2 Mar 21	11 Sep 18	4 Jul 18	1 Jun 20	25 Dec 20	13 Dec 19	1 Aug 21
15 May 20	31 Mar 21	3 Dec 20	19 Mar 18	19 Mar 21	13 Jul 22	7 Jan 22	16 Nov 20	31 Oct 18	30 Mar 18
2 Apr 18	7 Jul 18	17 Sep 18	26 Feb 21	22 Dec 20	6 Mar 22	3 Feb 21	16 Apr 22	14 Feb 18	17 Dec 19
16 Oct 19	17 Oct 20	15 Jul 18	1 May 18	19 May 20	3 Nov 20	31 Jul 21	9 Dec 21	28 May 19	19 Apr 21
16 Feb 18	19 Oct 19	20 Jan 18	20 Jun 19	27 Feb 18	20 Apr 18	14 Sep 19	26 May 22	6 Jun 21	12 Jun 22
18 Jun 20	4 Jun 20	12 Feb 22	4 May 19	20 May 21	6 Aug 20	12 Nov 21	23 Aug 18	5 Jan 18	12 Apr 18

The formula in B5:

```
=RANDARRAY(6,10,C2,C3,1)
```

RANDARRAY is delivering 6 rows and 10 columns of dates. The earliest date is in C2 (1JAN18); the latest date is in C3 (1AUG22). The 1 in the formula is the RANDARRAY component that asks if the result should be integers, or not. 1 or TRUE means yes, integers are desired. Blank, 0 or false would return decimal numbers.

Notice this! If a regular formula was used—instead of a dynamic array—absolute cell references would have been required for C2 and C3 in anticipation of dragging the formula down and to the right. Absolute cell references were not required here.

A Warning About Creating Fake but Realistic Data

RANDARRAY's results will be an even distribution of the range you request, and this can be a problem if you need data that either makes sense or at least isn't distracting because it's so nonsensical.

In the image below, RANDARRAY is generating 10 rows and 12 columns of data; Min = 1, Max = 100; all integers.

The formula in E2:

```
=RANDARRAY(10,12,1,100,1)
```

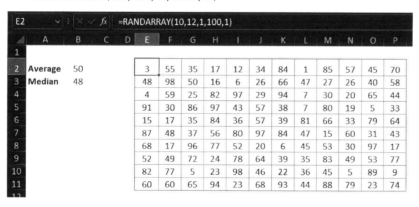

You can try this experiment:

1. Create a dataset with RANDARRAY in cell E2: =RANDARRAY(10,12,1,100,1)
2. Calculate the average: =AVERAGE(E2#)
3. Calculate the median: =MEDIAN(E2#)
4. Press the F9 key several times to recalculate and get different values

Did you try it? Did you notice that both numbers stay close to 50?

Having an even distribution of data is a problem if you need fake data representing, say, two years' worth of weekly tourism data in an area where November–February numbers are normally low. RANDARRAY can still be helpful in this type of situation. Instead of creating one single goofy set of values, you could generate three or four different sets of data representing different tourist seasons—with lower values generated for November through February.

Can **RANDARRAY** handle negative numbers?

Yes. RANDARRAY can handle negative numbers. In this example, RANDARRAY is being asked to provide 25 random temperatures between -3 °F and 10 °F. The formula in B3:

```
=RANDARRAY(5,5,-3,10)
```

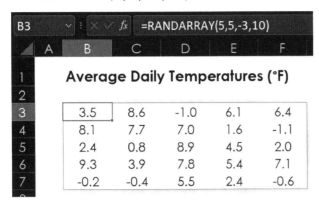

UNIQUE

There are many obscure ways to get a unique list of values from a range. I used to have a gig on TechTV where Leo Laporte would let me fill six minutes of airtime with Excel tricks. At the end of the six minutes, Leo would hold up my book and tell people to buy the book. One episode, I filled the six minutes with all the various ways to get a unique list:

- Create a Pivot Table with the field in the rows area.
- Use Advanced Filter and choose Unique Records Only.
- Make a copy of the data and use the Remove Duplicates command on the Data tab.

I am sure there were more methods.

All of those obscure methods can be replaced by the UNIQUE function. In the simplest use, ask for the UNIQUE of a column of names. You will get a list of each name that occurs one or more times in the list.

The list is not sorted. The names appear in the same order that they appear in the original range. If you want them sorted alphabetically, use =SORT(UNIQUE(A4:A15)).

UNIQUE with Two Criteria

When you have multiple columns of data, the UNIQUE function returns all combinations that appear. In the figure below, Mike was nominated in January and February but not in March. He appears in the results twice: once for January and once for February.

The operation of UNIQUE in this example makes it difficult to get a unique list from a rectangular range.

Below is the staffing schedule for a museum exhibit hall. You need to generate an access code for each person who is volunteering this month. A UNIQUE formula in B10 fails because the combination of Lou, Mike, Kelly, Hank, Hank, Raul, Raul, Hank never happens again.

B10				f_x	=UNIQUE(B3:H7)		
	A	B	C	D	E	F	G	H

	A	B	C	D	E	F	G	H
1	Volunteer Schedule for Museum Exhibit Hall							
2		Sunday	Monday	Tuesday	Wednesd:	Thursday	Friday	Saturday
3	Week 1	Lou	Mike	Kelly	Hank	Raul	Raul	Hank
4	Week 2	Kelly	Hank	Hank	Gary	Raul	Gary	Gary
5	Week 3	Gary	Raul	Yazmin	Hank	Lou	Quenten	Gary
6	Week 4	Hank	Kelly	Kelly	Lou	Lou	Raul	Lou
7	Week 5	Barb	Yazmin	Hank	Yazmin	Kelly	Quenten	Raul
8								
9		Complete list of people who need an Access code this month:						
10		Lou	Mike	Kelly	Hank	Raul	Raul	Hank
11		Kelly	Hank	Hank	Gary	Raul	Gary	Gary
12		Gary	Raul	Yazmin	Hank	Lou	Quenten	Gary
13		Hank	Kelly	Kelly	Lou	Lou	Raul	Lou
14		Barb	Yazmin	Hank	Yazmin	Kelly	Quenten	Raul

In March 2022, Microsoft gave us the TOCOL function. It will unwind the names from B3:H7 into a single column of data. You can pass the results of TOCOL to the UNIQUE and SORT functions like this:

```
=SORT(UNIQUE(TOCOL(B3:H7)))
```

When you do this, you produce a list of unique names that appear in the specified range.

Unique vs. Distinct

Consider the list shown in A2:A9 below. The UNIQUE function in C2 returns the list Apple, Banana, Cherry, Dill, Eggplant. A person brought up in SQL Land would call this a distinct list; someone who grew up in Excel Land would call it a unique list.

There are some folks in the distinct camp who would argue that there is nothing unique about Apple. It appears twice in the list. Those folks wish that UNIQUE would return the items that appear exactly once in the list: Banana and Dill. You can force UNIQUE to return the items that appear just once: Just add a TRUE as the optional third argument to UNIQUE.

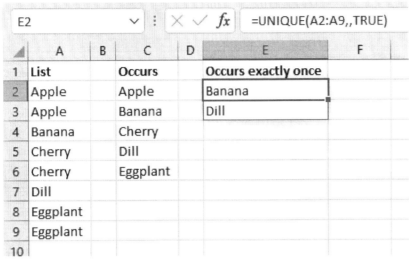

The @ Operator, Briefly Known as SINGLE

If you know that you are going to be in a dark alley and you might encounter a rogue Excel know-it-all who plans to make life miserable for you unless you can stump him with an Excel trick, you might consider asking him about a concept known as *implicit intersection*. During 17 years of 35 seminars a year, I've only run into two people who use it, and only one actually knew that they were using it.

Consider =A3:A15, which most would consider to be an "illegal" formula. If you enter that formula in rows 1, 2, 16, 17, or anywhere below that, you get a #VALUE error. But if you enter that formula anywhere in rows 3 to 15, Excel thinks you are trying to use implicit intersection and returns the value from that row.

	A	B	C	D	E	F	G	
1								
2		Sales						
3	Apple	2044			An odd formula of			
4	Cherry	6073						
5	Elderberry	4691			**=A3:A15**			
6	Guava	1954						
7	Iceberg	9581			entered anywhere			
8	Kiwi	5473		Kiwi	in rows 3 to 15			
9	Mango	6874			would trigger			
10	Orange	3582			implicit intersection			
11	Quince	9445						
12	Star fruit	9932						
13	Ugli fruit	2045						
14	Watermelon	3539						
15	Yuzu	1396						
16								

Go back to before dynamic arrays. If you entered =A3:A15 (or, more likely, =$A$3:$A$15) in D8, you would get Kiwi. If you entered the same formula in D14, you would get Watermelon. In the world of dynamic arrays, the formula =A3:A15 would spill the results.

Let's just guess that 7-thousandths of 1% of people have used implicit intersection in an average of three spreadsheets in their life. That means there are 151,260 spreadsheets stored on hard drives that need implicit intersection to keep working. According to Joe McDaid, Microsoft's Calc Team spent an inordinate amount of time making sure that those 151k spreadsheets would keep working after dynamic arrays. There are probably another 449k spreadsheets where the result is inadvertently using implicit intersection, and those 600k spreadsheets need to keep working.

Joe needed a way to allow people who loved implicit intersection to keep using it. For a brief time, Microsoft used SINGLE—in the formula =SINGLE(A3:A15) in this example—but in a later incarnation, it decided on using the @ symbol to indicate implicit intersection. Cell D8 in the above image contains the formula @A3:A15.

Here is an actual useful example from data analyst Mordechai Steinfeld. (If you regularly read Contextures or MrExcel, you have undoubtedly run across a few tricks that were discovered by Mordechai.)

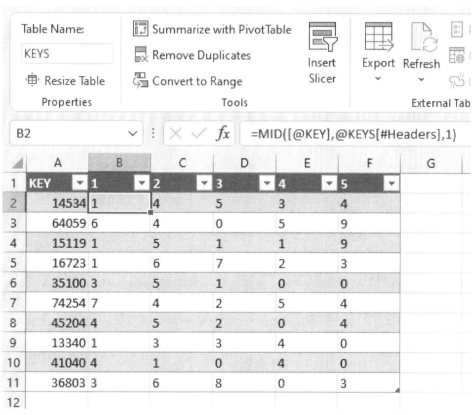

In this example, the reference to [KEY] is the entire column A. By using [@KEY], you get the key from this row. Then the reference to KEYS[#Headers] refers to the headers at the top of the table. By using @KEYS[#Headers], you get just the header in the column above the cell. The formula shown in B2 can be copied to B2:F11 and will parse the keys from column A into five digits.

🐉 Is There an Explicit Intersection?

Have you ever wondered about the term *implicit intersection*? Is there another kind of intersection? There is, but you can't see it. That is because the intersection operator is invisible. A space between two cell references indicates that you want the intersection of the references.

Here is a quick demo of explicit intersection.

In the figure below, select A2:E7. Then: Formulas | Defined Names | Create Names from Selection. The dialog defaults to using labels in the top row and left column. This is fine. Click OK, and you will very quickly create nine named ranges.

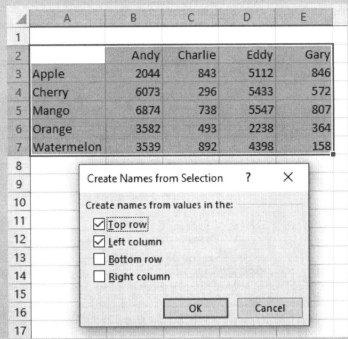

Excel creates five names from the labels in A3:A7. For example, a named range called Mango will refer to B5:E5.

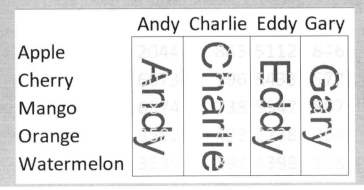

Another four names will be created from the columns. Eddy would refer to D2:D6.

Note: You can "see" the range names in the grid if you change the zoom level to 39% or lower. Of course, at 39% zoom, you can't make out much text. To create the screenshots above, I had to first enlarge everything to 72-point font and then reduce to 39% zoom. Finally, I changed the font color of the numbers to light gray so you can see the range names.

With those range names created, you can do fun things like =SUM(Charlie) or =AVERAGE(Cherry). To explicitly use the intersection operator, you can type =Charlie Cherry or =Cherry Charlie, and Excel will find the cell(s) at the intersection of the Charlie named range and the Cherry named range.

▲	A	B	C	D	E	F	G
2		Andy	Charlie	Eddy	Gary		
3	Apple	1	2	4	8		
4	Cherry	2	4	8	16		
5	Mango	4	8	16	32		
6	Orange	8	16	32	64		
7	Watermelon	16	32	64	128		
8							
9		62	=SUM(Charlie)				
10		30	=SUM(Cherry)				
11		4	=Charlie Cherry				
12							
13							
14		**explicit intersection!**					

Is there really a useful situation where you might use intersection? In the example below, the person is allowed to choose a name and a product. A pair of INDIRECT formulas create the equivalent of =Gary Orange.

C13				✕ ✓ *fx*	=INDIRECT(C9) INDIRECT(C10)		

▲	A	B	C	D	E	F	G	H
2		Andy	Charlie	Eddy	Gary			
3	Apple	2044	843	5112	846			
4	Cherry	6073	296	5433	572			
5	Mango	6874	738	5547	807			
6	Orange	3582	493	2238	364			
7	Watermelon	3539	892	4398	158			
8								
9	Choose a name:		Gary					
10	Choose a product:		Orange					
11								
12	Intersection of Gary and Orange				="Intersection of "&C9&" and "&C10			
13			364		=INDIRECT(C9) INDIRECT(C10)			
14								

Caution: The INDIRECT function is volatile. Using volatile functions severely slows down calculation of a workbook. You should never use volatile functions in any sizable worksheet. However, if you have a worksheet with only 37 cells and need an example to get out of a threatening situation in a dark alley, the use of INDIRECT is authorized.

The Spill Indicator

The results from dynamic array formulas might shrink or grow. Particularly if your formula is pointing to a range defined as a table, you can see more results as the table grows.

Here is a simple example. In the following figure, there is a date in A1. The formula in B2 will generate the numbers from 1 to the month number. Since the date is currently in May, you get the numbers 1 to 5.

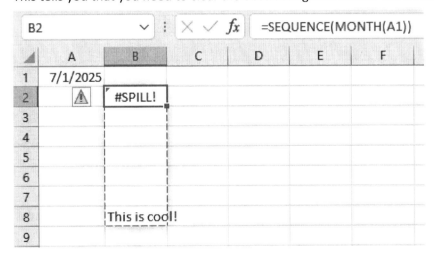

Two months later, once the date in A1 changes to July, Excel will want to return the numbers 1 to 7. There is not room to return all of the results. Instead of getting partial results, you will instead get the #SPILL! error. This tells you that you need to clear the obstructing cells before the answers will be displayed.

Chapter 11: Data Is Never 100% Clean (Not for Very Long)

♻Data quality is important. Sometimes, if you are building the worksheet to collect data, you can implement data validation to maintain some control over data quality. But more often, you are receiving data that you need to analyze, and you are at the mercy of the person who collected the data. You need to figure out what pitfalls are hiding in the incoming data—which means you need to clean it.

Let's say you and I have an aquarium maintenance service with a list of three clients:

Client	Address	Email	Aquarium
Angela Davies	10312 St. Ignasius Ct.	Angie.D@fake-email.com	100 gallon freshwater
Fara Santos	744 E Arlington Circle	Fara@fake-email.com	30 gallon freshwater; 55 gallon saltwater
Seductive Smile Dentistry	39 SE 22nd Ave 8th Floor	SSD-Teeth@fake-email.com	150 gallon saltwater; 200 gallon saltwater

Even a small dataset like this one can be wrong. Take a moment and think about ways that this data might be untrustworthy. Here are a few:

- Angela Davies no longer has an aquarium.
- Seductive Smile Dentistry has moved to a different address but still has the two aquariums.
- Yesterday, Fara Santos added a 100-gallon saltwater aquarium.
- A new client, Silva-Azio Realty, isn't on the list.

Now, let's say we have a dataset of 500 rows, and some entries look like this:

Client	Address	Email	Aquarium
Alice Boyton	4749 Arthur Avenue	AliceBee@fake-email.com	100 gallon saltwater; 200 gallon saltwater
Alice Boyton	4749 Arthur Avenue	AliceJean@fake-email.com	200 gallon saltwater
Alice J. Boyton	4749 Arthur Avenue	AliceBee@fake-email.com	
Angela Davies	10312 St. Ignasius Ct.	Angie.D@fake-email.com	100 gallon freshwater
Collette Kurian	1981 Kemper Lane	Casa-Kurian@fake-email.com	150 gallon
DeniseClay	11208 112th St	Denise88@fake-email.com	100 gallon freshwater
Fara Santos	744 E Arlington Circle	Fara@fake-email.com	30 gallon freshwater; 55 gallon saltwater
Judith Merriman	553 W Lake Rd #1701	Judy@fake-email.com	90 gallon saltwater
Kenwood Library	3442 Cannon Ave	KWD-Library@fake-email.com	500 gallon freshwater (enter on Criss Drive)
Latrice Chanceler	914 Brentwood Drive		2 29 gallon Fresh Water aquariums
Marco			150, 30, 30
Maureen C. Mellon	309 Red Prince Dr.	65-gal salt	Maureen@fake-email.com
Red Car Auto Body; 8722 N Industrial Pkwy		RCAuto@fake-email	aquarium is in the lobby
Ricardo H. Hobbs	2231 Joseph Street	fake-email.com	
Seductive Smile Dentistry	39 SE 22nd Ave 8th Floor	SSD-Teeth@fake-email.com	150 gallon saltwater; 200 gallon saltwater
Silva-Azio Realty	917 SE 30th Ave	SAR@fake-email.com	75 gallon freshwater
Venita Tate			

A few of the problems:

- There are three entries for Alice Boyton, and one of them is Alice J. Boyton.
- For Red Car Auto, there's a note in the Aquarium section.
- Emails and addresses are missing.
- Red Car Auto Body's address is in the same cell with the name.
- Venita Tate has a name and no other data.

- Maureen C. Mellon's email and aquarium data are reversed.
- Ricardo H. Hobbs's email address is incomplete.

Imagine what the other 483 entries look like. 😖

Deciding What's *Clean Enough*

An effort to cleanse our aquarium maintenance data can and should be made. But how much effort should be put into it? There will be some folks who insist that anything and everything should be done to get this list pristine. But that's not realistic—especially when you consider that the real world outside keeps moving. (While you are cleaning the data, Silva-Azio Realty might split up, leaving a useless phone number, and the space may be taken over by a chiropractor who plans to keep the aquarium.)

It's critical to ask questions about your situation. Questions you might ask about the aquarium client data:

- What am I trying to do with this data?
  - Notify the freshwater clients of a product that can be lethal to their fish?
  - Mail out *Happy New Year* postcards?
  - Get a rough count of how many freshwater vs. saltwater aquariums we service?
- What's at stake? After making efforts to clean up the data and there's still crap entries, *so what*?
  - Risk terrifying the wrong clients while failing to notify all of the relevant clients? Could this result in lawsuits, lost business, and bad reviews?
  - Alice Boyton will get three postcards, and other people won't get any?
  - The owner tells a potential client you serve 40% saltwater tanks but it's actually 43%? That's not a big deal.
- How bad is the data, and what will it honestly take to get it clean?
  - 5 days?
  - 1 hour?
  - You'll never get it handled because crap data is coming in faster than you can clean what's already here?

A Story: We Just Can't Clean All This Data

I had a job cleansing critical data to clear errors related to insurance licensing. After a month, my director asked how many I was able to cleanse in a day. I told him, "Maybe 10 because of all the research. Then, after I make whatever corrections, the company database updates overnight. The next morning, I check to see which errors cleared and which hadn't." It was rare for all 10 to have cleared. Some days 0 errors would clear.

He asked, "How many errors are there? How do you know when you'll be done?"

"I don't know," I replied.

He determined that the company was processing thousands of transactions per day, and dirty data was coming in faster than I could clean it—at a rate of 0 to 10 corrections per day. So, he took me off of that job and put me on something else, **accepting the reality that there would be problems and angry customers**.

It would have been unrealistic to suggest putting more people on the job because it required a deep understanding of the business, the data, the reports, the product line, and state regulations in order to do the research and attempt to clear the errors. Meanwhile, the business kept chugging along, and new transactions were entering the company database from all over the world via the call center and online—24 hours per day.

The solution in this case was to **give priority to the customers who called in with problems** and handle them as they came in.

Chapter 12: Data Validation: Controlling Inputs and Maintaining Data Integrity

Consider these common issues that make datasets hard to work with:

- Analysis on the Great Morning Cafe account is wrong because some entries are under Great Morning Coffeeshop and others are under GM Café.
- Survey results are messy because a field accepted Y, N, Yes, No, nope, maybe, absolutely, 6, and T.
- A field for customer birthdate includes dates that were just three days ago.
- An item number is sometimes H377T and sometimes H-377-T.

Controlling inputs and maintaining data integrity are essential topics in guerilla data analysis. Far too often, when the stakes are high, this aspect of spreadsheet development is overlooked. In extreme cases—such as where there's a serious legal matter—forensic accountants are called in to try to determine if a transgression involves poor spreadsheet integrity or a deliberate decision to hide illegal activity in a mess of confusion.

For most of us, messy data turns simple analysis into hours of data cleansing. One hour's worth of making subtotals and basic graphs is held off by a full day of tussling with ornery data, detecting and fixing things like:

- Every possible abbreviation and misspelling of California
- Variations of vegetarian, such as veg and veggie
- Determining if veg = vegan or veg = vegetarian

This is especially a big deal since so many people are working with data and Excel in so many different ways—with varying levels of skill and awareness. The upshot is that inconsistent and nonsensical inputs make for sloppy spreadsheets that impact everything from the global economy to a fantasy football league or budgeting for a road trip.

To help you control and minimize input errors, Excel has useful features in the Validation section on the Data tab.

Data Validation Overview

The figure below shows coffee orders from your accounts. There are official/formal lists in column G, with the formal account names and available coffees. You'd like to do some summaries and analysis, make some Pivot Tables, and write some formulas.

WAIT! There are problems:

- In B4, the year is listed as 2021, but the current year is 2022.
- In C4, DE03 should be DE3, as represented in the Coffee list in G10.
- In A5, GM should be GM Café.
- In D7, there should not be a fractional amount. The rule in the text box on top says orders must be in 1-pound increments.
- In A10, A&D should be Andi & Dandy.

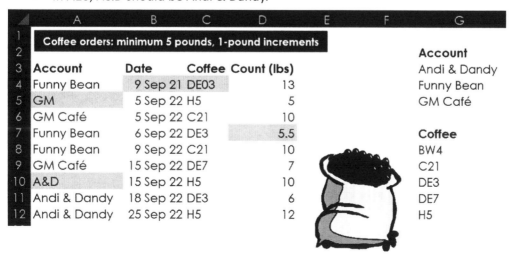

You would like to use the data in the image above to do a lot of things, such as calculate the total pounds by account, regardless of the coffee type. But you can't do it with these problems.

Data validation helps prevent problems **before** you get a mess like this. So, you have to think ahead to how the data could get corrupted and toss you face-first into the struggle of cleaning the data later.

Implementing Dropdown Lists

First, convert the Account and Coffee data ranges into tables because these tables are going to be the source for the dropdown lists.

To put the Account dropdowns in place:

1. Place your cursor in A4. That's where you'd like the first dropdown list to be.

2. Select Data | Data Tools | Data Validation.

3. In the Data Validation dialog, under Allow, select List.

4. Tick In-Cell Dropdown.

5. Click the Edit Reference icon at the far right of the Source field. The Data Validation window minimizes and allows you to select the range where you've stored the dropdown entries—in this case, G3:G5.

6. After you've selected the data, click the Edit Reference icon again, and the Data Validation dialog will be full-sized again.

7. Click OK.

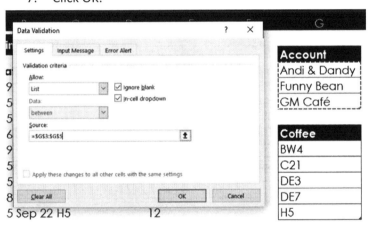

As shown here, the dropdown list is in place, and you can copy it down the column.

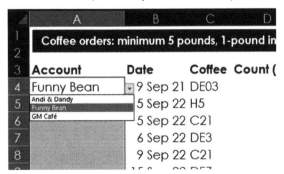

Follow these same steps to apply dropdown lists in the other cells in the Coffee column.

New in 2022: AutoComplete in Validation Dropdown Lists

A new feature appeared for Office Insiders in early 2022. This feature may have made it to a wider Microsoft 365 population by the time you read this. Say that your list includes Apple, Fuji Apple, and Pineapple, as well as other fruits. If a person starts type A, the list will be limited to Apple and Fuji Apple. Even though Pineapple might seem to be a possible match for App, it will not be shown in the shorter list.

Controlling Dates

To restrict valid dates to Q4 of 2022, here's how you'd set up that data validation:

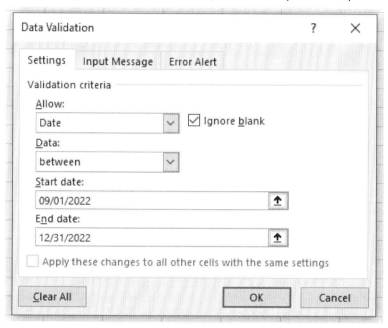

Reasonable Numbers

In the Count (lbs) column, acceptable values are whole numbers ≥5. But let's say that orders are rarely over 20 pounds. So, further restrictions can be applied to prevent any extreme numbers. To give yourself some room, allow numbers between 5 and 40.

Here is how the Data Validation dialog is set up:

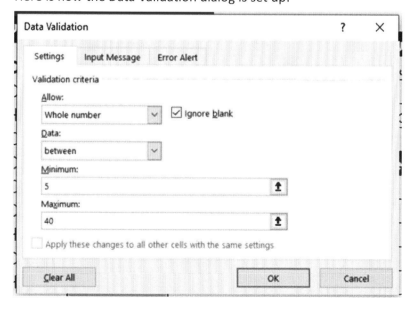

You should check out the Input Message and Error Alert tabs in the Data Validation dialog. They might come in handy. Actually ... let's have some fun and do one more thing.

For the Counts (lbs) column, add an error message guiding users to input a whole number ≥5 and for any values >40 to contact Fabiona for approval. On the right side of the figure below, Excel did not accept the 55 and gave the error message.

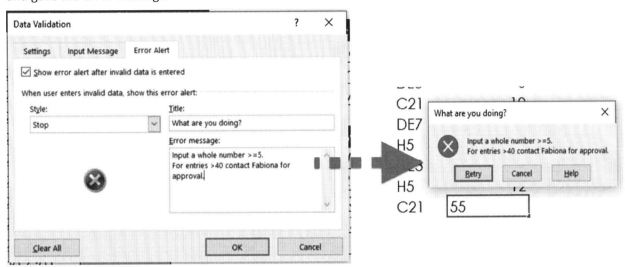

Data Validation Cautions

As you set out to build solutions using data validation, there are some areas that you need to be aware of. Some are limitations with the feature. Some are limitations with the humans using the worksheets you build.

Lists Are Case-Sensitive

This is especially important where there isn't an in-cell dropdown and the user doesn't get a list of available options. If you want to restrict a cell entry to Yes or No, you have to consider the options that a user might attempt: Y, Y, n, y, Yes, No, YES, NO, ...

If any or all of these are acceptable, you need to list them in the Source Field in the Data Validation dialog. The image below shows the configuration for a list of acceptable entries and is not an in-cell dropdown list. Note that the entries are separated by commas.

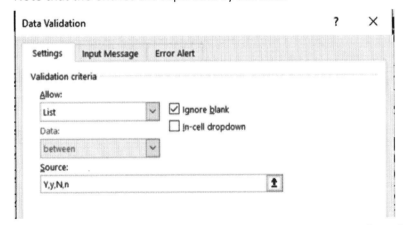

Considering the User Experience vs. the Analyst's Needs

When setting data validation restrictions, you have to balance the user's experience with the ease of analysis later. If you only accept Y or N and don't include a descriptive error alert, the user might input Yes, get an error, and then try YES and get another error. The user might then give up and leave the field blank. One preemptive strategy is to use an input message to tell people that you only accept Y and N. This message appears as a tooltip when a user selects the cell, as shown here.

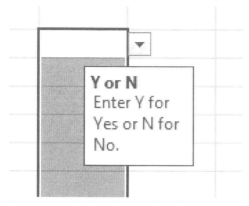

So, you might decide to allow Y and y and include an error alert stating that Y or N is needed, but you include y and n as tolerable options. Then when you do your analysis, you'll have to convert every y to Y for consistency and accuracy. Making that conversion is better than having no validation and enduring the misery of sifting through nonsense before you can do your analysis.

Adding New Rows

In a range (as opposed to a table), data validation isn't automatically applied to include new rows. If your validation goes down to row 10, row 11 will not include validation. One solution is to think about how many rows of data the user might need. Maybe you're building a form where the number of entries rarely exceeds 25 and is never more than 30. You can prebuild, say, 35 rows with the data validation in place.

If your data is in a table, life will be easier. In the image below, I've converted the coffee data to a table. Row 14 is just below the table.

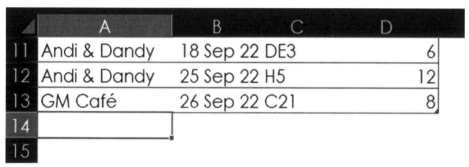

If you are in D13 and want to add a new row, you can hit Tab, and a new row will be added—and it will include any data validation and formulas that are applied to the table. Hitting Tab is easy to forget. A user might start adding data in A14, and the dropdown list will not show until the entry has been made. However, the data validation will still apply.

When you try a new but invalid entry, the error alert pops up, and the table shows a new row. However, because this is an error, when you click Cancel, the row will go away, and cell A14 will empty out.

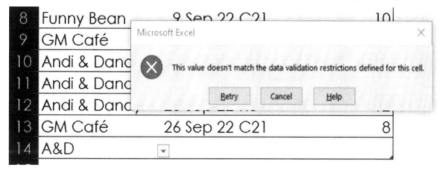

WARNING! It's Possible to Bypass Data Validation by Deleting or Pasting over Cells

Whether it's done by accident or deliberately committed by a diabolical user, one way around data validation is to delete or paste over the cells. Unfortunately, this is one problem that doesn't have an easy or standard solution.

Data Validation Conclusions

Data validation is an invisible protective layer in a spreadsheet that helps keep people out of trouble. Sadly, it's overlooked. I've offered data validation workshops, and the most registrations has been one. Yes. Just one brave soul.

But I can fill up workshops on Pivot Tables or Power Query. I've also had a client insist that I build a form with the right formulas and layout but skip the data validation in order to save time and money. I declined because it would be thoroughly irresponsible to create an expense report file that someone can fill with inconsistent, incomplete, and just plain wrong values and then turn it over to their vice president for approval and reimbursement.

That's not a situation that can be dismissed as, "Well, it's that person's responsibility to work it out with the VP." My worry is when the vice president sees the problems, it'll be easy for them to blame "that stupid consultant" who built the form.

At some level, we have to protect our reputation. We can't control everything, but if there's something foreseeable that can be avoided, it's our responsibility to do so.

Please. I beg you. Take data validation seriously. When you're building a document, think about the ways that it can be corrupted by a user:

- Addition of notes in a field that should have a Y or N
- Text where only numbers should go (think of accidentally typing an account name into the account number field)
- Inconsistent formatting and abbreviations (e.g., NorthEast, NE, North East, northeast)
- Numbers that make no sense (e.g., -15 years old or 1.22 cars)
- Misspellings (e.g., Norheast)

Smart use of validation can eliminate or greatly reduce these problems, make analysis easier, and increase the trust we have in our results.

Chapter 13: Protecting Sheets and Cells

After your workbook is all set up—when the layout is how you want it and the formulas are accurate—it might be wise to protect your hard work, especially if the workbook was built for other people to use.

In this example, an order form was created for people to input their orders.

In the image below, the order form is on the left, on the Order Form sheet. On the right, the Pricing worksheet shows the price of each available fishing lure.

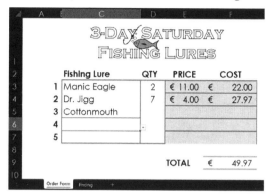

On the Order Form sheet, in E3:E7, an XLOOKUP is retrieving the prices from the Pricing sheet. Here is the formula in E3:

```
=IF(COUNTA(C3:D3)<2,"",XLOOKUP(C3,prices[Lures],prices[Prices]))
```

Here is the formula that multiplies the price and quantity in F3:

```
=IF(COUNTA(C3:D3)<2,"",D3*E3)
```

Dropdown lists are being used in C3:C7, and you can see the dropdown arrow in C6.

Locking Down an Entire Sheet

NOW! You want to protect the Pricing sheet to prevent users from typing in the wrong places, accidentally typing over the formulas, tampering with the formulas, changing the prices, or adjusting the lovely logo.

On the Pricing sheet: Review | Protect | Protect Sheet. This opens the Protect Sheet dialog, where you'll get options for:

- Adding a password. Be careful with this option. If you forget the password, it's gone. And it's getting increasingly difficult to break into a workbook or worksheet that's password protected.

- What you will allow the users to do (e.g., change formats, sort, delete columns).

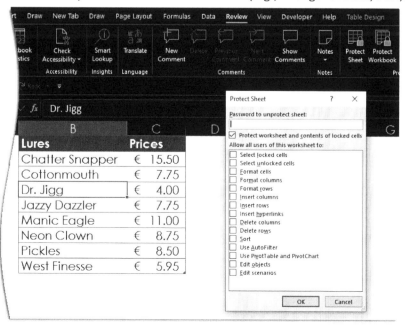

In this example, none of the "Allow" boxes are ticked. If a user clicks on this page, the only thing they can do is look. They won't be able to select a cell, sort, filter … *nothing*.

Locking and Unlocking Cells

Protecting the Order Form sheet is a little more involved than protecting the Pricing sheet because users need to be able to input data.

The first thing you need to know is that all cells in an Excel workbook are locked by default.

Click on the logo to select it. Then right-click on the selected logo and choose Size and Properties.

You'll see that the option for Locked is ticked. This means if you protect the sheet, the user will not be able to move it, alter it, or delete it unless you go to the Protect Sheet dialog and tick the Edit Objects box.

Cells are also locked by default. Thus, before protecting the sheet, it's necessary to *unlock* any cells that the user should have access to.

Highlight C3:D7 | right-click | Format Cells.

The Format Cells dialog opens.

Untick Locked | OK.

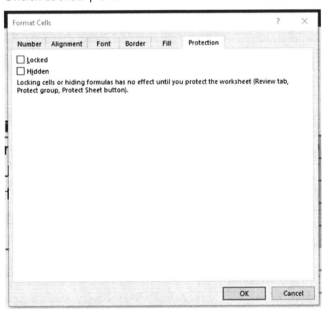

As it says in the dialog, the formatting won't have any effect until the sheet is protected.

With the Order Form sheet visible: Review | Protect | Protect Sheet.

In this case, at a minimum, the user needs to select unlocked cells. Tick the box for that option, as well as any others that you deem appropriate. Click OK.

Unprotecting a Sheet

To remove protection from a sheet: Review | Protect | Unprotect Sheet.

Chapter 14: Octopus Spreadsheets

Skirmish

⮫ Often when clients contact me for Excel help, they're dealing with a workbook that's got lots of parts and pieces and data everywhere. Some parts are connected and others aren't—but should be. This is the dreaded octopus spreadsheet.

Together, the client and I have to decide if we:

- Get rid of the octopus, set the octopus free back into the ocean, and build something integrated from scratch OR
- Keep the octopus and carefully add another tentacle.

Where Did the Octopus Come From?

How do octopus spreadsheets develop? Here's an example.

Let's say you have a small business with four departments. Someone creates a workbook to calculate payroll. A year later, you decide to calculate monthly overhead and how much each department should pay toward overhead. That gets added to the payroll workbook since payroll data will help the overhead calculations.

Later, a few people are allowed to take an advance on their salaries, and you need to track how much they borrowed, how much has been paid back, and what's still due.

The pieces are on separate sheets, and changes need to be made in multiple places instead of one. CONGRATULATIONS! BOO! You've got an octopus workbook. ☹

Now what?

To Jettison or Not to Jettison the Octopus … That Is the Question

Here are a few things you face when you're wrapped up and being squeezed by a big ol' wet octopus spreadsheet:

- **Time:** What kind of time do you and the client have? Carefully integrating a new tentacle or retrofitting the workbook to be better integrated might take a week, but a complete development from scratch might take two months.
- **Cost:** Does the client have the money available for a two-month build?
- **Effort:** A complete build can create upheaval and lots of testing, tweaking, rebuilding, and more testing and tweaking. Sometimes, there isn't enough bandwidth to run the business and be supportive of the testing and tweaking.
- **Approval process:** I've had multiple situations where the client can't get approval for a new build, but the person will personally pay for a quick improvement.
- **Acceptance/resistance to change:** This is the biggie! There might be money and willingness, but then you get the word: "I know this needs to be overhauled, but people have been looking at the spreadsheet this way for five years, **and *they are not* going to want anything different**."

In any of these cases, you're limited to what you can improve and integrate on the back end.

Avoiding the Octopus

To avoid or reduce the chances of birthing an octopus spreadsheet, here are some suggestions:

- Think ahead as best you can and set things up for easy integration.
- Keep data in as few places as possible.
- Use formulas with relative, mixed, and absolute cell references to make data dynamic.
- Use tables.
- Learn Pivot Tables!
- Learn Power Query.

Chapter 15: INDIRECT

INDIRECT is pretty slick because it lets you assemble parts of a formula and have Excel treat it like a single formula.

In the example below, instead of using the formula =E3 to retrieve Beijing, cell B2 uses:

```
=INDIRECT(B4&B5)
```

It treats E and 3 as if they're the cell reference E3.

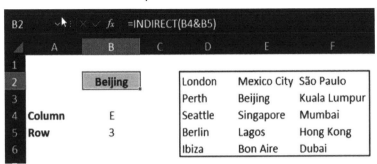

Where's the thrill in that? Okay, I'll show you.

In this example, there are three centers on three different worksheets in three different tables. Each table is named for a city.

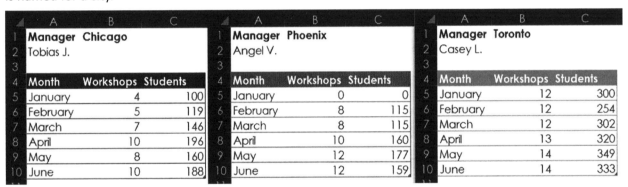

The Workshop Summary sheet (on the left side of the image below) has a dropdown list in B1, and the INDIRECT function is being used to retrieve data from the respective worksheets and tables. On the right side of the image, the underlying formulas are shown by using the Ctrl+` keyboard shortcut.

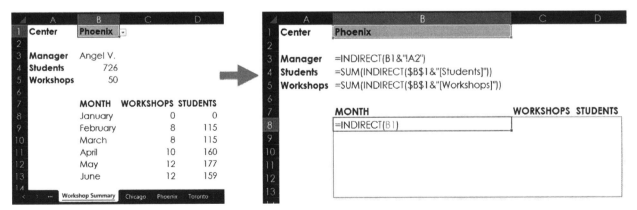

If you created a formula in B3 to retrieve the name of the manager in Phoenix, that would be:

```
=Phoenix!A2
```

The exclamation point tells Excel to go to the sheet named Phoenix and then get whatever is in cell A2. The result is Angel V.

But you want something dynamic so that you can use the dropdown list to easily retrieve data from any sheet: Chicago, Phoenix, or Toronto. And that's where INDIRECT comes in.

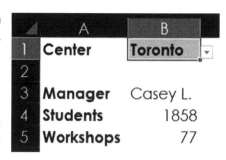

In B3 on the Workshop Summary sheet:

```
=INDIRECT(B1&"!A2")
```

This formula says "Take whatever is in cell B1 and combine it with "!A2" to create Phoenix!A2." When you wrap that in INDIRECT, Excel treats it like a normal formula. When you change B1 to Toronto, BOOM!

Cell B4 refers to the tables. The dull, static version would be:

```
=SUM(Toronto[Students])
```

That generates a sum of the Students column in the Toronto table. The sexy, dynamic variation is:

```
=SUM(INDIRECT($B$1&"[Students]"))
```

The same is happening in B5:

```
=SUM(INDIRECT($B$1&"[Workshops]"))
```

Did you notice the line drawn around B8:D13? =INDIRECT(B1) in B8 returns the entire table, taking advantage of Excel's dynamic arrays. It's returning the entire table named whatever is in cell B1.

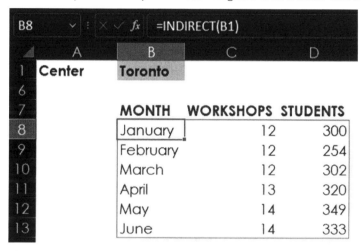

The thrills and excitement don't stop here!

Let's say workshop data from Lagos has arrived and needs to be added to the file:

1. Add a sheet named Lagos with the manager's name in cell A2.

2. Add the workshop data in a table named Lagos with the column headers MONTH, WORKSHOPS, STUDENTS.

3. Add Lagos to the dropdown list.

4. Shout "HALLELUJAH!"

You don't have to write more formulas. As long as you keep the layout and naming consistent (steps 1 and 2), INDIRECT takes care of everything else.

Here is a note from the Calc Team's Joe McDaid about INDIRECT:

INDIRECT can solve some problems that no other function can solve. However, it has some problems that are worth pointing out. (1) It can't be used to point to another workbook, unless both workbooks are open at the same time. (2) It is volatile. That means everything in the calculation chain that happens after the INDIRECT must be recalculated every time, potentially slowing down the workbook. (3) It does not adjust if something above the reference is inserted. (Although sometimes this is a positive thing!)

Chapter 16: OFFSET

At its most basic, OFFSET asks for a starting point and retrieves data that's a number of rows and a number of columns away. For example, in the figure below, the formula =OFFSET(B5,4,2) in cell B1 causes the following to happen: Starting in B5, go four rows down and two columns to the right. The result is cell D9: Saturn.

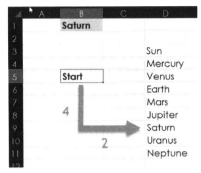

This is pretty bland. However, when combined with other functions, OFFSET provides dynamic formulas. Here's its syntax:

```
=OFFSET(reference, rows, column, [height],[width])
```

Using OFFSET to Sum a Range

When used with [*height*] or [*width*] values, OFFSET must be nested inside another function—such as SUM, AVERAGE, MAX, or MIN—that's doing work on the range of cells.

> **Note:** A pair of square brackets ([ ]) around an argument means that the entry is optional.

The following dataset has a count of colors sold, displayed by month:

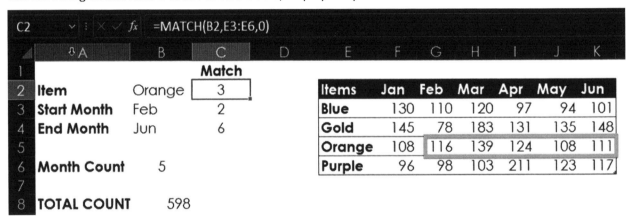

The goal is an integrated layout that lets you input an item, a start month, and an end month and get the sum. The image shows that you're interested in Orange items for February through June. B8 shows the total is 598.

The formulas in C2:C4 are helper columns, making it easier to build the OFFSET function when you're ready for it in B8:

- In C2, =MATCH(B2,E3:E6,0) finds the row number of the item.
- In C3, =MATCH(B3,F2:K2,0) finds the column number of the first month.
- In C4, =MATCH(B4,F2:K2,0) finds the column number of the ending month.

To find the number of Orange items that were sold February through June, the formula in cell B8 will give you the answer:

```
=SUM(OFFSET(E2,C2,C3,1,B6))
```

Here is a deconstruction of the formula and what it's doing:

Formula Component	Description	Value
=SUM(	Opens the SUM function	
OFFSET(	Opens the OFFSET function	
E2	Starts at cell E2	Items
C2	Specifies the number of rows to go down from E2	3
C3	Specifies the number of columns to go to the right of E2	2
1	Specifies the height of the final range	1 (row)
B6	Specifies the width of the final range	5 (columns)
)	Closes the OFFEST function	
)	Closes the SUM function	

Chapter 17: Recognizing Patterns

Skirmish

♻ Being able to recognize patterns in your data is an important skill.

The dataset below includes data about apartment buildings, tenants, car parking assignments, etc. And it's all over the place.

Goal: Fill in the Apartment Building column. Example: In A5, Riverwalk is the apartment building, and it needs to be in C2, in the same row as the tenant's first name; A9 says Queen Court Apartments, and it needs to be in C6.

	A	B	C
1	Tenants	Units & Notes	Apartment Building
2	Chance		
3	Upshaw		613
4		Car park: H-13	
5	Riverwalk		
6	Flavius		
7	Ruszala		1214
8	Studio Apartment	Notify for 1bdrm	
9	Queen Court Apartments		
10	Chicken		
11	Romero		1705
12			
13	QCA		
14			
15	Issac		
16	Cormondy		308
17	Issac@fake-email.com		
18	Seabreeze		
19	Nigel		
20	Turner		831
21			
22	RW Apartments		
23	Esme Romero		
24			1515
25	Parking space: 4	Parking space: 6	
26	Sea Breeze Apartments		
27	Chance		
28	Rudder		944

Problems with the data:

- The records aren't consistent.
- The names of the apartment buildings aren't consistent.
    - A9 has Queens Courts Apartments
    - A13 has QCA
    - A5 has Riverwalk
    - A22 has RW Apartments
- Tenant names aren't consistent.
    - Chance Upshaw's name is split across A2 and A3.
    - Esme Romero's whole name is in a single cell, A23.
- Row 14 is completely blank.

But notice a pattern: Wherever there is an apartment number, the apartment building's name is two rows down and one column left.

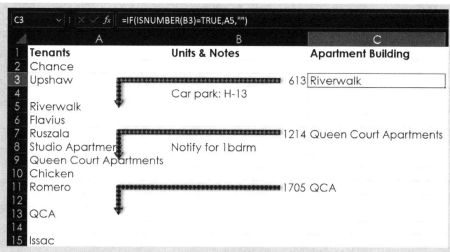

To retrieve the apartment names, use this formula in C2:

`=IF(ISNUMBER(B3)=TRUE,A5,"")`

The formula says: "If the value in B3 is a number, then retrieve the value in A5; otherwise, stay empty."

Dragging the formula down the column takes advantage of the relative cell references.

Chapter 18: Data Types and Stock History

My take on the Excel Data Types feature might be different than most. As of early 2022, I think everything we've seen in Data Types is a beta-style proof of concept. Ten years from now, no one will be using Data Types the way we are using it now. The real power will be using Data Types to query your own company data.

But before we get there, let's see where we started and where we are now:

- **The original release:** Microsoft introduced Geography and Stock as Data Types options. They have a lot of "gee-whiz" coolness about them. Enter some cities in some cells, and Excel can magically tell you the population or mayor of those cities. Enter some stock symbols and retrieve the current day's high, low, open, close, and a slightly delayed stock price. You could use a formula to retrieve the information from the data type and populate a cell. The formula could even return a picture. Or, instead of returning the data to the grid, you could view a Data Card to browse all of the information that Excel knows about a city. You can access information in the data type entity for sorting or filtering or XLOOKUP without actually bringing that data into the grid.

- **The second release:** Wolfram options were added to the Data Types feature. These were very important additions. A field can now return an array of values, including an array of other entities. There is a lot of functionality in the phrase "return an array of other entities." The "array" part means that an answer can contain several items. The "other entities" might mean that the answer will be another entity, and that entity will have a bunch of fields as well. After May 2022, these Wolfram data types will only be available in Home editions of Excel.

In the original release of Data Types, you could ask who is the mayor of Portland and get a single answer. That single-cell answer might list that the leader of a city is both Bob as mayor and Freda as city manager. But that data is in a single cell, and it is plain text in a single cell.

The second release of Data Types now lets you ask for the members of the Ohio Players music act. This question will return an array of several people. Each returned value in the array is also a data type. That means you can find out that Billy Beck was a member of the Ohio Players. And then you can ask where Billy Beck was born. The answer will be a Location entity of Youngstown, Ohio. Then you can ask who else was born in Youngstown, Ohio. Among the 100 people in that array of People entities is drummer Sonny Parker. Where did Sonny Parker die? The answer is another Location entity: New York City. What's the average temperature in New York City in February? 31.892 degrees. You can continue to drill down and down and down through this vast Excel encyclopedia.

I would frequently demo the original release of Data Types in my live seminars. I would always ask people what they would like to see in Data Types. Three common answers:

- **Currency exchange rates:** Done! Microsoft switched their stock price vendor to someone who offers currency rates as well.

- **Weather:** Done! The Wolfram location data includes weather history for each city. But be careful: Since Wolfram is a scientific data source, the answers are in Celsius instead of Fahrenheit.

- **Our own company data:** I laughed when someone suggested this. "Well, THAT will never happen!" But I sent a note to the Excel project managers, saying that someone had the crazy idea of storing their own company data in a data type. I was surprised when they said, "We've thought of that, and we aren't ruling it out." As of early 2022, Microsoft has made four attempts to offer this. One is with Power Query. Another is with Power BI. The third is a custom function through a JavaScript API. The fourth is a full-blown data type through a JavaScript API. These are getting very close to what I think they need to be.

Original Release Data Types

Let's walk through examples using original release Data Types.

Finding the Population of Portland and Other Cities

Open a blank workbook. Type a few cities in A2, A3, and so on. You can help Excel a bit by typing City in A1, but this is not required.

	A	B
1		
2	Portland, OR	
3	Chicago, IL	
4	Akron, OH	
5	Cape Canaveral, FL	
6		
7		
8		

With the city cells selected, go to the Data tab and choose Geography from the Data Types gallery.

Excel will successfully convert the text Portland, OR to a data type entity. A tiny "unfolded map" icon appears in each cell, and you lose the state part of each city entry.

	A
1	City
2	🗺 Portland
3	🗺 Chicago
4	🗺 Akron
5	🗺 Cape Canaveral
6	

Tip: The original release of Data Types has a neat feature that has not been picked up by the second release or custom data types. The original release of Data Types looks at the surrounding cells to try to figure out context. In the image below, if you have a lone cell that says Paris and convert to Geography, Excel will ask you which Paris you want. But if you surround Paris with names of other European cities, you will get Paris, France. If you surround Paris with names of other Kentucky cities, you will get Paris, Kentucky. This was a cool feature, but it was not picked up with the second release of Data Types, so you might see it abandoned eventually.

Asks   **Paris, France**

	A	B	C	D	E	F
1						
2	Paris		Lexington		London	
3			Louisville		Frankfurt	
4			Paris		Paris	
5			Bowling Green		Brussels	
6			Owensboro		Istanbul	
7			Convington		Milan	
8						
9						

Paris, Kentucky

Caution: After converting text to a data type, Excel replaces the original text with the .Name property of each entity. As shown below, if you are producing a report of all of the Springfields in the United States, this will be confusing. It might make more sense to keep your original text in column A, copy that text to column B, and convert column B to a data type.

C2 f_x =B2.[Admin Division 1 (State/province/other)]

	A	B	C	D
1	Before Data Type	After Data Type	State	Population
2	Springfield, Missouri	Springfield	Missouri	169,176
3	Springfield, Massachusetts	Springfield	Massachusetts	155,032
4	Springfield, Illinois	Springfield	Illinois	114,694
5	Springfield, Oregon	Springfield	Oregon	62,979
6	Springfield, Ohio	Springfield	Ohio	58,662
7	Springfield, Virginia	Springfield	Virginia	31,339
8	Springfield, Pennsylvania	Springfield	Pennsylvania	24,199
9	Springfield, New Jersey	Springfield	New Jersey	17,517
10	Springfield, Tennessee	Springfield	Tennessee	16,957
11	Springfield, Vermont	Springfield	Vermont	9,062
12	Springfield, Florida	Springfield	Florida	8,075

Pulling Data Out of a Data Type Entity

As shown below, in B2, type =A2 and a period. Excel provides a list of available fields. Choose from the list. For example, =A2.Population.

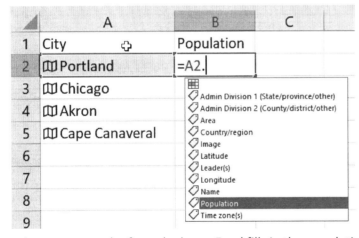

When you copy the formula down, Excel fills in the population for each entity.

B2 f_x =A2.Population

	A	B
1	City	Population
2	Portland	652,503
3	Chicago	2,746,388
4	Akron	198,006
5	Cape Canaveral	10,449

Using Data in a Data Type Entity Without Displaying It in the Grid

If you convert your data to a table, you can choose to sort by a field that is not displayed in the grid. Open the Filter dropdown, and you can select a field to use for sorting.

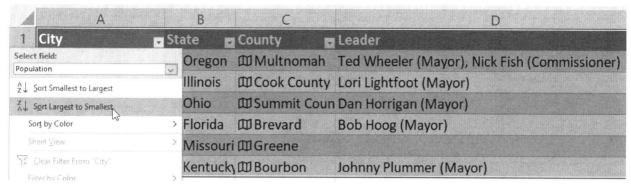

You can also use the XLOOKUP function to pull data out of data types.

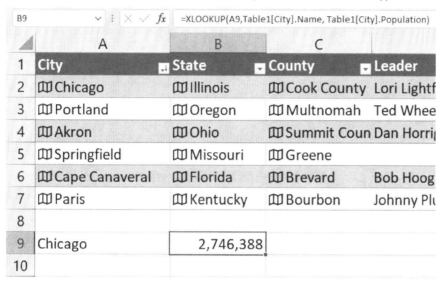

Original Release Data Types for Stocks and Currency Exchange Rates

You can pull current day trading information for publicly held companies and exchange rates. In this figure, the formula =B2.Price returns the current stock price to a cell.

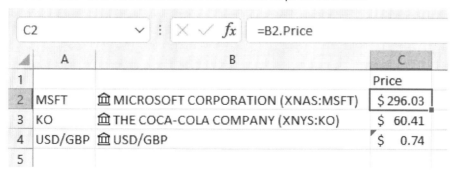

There is quite a bit of data available for a company. But you quickly realize that while you can get the previous day's close and the 52-week high and low, you cannot get daily history by using data types. To get this, you need to use the STOCKHISTORY function, discussed on page 144.

	A	B
1	🏛 MICROSOFT CORPORATION (XNAS:MSFT)	Formula
2	$ 301.60	=$A$1.[Previous close]
3	$ 296.03	=$A$1.Price
4	$ 304.11	=$A$1.High
5	$ 295.61	=$A$1.Low
6	$ (5.57)	=$A$1.Change
7	-1.85%	=$A$1.[Change (%)]
8	$ 296.31	=$A$1.[Price (Extended hours)]
9	0.09%	=$A$1.[Change % (Extended hours)]
10	$ 0.28	=$A$1.[Change (Extended hours)]
11	57,984,403	=$A$1.Volume
12	$ 349.67	=$A$1.[52 week high]
13	$ 222.42	=$A$1.[52 week low]
14	31,663,366	=$A$1.[Volume average]
15	$ 7,507,980,000.00	=$A$1.[Shares outstanding]
16	$ 2,222,588,000,000	=$A$1.[Market cap]
17	0.91	=$A$1.Beta
18	USD	=$A$1.Currency
19	Microsoft Corporation is a technology compar	=$A$1.Description
20	181,000	=$A$1.Employees
21	Nasdaq Stock Market	=$A$1.Exchange
22	XNAS	=$A$1.[Exchange abbreviation]
23	1 Microsoft Way, REDMOND, WA, 98052-6399	=$A$1.Headquarters
24	Software & IT Services	=$A$1.Industry
25	Stock	=$A$1.[Instrument type]
26	1/21/2022 23:51	=$A$1.[Last trade time]
27	MICROSOFT CORPORATION	=$A$1.Name
28	MICROSOFT CORPORATION	=$A$1.[Official name]
29	33.71	=$A$1.[P/E]
30	MSFT	=$A$1.[Ticker symbol]
31	1993	=$A$1.[Year incorporated]

Second Release Data Types: Wolfram

Microsoft signed an agreement with the Wolfram database to use a lot of their information in Excel. This is automatically included in Home editions of Office. It was briefly available in Enterprise and Education editions of Office, but this support was removed on May 31, 2022.

The most important improvements in the second release of Data Types:

- A field might contain an array of answers.
- Any answers might also be data type entities themselves.

Here is an example. A3 contains the music act Ohio Players. You can tell it is a music act because of the music note icon. In cell B3, you ask for =A3.members, and the result is nine cells that have a Person data type entity.

	A	B
	B3 ⌄ ⋮ ✕ ✓ *fx*	=A3.members
3	♫Ohio Players	👤Billy Beck
4		👤Clarence Satchell
5		👤Walter Morrison
6		👤Leroy "Sugarfoot" Bonner
7		👤Marshall "Rock" Jones
8		👤Ralph "Pee Wee" Middlebrooks
9		👤James "Diamond" Williams
10		👤Dutch Robinson
11		👤Greg Webster
12		

Returning new entities as the answer to the formula would allow you to ask further questions about each person in the band. If you go to C3 and ask for =B3.[place of birth], you will learn that Billy Beck was born in Youngstown, Ohio. Change that formula to =B3#.[place of birth], and you will see the place of birth for each member.

Note: The #FIELD! error means that the information is not available in the data source.

	A	B	C
	C3 ⌄ ⋮ ✕ ✓ *fx*	=B3#.[place of birth]	
3	♫Ohio Players	👤Billy Beck	🏢Youngstown
4		👤Clarence Satchell	🏢Cleveland
5		👤Walter Morrison	🏢Dayton
6		👤Leroy "Sugarfoot" Bonner	🏢Hamilton
7		👤Marshall "Rock" Jones	🏢Dayton
8		👤Ralph "Pee Wee" Middlebrooks	#FIELD!
9		👤James "Diamond" Williams	#FIELD!
10		👤Dutch Robinson	🏢United States
11		👤Greg Webster	#FIELD!

You will notice that Youngstown in C3 is returned as a Location data type entity. To find out who else was born in Youngstown, use the formula = C3.[notable people born in city] to get a list of 100 notable people born in Youngstown.

Tip: At this point, you are running out of vertical room for the 100 answers. Particularly if you want the list of notable people from Youngstown, Cleveland, Dayton, and Hamilton, the spreadsheet will get very tall very quickly. An easy alternative is to wrap the formula in the ARRAYTOTEXT function. This will return the names as text and concatenate the whole list into a single cell. You lose the ability to drill down further on Ed O'Neill, but this makes it possible to see the list. ARRAYTOTEXT is a shorthand way of writing TEXTJOIN(", ",,C3.[notable people born in city]). And it is easier than using TEXTJOIN.

	B	C	D
D3		f_x	=ARRAYTOTEXT(C3.[notable people born in city])
3	Billy Beck	Youngstown	Ed O'Neill, Omarosa Manigault, Jim Cummings, Maurice Clarett, Kelly Pavlik, Bc
4	Clarence Satchell	Cleveland	Kid Cudi, Halle Berry, Dolph Ziggler, Tracy Chapman, Mehmet Oz, Drew Carey, J
5	Walter Morrison	Dayton	Martin Sheen, Allison Janney, Nancy Cartwright, Roger Clemens, Jonathan Wint
6	Leroy "Sugarfoot"	Hamilton	Ray Combs, Steve Morse, Roger Troutman, Eric Lange, Joe Nuxhall, Robert McC
7	Marshall "Rock" Jc	Dayton	Martin Sheen, Allison Janney, Nancy Cartwright, Roger Clemens, Jonathan Wint

What Does It Take to Be a Notable Person?

I've lived a few places in my lifetime. I always enter a city I know and ask for the list of notable people. As you would expect, notable people include famous actors, singers, some politicians. They also include pro sports players. College football coaches. Serial killers. Sadly, Excel book authors and YouTube creators have not made these lists—yet. I have no problem with Willie Mays, Hank Aaron, Barry Bonds, or Derek Jeter being on a list of notable people. They are all Hall of Fame baseball players. But Horace B. Phillips? He managed the Pittsburgh Alleghenys back in 1871, when baseball was barely a pro sport. Horace makes the list? I guess I am just jealous.

	A	B	C
1	Salem	John Allen Campbell	
2		Rich Karlis	
3		Horace Phillips	
4			
5		Horace B. Phillips (May 14, 1853 – February 26, 1896) was an American manager in Major League Baseball for eight seasons, from 1879 to 1889.	
6			

Data Types: Navigating the Data Card

If you click on the icon to the left of the data type, Excel displays a Data Card. Here is the Data Card for Microsoft.

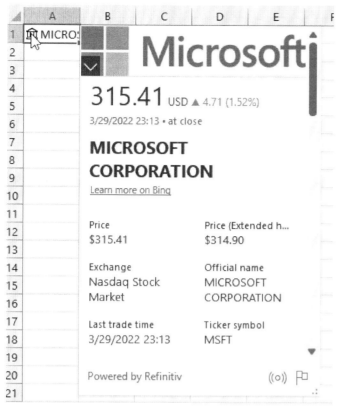

Back in the original release of Data Types, the Data Card was nearly useless. It was very narrow. You could not print it. With each answer being a single answer, there was not a lot to discover.

With the second release of Data Types, the Data Card has improved. You can resize it. There are now separate symbols for "put this in the grid" vs. "drill down a level and show me this entity."

To show the Data Card, either click on the icon in the left edge of a cell or select the cell and press Ctrl+Shift+F5.

You can resize a Data Card by using the dots in the lower-right corner.

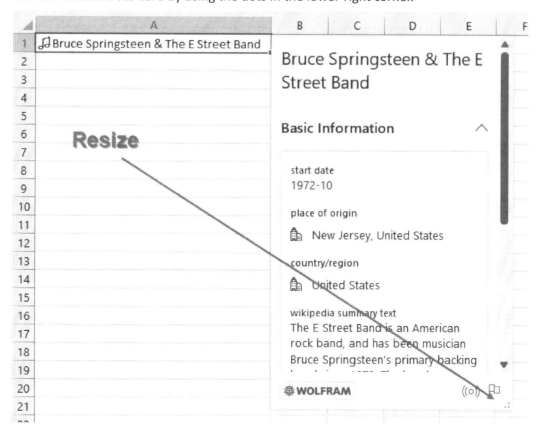

In the image below, the symbol on the right is the Extract to Grid symbol. The symbol on the left lets you drill down right in the card.

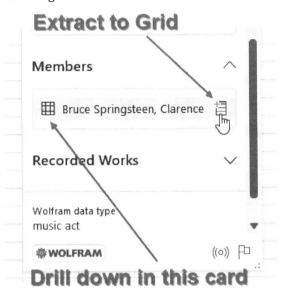

If you drill down on Members in the image above, you are shown an array of a dozen Person entities.

members

⍺ Bruce Springsteen
⍺ Clarence Clemons
⍺ Max Weinberg
⍺ Nils Lofgren
⍺ Steven Van Zandt
⍺ Charles Giordano
⍺ Danny Federici
⍺ David Sancious
⍺ Garry Tallent
⍺ Patti Scialfa

Click on the icon for Clarence Clemons. You will learn that Clarence Desmond Clemons was born January 11, 1942, in Chesapeake, Virginia. Click on the icon for Chesapeake. Click on other notable people born there. Choose one. Choose one of their films. Choose the cast of the film. And so on. When you finally decide to extract to grid, the Excel formula will show the path that you took to get there, as shown below.

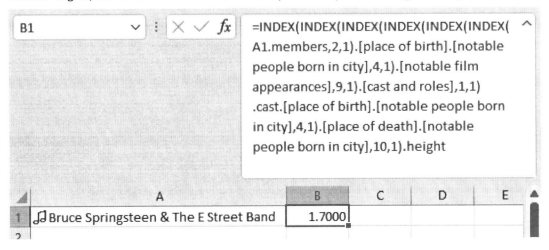

Custom Data Types: Features Needed

When you buy a photo frame at the store, there is already a picture of someone in the frame. No one actually keeps that photo of someone else in the frame. You take that slip of paper out and put in a photo of someone you care about.

For the past several years, Microsoft has been building the architecture behind Data Types using someone else's data. In 2021, Microsoft gave us four ways to use our own data in Data Types instead of using someone else's data. I predict that soon, no one will care about finding out Clarence Clemons's hometown. Ninety-nine percent of the people using Data Types will be using their own data in Data Types.

Microsoft has four ways for us to create data types—and I'll talk about them below, in the section "Custom Data Types: The Choices Available Today." Before we get to the four ways, let's consider a rating scale of which Data Type features are most important. Here is my rating scale of what I need in custom data types, from most important to least important:

1. I need to be able to show an image as a field in the data type. I store an image URL, and the data type returns the image to the grid.

2. I need to be able to store an array of entities as a field.

3. I need to be able to drill down into an entity and get fields from the sub-entity.

4. I would like to be able to type "Excel Skirmishes" into a cell, press a button (in or near) the Data Types gallery, and have Excel figure out that I am talking about this book.

5. I need to be able to embed the data type in the worksheet. If I send the workbook to someone else, they should be able to query the data type.

6. It would be nice if I could customize the icon that appears to the left of the entity.

Custom Data Types: The Choices Available Today

There are four ways to create custom data types today:

*   **Power Query:** You can use Power Query to group several columns into a data type. It is super-easy to set up. It does not support features #1, #2, #3, #4, or #6 in my list above.

*   **Power BI:** If you have E3 or E5 subscriptions to Office 365, you can create a new data type in Power BI. This is the only option that meets #4 above. But it does not handle #1, #2, #3, or #6.

*   **Custom function using JavaScript API:** This one gets really close. It does handle #1, #2, and #3. It won't use the Data Types gallery, but you could create a data type by using =Foo.BookName("Excel Skirmishes"). It handles #5. It does not offer #6.

*   **Task pane using JavaScript API:** This one is probably the best. It handles #1 through #5 with the exception that you are using a button in a task pane instead of a data type in the gallery. What about #6? there is still no way to customize the icon.

The sort of bad news is that the JavaScript API is going to require someone in your IT department to build out a structure for you. This isn't something that you are going to build yourself. But the extra effort is worth it, particularly once you are able to, for example, show your company product catalog and drill down to show images, features, and more.

Building these is beyond the scope of this book, but this video will get you started:

Chapter 19: Graphing

Much can be accomplished by building and customizing graphs in Excel. Following are some tips on working with Excel graphs and going a little beyond out-of-the-box graphing.

Graphing a Histogram Using the FREQUENCY Function

Making graphs in Excel is fairly straightforward, but this first example addresses how to handle a simple graph when the source data makes the graph less than useful. In this example, it'd be nice to get a summary of the ages of the guests. The image below shows that there are 107 total entries. We don't care about the individual ages; instead, we want five broad areas, formally called *bins*.

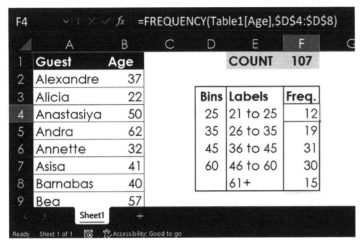

The bins you want are the labels in E4:E8. Cells D4:D8 show how the bins need to be set up in preparation for using the FREQUENCY function to build a graph. The first bin should include everyone up to age 25.

In cell F4, the FREQUENCY function is used:

```
=FREQUENCY(Table1[Age],$D$4:$D$8)
```

Syntax:

```
FREQUENCY(data_array, bins_array)
```

Take special note of the range D3:F8. I learned from my friend, longtime Excel MVP and chart master Jon Peltier, that this range is called a *staging area*. This area simplifies creating a chart because:

- It summarizes what you want to graph.
- It minimizes the number of formulas you have to write. The alternative would be to set up a lookup range with the ages and then add formulas in column C that would retrieve the labels using XLOOKUP or VLOOKUP. And then you'd need a Pivot Table to get the bin totals.
- It is easier to troubleshoot or modify later than if you'd written complicated formulas against the original data.

Ready to make the graph? Let's do it!

With your cursor on any cell within the staging area: Insert | Charts | click the arrow next to the column chart icon | select the first 2-D Column option.

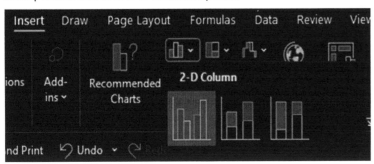

And there is the chart!

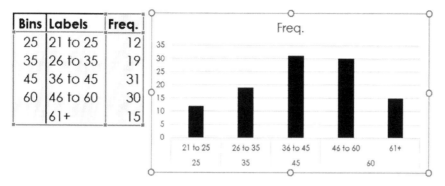

Bins	Labels	Freq.
25	21 to 25	12
35	26 to 35	19
45	36 to 45	31
60	46 to 60	30
	61+	15

One problem: You don't want the bins data in the chart. To get rid of them: Select the chart | Chart Design tab | Data | Select Data.

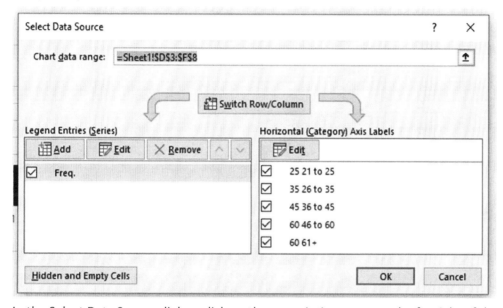

In the Select Data Source dialog, click on the up-pointing arrow at the far right of the Chart Data Range box. Highlight E3:F8.

Click the arrow to return to the Select Data Source dialog | OK.

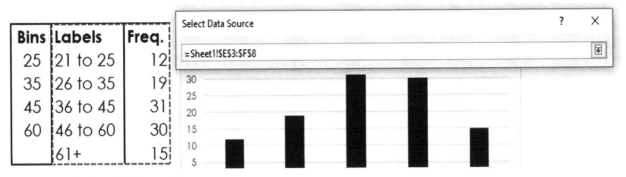

Bins	Labels	Freq.
25	21 to 25	12
35	26 to 35	19
45	36 to 45	31
60	46 to 60	30
	61+	15

HALLELUJAH! There's the graph.

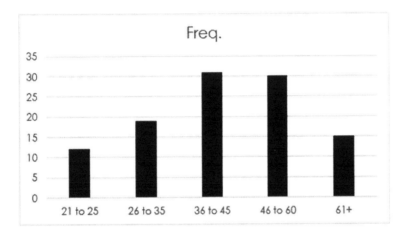

Note: Clever readers might point out that this change could have been avoided if E4:F8 had been selected (omitting the bins data) before making the graph. That's an important point. Because we selected a single cell within the staging area, Excel made a graph with the entire surrounding range of data.

From here, there are a lot of customizations that can be made.

Changing the Chart Title

To change the chart title, you can simply type over the original title.

But you can also create a dynamic title:

1. Type Age Range into H1.
2. Select the Freq. title in the chart.
3. Place your cursor in the formula bar, and it'll empty out.
4. Type = and then use your cursor to select cell H1.
5. Press Enter.

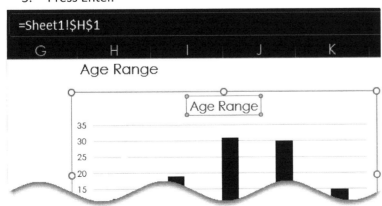

Then, if you want to change the title to something else, change it in H1.

Changing the Font on the X-axis

To change the font on the X-axis, click on one of the labels at the bottom of the chart | Home | Font.

Then make whatever customizations feel good to you. (If this doesn't feel good, there's no point.) For example, in the following image, I made the font bold and increased the size to 12 points.

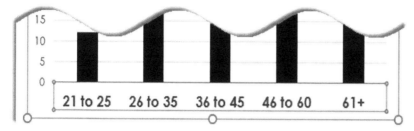

You could, for example, get rid of the gridlines. Click on one of them, and they will all get highlighted. Press Delete, and the gridlines go bye-bye.

Preventing the Chart from Moving or Changing in Size

This is important. I'm serious.

When you're developing a spreadsheet, objects like graphs, shapes, and images will start moving around and changing shape when you insert or remove rows and columns or change the height of a row or the width of a column.

The image below shows that I inserted four columns, and the chart stretched out. ☺

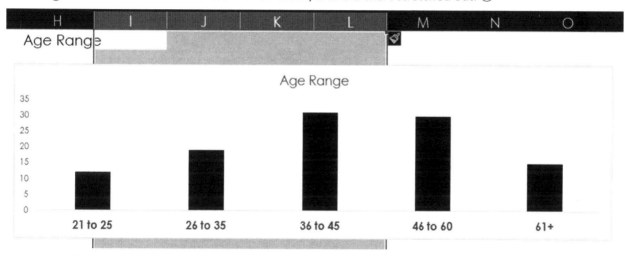

To prevent this:

1. Hover over the chart | right-click | Format Chart Area.

2. In the Format Chart Area pane, Select Chart Options.

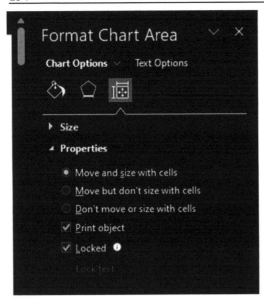

3. Click on the third icon (the four-way arrow inside the square).

4. Click the radio button Don't Move or Size with Cells. (The default for objects is Move and Size with Cells.)

> **Tip:** While we're here, something you should know about is the Print Object option. Let's say this sheet needs to be printed and given to someone who doesn't need the chart. You could delete the chart or move it onto another sheet. Or you can untick the Print Object box and then print.

Adjusting the Width of the Columns in the Chart

To make the chart columns wider:

1. Select one of the columns, and all of them will get selected | right-click | Format Data Series.

2. In the Format Data Series pane, select the three-columns icon and then adjust the Gap Width option to the width that you prefer. In the image below, the Gap Width setting has been reduced to 25%.

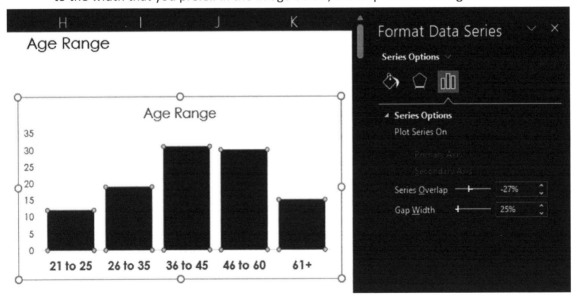

Using Chart Features

This next example will take you into more customization features that you should know about. This data represents average daily views of your videos online:

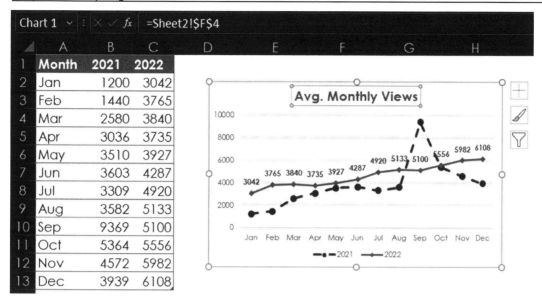

Note: Some of the real-deal graphics people—like Mynda Treacy, Ann Emery, and Jon Peltier—might wonder, "Why did you make such an ugly chart?" My response: The objective is to show you where chart-making things are, not to make a presentation-ready chart. So, let's get on with the gettin' on.

To start working with this chart, place your cursor anywhere in the dataset (A1:C13). Then: Insert | Charts | select the line charts to expand the options menu | select the first chart (as shown below).

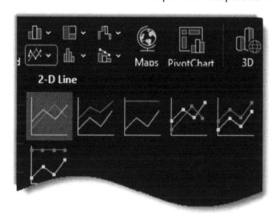

Here is the default chart:

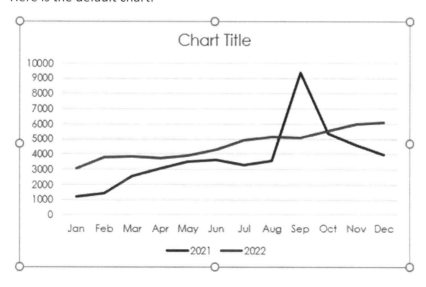

Next, you'll see what customizations you need in order to make the chart look like the one at the start of this section.

Reducing the Congestion on the Y-axis

Click on the values 0 to 10,000 along the left side of the chart. A box will surround those values, and the Format Axis pane will open.

Click the three-columns icon | change the Major option under Units to 2000.

This reduces the clutter in the axis, showing values in increments of 2000 instead of the default 1000.

Adding Markers to the Lines

Select the blue 2021 line. In the Format Data Series pane, click on the paint can icon | select Marker | change the selection from Automatic to Built-in | use the Type option to choose the marker that suits your fancy. (The chart in this example uses the circle marker and a Size setting of 8.)

Repeat these steps to add markers to the 2022 line.

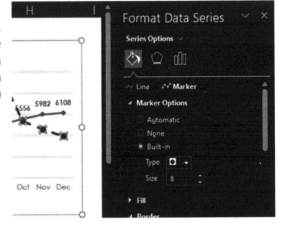

Change the 2021 line to a dashed line | scroll down to Dash Type and select the option you like.

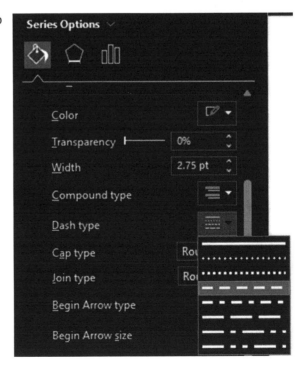

Adding Data Labels to the 2022 Line

This time, select the 2022 line, and the three icons appear to the right of the chart. Click the first icon, and the Chart Elements pane opens. Tick the Data Labels option and click the arrow to open the pane that gives you the options for where the data labels will be placed. Choose Above.

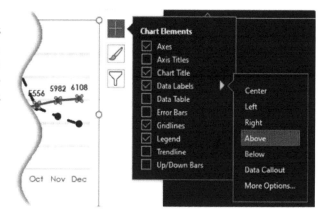

Adjusting the Gridlines

Say that you don't want to completely remove the gridlines but want them to be less intense. You can select one of the gridlines to select them all. Then, in the Format Major Gridlines pane:

- Make them thicker by adjusting the width to 3 points.
- Increase the transparency to 91%.

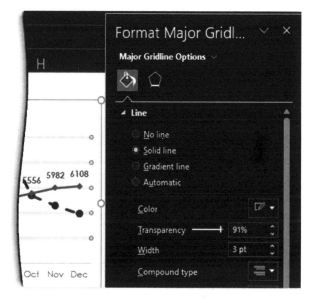

Changing the Chart Title

The last step is to change the chart title by following the steps in the earlier example on page 192. But where is the cell that the chart tile is connected to?

With the title highlighted, look in the formula bar. The chart title is tied to cell F4, which is behind the chart. Putting a cell behind a chart when you don't need that value always visible is one way to reduce visual clutter. You could move it to another sheet, but that could be inconvenient. Just set the chart on top of it. 😄

The image below shows all these changes implemented.

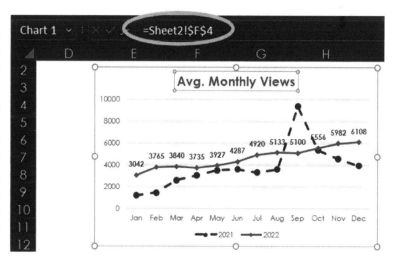

Chapter 20: The Dangers of Just Diving In

⏎ You just received some data. Now you need to do some basic summaries and a little analysis. But can you trust this data? That's the first thing you need to consider.

Do not just dive in.

It's like you're looking at beautiful blue water 10 feet below. Soft waves caress the white sand. You tell yourself, "THIS is the definition of Saturday morning" as you look down to admire your bathing suit that cost so much money that you refuse to tell anyone the real price. Seagulls and pelicans sail overhead.

3

2

1

SPLASH

Straight into a smack of stinging jellyfish! Now a seal has started barking at you as you desperately swim ashore, scraping along the spines of sea urchins. ☹

Check things out before you dive.

Before Diving into the Data

Let's say your data has 8000 rows and a column with city names in it. You scroll down, and in cell B3928 you've got the value 60643. You scroll further, and there's 60657.

Oh no! Rather than containing the city name, Chicago, some entries have Chicago zip codes. And then you see 80201, 75043, 75088, 84110, 2115, 6340. ☹ More zip codes, but Excel has clipped off the leading zeros; 2115 should be 02115 for Boston, and 6340 should be 06340 for Groton, Connecticut. A U.S. zip code is either five or nine digits (e.g., 60657 or 60657-2805).

Imagine that you've gotten started with your work, and some things don't add up. Totals for Chicago are low because of 30 entries that don't have the word *Chicago* but have zip codes instead.

Here are some things you might consider **BEFORE** starting your work:

- How many of the 8000 rows have numbers instead of city names, and are all of those numbers zip codes?
- Are there **any other inconsistencies**, e.g., city name and zip code in the same cell or alternative names like The Bronx instead of New York?
- Are there **blank cells**? How many are there, and **do they matter**?
- Are there duplicates in your data that should not be there?
- Are there **blank rows or columns**? These will cause problems if you need to use Pivot Tables, tables, or Power Query.
- Is there data that you don't need?
  - Maybe there's a birthday column and social media links that you won't ever use. Get rid of them.
  - Maybe you're interested in Chicago, Boston, Salt Lake City, and Denver. Delete entries for Groton, New York, Spokane, and New Orleans.

- Are there **extraneous rows of subtotals** that are preventing the data from being contiguous? Get rid of them!
- Are there **formatting** problems? 2115 is a Boston zip code, and the leading zero has been clipped off.
  - The zip code should be 02115.
  - Everything you do with this data has to guard against losing those leading zeros because 02115 and 2115 are not the same.
- **Do the dates make sense?** If you're looking at new registrations, does a date from 30 years ago make sense? Maybe that person input their birthday.
- **Are you missing too much critical data?** Maybe you need to send mail to 8000 people but only have 3200 home addresses. Is 3200 enough to move forward? It might be or might not be. How much effort would be involved in finding the other 4800 addresses? Is it worth the effort? Depends on what's at stake.
- Do you have **data that's just plain useless**? Maybe you have the name *Phil*. No last name, no address or account number or email address. Or, maybe you have incomplete email addresses, like Cricketfan119@c.

You've got to identify these types of things early on and make some decisions:

- Do you clean up the data?
- What is your strategy?
- What is the acceptable level of "clean enough"?

Sometimes things cannot be cleaned up. Or you don't have enough detail or enough information. In those situations:

- You have to know that the data is wrong or incomplete.
- You also need the story about how you know it is wrong—and that you are digging into the problems.
- You should know why the data is wrong and what adjustments can be made until the data can be corrected.

Another part of *don't just dive in*: How big is the job ahead of you? How many cells already have data in them? In Chapter 1, we offer some tips on using COUNTA to figure out how many empty cells need to be entered.

Go through your data. Check the quality. Check the completeness. Check for consistent formatting. Know where the data can't be trusted. And have an explanation.

Many times I've been in situations where I've been asked to help people. Maybe they need to merge two datasets. In almost every situation, I find problems with the data quality—duplicates, incomplete entries, inconsistent entries (e.g., some names have the first name and the last name and then other names are a last name, professional designation, first name). Those types of things stand in the way of what you're trying to accomplish.

I can tell you stories about working with students or clients and how I saw something that they didn't see. But I am not immune. I have my own bad experiences with diving straight in and regretting it.

One time I had 30,000 addresses. I started moving things around and cleaning things up. And then realized a bunch of the addresses—maybe 1000 of them—were Canadian addresses. Canadian addresses don't have the same format as U.S. addresses. Suddenly I was faced with having to go back into the work that I'd thought was done and write formulas to identify Canadian addresses before I went any further. Had I checked that out before I got started, I could have saved myself a lot of time and heartache. Don't just dive in.

Bottom line:

- Explore your data before you dive in.
- Get clear on your objective(s).
- Clear unnecessary stuff out of the way.
- Ensure that you have access to your original data.

Only then is it safe to enter the water and avoid the seals, jellyfish, and sea urchins.

Before You Dive In: Data Profiling Tools in Power Query

Power Query gives you a quick way to test the quality of your data.

Say that you surveyed 8000 university students and have their results in the spreadsheet shown here.

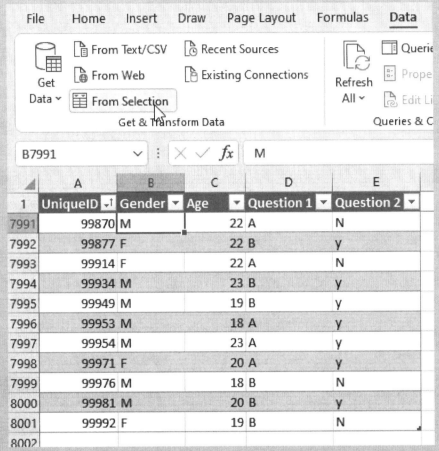

The View tab in Power Query has three data profiling tools built in. Select one cell in your table. From the Data tab, choose From Selection in the Get & Transform Data group. (This was formerly called From Table/Range and From Sheet. Look for the icon and position shown above.)

Once in the Power Query editor, go to the View tab. Turn on three settings: Column Quality, Column Distribution, and Column Profile.

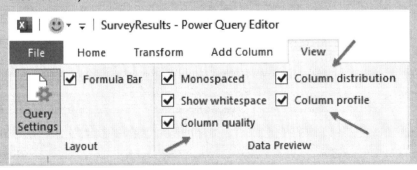

Caution: Do not skip this step. Initially, the profiling tools are based on just the first 1000 records in the data. Look in the lower left of the Power Query editor grid. There is a sentence that says "Column profiling based on top 1000 rows." This means that the tools are only analyzing the first 1000 rows in the dataset. Click that sentence, and a menu pops up. Choose Column Profiling Based on Entire Data Set.

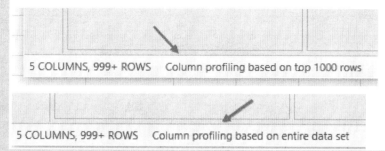

Here are the Column Quality statistics. You can see that there are no empty answers for most questions, but the <1% means that there are some empty answers for Question 2 on the right side of the data.

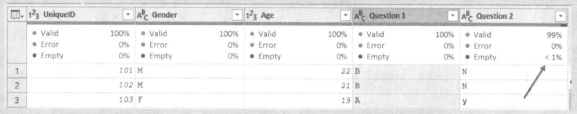

Below, I've turned off Column Quality and turned on Column Distribution.

There are some red flags here:

- The UniqueID column should have 8000 unique entries, but it only has 7996 unique. This means a couple of people managed to answer twice.
- The instructions said to use M/F for gender. But you have six entries.
- The people answering were selected because they were aged 18 to 22. There were five answers with nearly equal distribution but three answers that were only answered once.
- Question 1 was multiple choice with A/B/C/D answers. This looks good.
- Question 2 was Yes/No. The instructions said to enter Y or N. But there were seven different answers given there.

Both Column Quality and Column Distribution show an overview for all columns at one time.

The Column Profile option shows more information, but only for one selected column. In the figure below, Column Distribution is toggled off, and Column Profile is on. Click on the Gender column. At the bottom of the screen, you can see that most people answer F or M, but there were a smattering of Male and Female answers, and even the typos Fe and Mail.

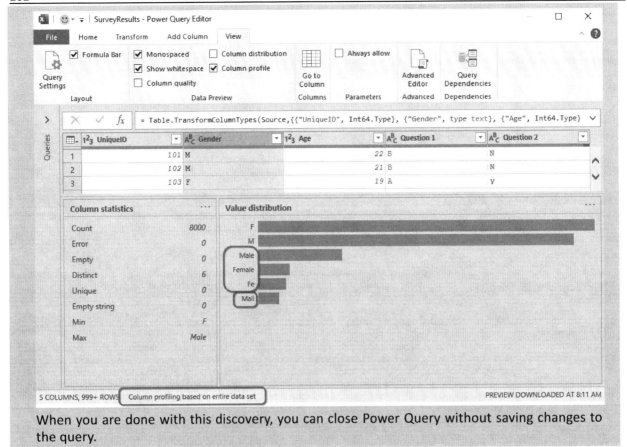

When you are done with this discovery, you can close Power Query without saving changes to the query.

Chapter 21: The LET Function

LET is a new function that simplifies complex formulas, but it also requires a different way of thinking. You have to think like a programmer—i.e., think several steps ahead, assign variables, and then write formulas using those variables.

Here's a very basic LET formula:

```
=LET(x,3,11*x)
```

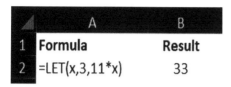

In this formula:

- x is the variable.
- 3 is the value being assigned to x.
- The formula 11*x multiplies 11*3 for the result 33.

No one would ever need such a formula because =11*3 works, but this example shows the raw components of LET, which has the following syntax:

```
=LET(variable1, variable_value1, calculation_or_variable2 …)
```

Why use LET? There are two main reasons:

- To repeat/reuse/recycle big chunks of formula
- To identify portions of a complex calculation for easier readability

Note: LET supports up to 126 pairs of variables and variable values.

LET for Reusing Parts of Formulas

Think about this: You have to write a formula that can be summarized as:

1. Do complicated calculation X.
2. See if complicated formula X meets certain criteria.
3. If it does, do complicated calculation X again. If it does not, don't do anything.

The formula could look like this:

```
=LET(X,complicated calculation, C, criteria to check for, IF(X meets C,X,""))
```

The formula has to calculate X twice if the criteria are met. It's going to be in the larger formula two times, and that might be problematic if that calculation is long, with a lot of parentheses, operators, and functions. That's double the challenge of getting the formula to work, double the places to look if the formula doesn't work, and twice the effort if the formula needs to be modified.

Time for a LET and some recycling.

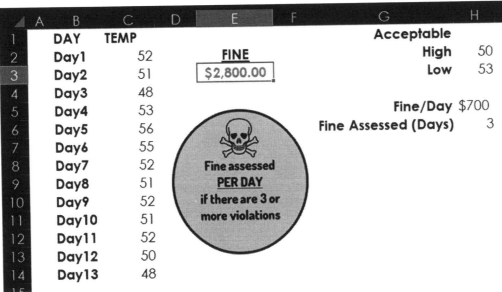

In the image above, you need to determine if a fine is applicable, and if so, what the fine amount is. The criteria:

- Acceptable temperatures are 50 to 53 degrees.
- If the temperature is outside that range for more than 3 days, a fine is assessed, each day. (For example, if there are 3 days of bad readings, no problem. If there are 4 days of bad readings, a fine is assessed for all 4 days.)
- The fine is $700/day.

A visual check reveals unacceptable readings on days 3, 5, 6, and 13. That's 4 days, and 4 > 3. Therefore, 4 days * $700 = $2800 fine.

Here is the formula used in E3:

```
=LET(Limit,H6,Bad,COUNTIFS(C2:C14,">"&H3)+COUNTIFS(C2:C14,"<"&H2),
Fine,H5,IF(Bad>Limit,Bad*Fine,"😊"))
```

- **Limit:** H6
- **Bad:** COUNTIFS(C2:C14,">"&H3)+COUNTIFS(C2:C14,"<"&H2)
- **Fine:** H5
- **Final calculation:** IF(Bad>Limit,Bad*Fine,"😊")

Notice that Bad is in the final calculation twice. Imagine what the formula would look like without LET because that entire piece of the formula would be in the overall formula two times.

Now. I know what you're thinking: What's the deal with the happy-face emoji? Change Day3 to 50, and here ya go:

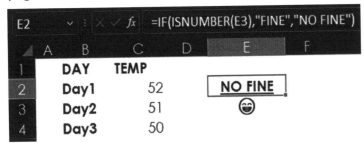

Happiness and joy!

By the way, cell E2 uses IF and ISNUMBER to check if E3 contains a number or not:

```
=IF(ISNUMBER(E3),"FINE","NO FINE")
```

LET for Easier Readability

Let's say a formula has to be written based on a compensation plan that goes as follows:

- **Product line A:** You get $95 on transactions ≥$500.
- **Product line B:** You get 12% on all transactions.
- **Product line C:** You get 6.55%.

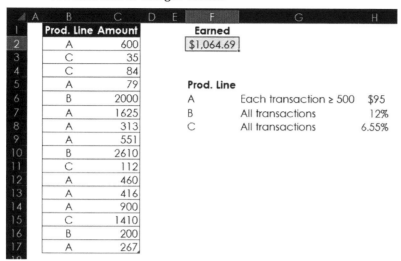

It's possible to build a single massive formula to calculate what's been earned based on the transactions in the image above. That would be messy and should get you thinking about using helper columns (see page 18). You could create a lookup table, and that would be effective, but if your workbook is already cluttered, a lookup table could add to the clutter.

In a situation like this one, the LET function can be a good choice because it will allow you to build a single formula that's readable and doesn't take up the space that helper columns and lookup tables require.

Here is the formula in F2:

```
=LET(ProdA,COUNTIFS(Table1[Amount],">="&500,Table1[Prod. Line],"A"),
        ProdB,SUMIFS(Table1[Amount],Table1[Prod. Line],"B"),
        ProdC,SUMIFS(Table1[Amount],Table1[Prod. Line],"C"),
        (ProdA*H6)+(ProdB*H7)+(ProdC*H8))
```

Here is a deconstruction of the formula and what it's doing:

Formula Component	Description
=LET(	Opens LET
ProdA	Variable for product line A
COUNTIFS(Table1[Amount],">="&500,Table1[Prod. Line],"A"),	Counts the number of transactions that are greater than $500 **AND** product line = A
ProdB,	Variable for product line B
SUMIFS(Table1[Amount],Table1[Prod. Line],"B"),	Sums the amounts for product line B
ProdC,	Variable for product line C
SUMIFS(Table1[Amount],Table1[Prod. Line],"C"),	Sums the amounts for product line C
(ProdA*H6)+(ProdB*H7)+(ProdC*H8)	Calculates earnings based on the compensation plan
)	Closes LET

Caution: The variables in LET formulas have restrictions:

- Cannot start with a number
- Cannot resemble a cell reference
- Can use the underscore but cannot include other characters, like space, comma, slash, hyphen, period

Acceptable	Unacceptable
A	E17
G3B	12
S_E	1YR
YR_1	YR-1
City_Pop	Y 1
	Y.2
	City_Pop.

Chapter 22: Warnings About Machine Learning–Driven Features in Excel and Power Query

Skirmish

🐍Artificial intelligence and machine learning are showing up everywhere. They're being used to simplify tasks, identify patterns or extreme values, manage things that are too enormous for people to handle efficiently, and make decisions that are too complex for humans to make sense of.

However, technologies like these aren't infallible. Think of your email inbox and emails that end up in your spam folder, or think of auto-correct turning *cty* into *cry* instead of *city*. **AI gives us a new job of monitoring what it's done.** My friends who have self-driving cars have told me about long trips they've taken while admitting, "but the car will drive through puddles with no concern that there's a deep pothole under that water." Similar issues are showing up in Excel.

This chapter looks at several machine learning features that can be helpful, but remember: **You have the added job of checking the accuracy of the results.**

Flash Fill

Here is a list of guests, where the goal is to convert the names to the format shown in column C. For example, Amée Romero is being converted to Romero, A.

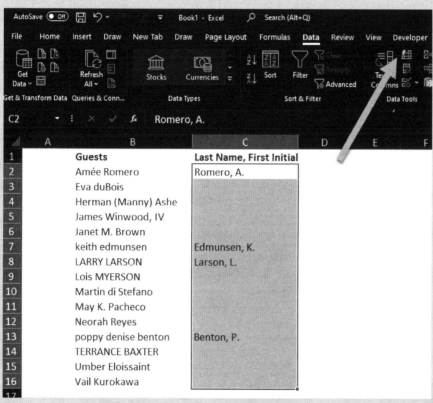

However, if you review the data, you see that there are problems that need to be cleaned up, like Larry Larson being ALLCAPS and Poppy Denise Benson being all lowercase.

Flash Fill can help!

The image above shows that a few names were manually entered to train Flash Fill on the desired result; the range for the results is highlighted; the arrow shows Flash Fill in the Data tab.

Here is the result! OH LORD!

B	C
Guests	**Last Name, First Initial**
Amée Romero	Romero, A.
Eva duBois	Dubois, E.
Herman (Manny) Ashe	Ashe, H.
James Winwood, IV	Iv, J.
Janet M. Brown	Brown, J.
keith edmunsen	Edmunsen, K.
LARRY LARSON	Larson, L.
Lois MYERSON	Myerson, L.
Martin di Stefano	Stefano, M.
May K. Pacheco	Pacheco, M.
Neorah Reyes	Reyes, N.
poppy denise benton	Benton, P.
TERRANCE BAXTER	Baxter, T.
Umber Eloissaint	Eloissaint, U.
Vail Kurokawa	Kurokawa, V.

For the most part, Flash Fill did a great job. But notice:

- James Winwood, IV was converted to nonsense.
- Martin di Stefano's result is wrong because di Stefano is the full last name.
- Eva duBois spells her name that way, but Flash Fill converted her last name to Dubois.
- Question: Should the third entry convert to *Ashe, H.* or *Ashe, M.*? (Someone might have to call Manny and ask him his preference.)

If you had a list of 500 names and needed them all converted, Flash Fill could be a huge help by handling basic entries. But **you have to know your data and anticipate blunders.** One solution would be to segment the data:

- Isolate the basic entries and convert them.
- See if you can group together and convert any similar entries, such as two-part names like:
  - di Stefano
  - de Luca
  - Van Patten
  - Le Beouf
- Identify any entries requiring manual corrections because there are too few in the dataset for Flash Fill to find a pattern, e.g.:
  - James Winwood, IV
  - Dr. Celia Boudreaux, DDS
  - MarionLPayton
  - Herman (Manny) Ashe
  - Zappy's Tea Room & Spa

Providing Feedback to Flash Fill

In some situations, crap data has only two variations. In such a case, you can have Flash Fill handle two rules.

Here are the steps:

In the image below, type Andy N. White in D2.

◢	A	B	C	D
1	**First Name**	**Middle Initial**	**Last Name**	**Full Name**
2	Andy	N	White	Andy N. White
3	Barb		Black	
4	Chris	A	Smith	
5	Diane		Jones	
6	Ed	P	Williams	
7	Flo		Abercrombie	
8	Gary	I	Butler	

Click D3 and press Ctrl+E to invoke Flash Fill. Excel will add a period after the middle initial, even in the rows where there is no middle initial. The Excel status bar will say "Flash Fill Changed Cells: 25." As long as this message is displayed and as long as the symbol shown in E4 is visible, Flash Fill is waiting for you to react.

◢	A	B	C	D	E
1	**First Name**	**Middle Initial**	**Last Name**	**Full Name**	
2	Andy	N	White	Andy N. White	
3	Barb		Black	Barb . Black	
4	Chris	A	Smith	Chris A. Smith	
5	Diane		Jones	Diane . Jones	
6	Ed	P	Williams	Ed P. Williams	
7	Flo		Abercrombie	Flo . Abercrombie	
8	Gary	I	Butler	Gary I. Butler	
9	Hank		Cairns	Hank . Cairns	
10	Ike	V	Deon	Ike V. Deon	

Flash Fill is Waiting for you to respond.

How do you react? You find a cell that follows the second rule and fix that cell. In D3, you could change the space-period-space between Barb and Black to just a single space.

As you make this change, an outline appears around D2:D27. This outline is alerting you that Flash Fill is watching your reaction and will attempt to fix other cells with the same problem.

◢	A	B	C	D	E
1	**First Name**	**Middle Initial**	**Last Name**	**Full Name**	
2	Andy	N	White	Andy N. White	**You fixed**
3	Barb		Black	Barb Black	
4	Chris	A	Smith	Chris A. Smith	
5	Diane		Jones	Diane Jones	
6	Ed	P	Williams	Ed P. Williams	
7	Flo		Abercrombie	Flo Abercrombie	**Excel fixed**
8	Gary	I	Butler	Gary I. Butler	
9	Hank		Cairns	Hank Cairns	
10	Ike	V	Deon	Ike V. Deon	
11	Jared	O	Jones	Jared O. Jones	

The message in the status bar changes. Now it says "Flash Fill Changed Cells: 10." Click on the symbol in E4, and you can choose Select All 10 Changed Cells. In the image below, the 10 changed cells are selected and shaded so you can see what just happened.

4	Chris	A	Smith	Chris A. Smith
5	Diane		Jones	Diane Jones
6	Ed	P	Williams	Ed P. Williams
7	Flo		Abercrombie	Flo Abercrombie
8	Gary	I	Butler	Gary I. Butler
9	Hank		Cairns	Hank Cairns
10	Ike	V	Deon	Ike V. Deon
11	Jared	O	Jones	Jared O. Jones
12	Kelly		Clarkson	Kelly Clarkson
13	Lou	O	Manalti	Lou O. Manalti
14	Mike	E	Miller	Mike E. Miller
15	Nan	B	Blanks	Nan B. Blanks
16	Otto		Jelen	Otto Jelen
17	Paul		Lewis	Paul Lewis
18	Quenten	E	Tee	Quenten E. Tee
19	Raul		Smith	Raul Smith
20	Sam		Snead	Sam Snead
21	Tracy	I	Ulman	Tracy I. Ulman
22	Uma		Thurman	Uma Thurman
23	Vera	O	Wang	Vera O. Wang
24	Will		Wheaton	Will Wheaton
25	Xavier	F	Ferdinand	Xavier F. Ferdinand

Sheet1   +

Ready   Flash Fill Changed Cells: 10   Workbook Statistics   🔢

In this example, you adeptly used Flash Fill to fix two different patterns. Flash Fill was your trusty assistant, waiting for you to teach it the second rule.

In this example, everything worked perfectly. There are certainly other examples where Flash Fill goes insane, finding some pattern that you never expected it to find. But for something simple like "Join these names together, adding a period when there is a middle initial," it works great.

Power Query's Column From Examples

Power Query offers Column From Examples (CFE) as a machine learning feature to help you get what you want from your data by entering a few examples. In the image below, CFE did a great job peeling the street directions from the addresses. It needed just one example and extracted E, SW, NE, etc. for the Zone column. In rows 11 and 13, the decimal point was also brought over, but that's easy to clean up.

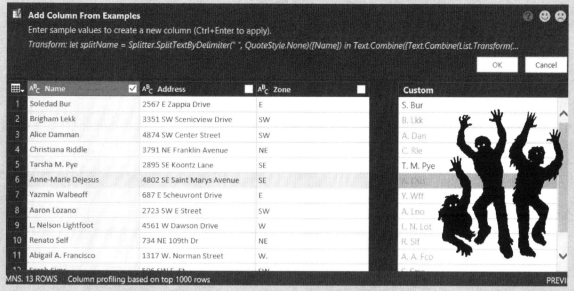

The names are another issue.

I typed examples for row 1 (S. Bur) and row 5 (T. M. Pye). When you use CFE, with each example that's typed in, Power Query builds and revises a formula. The gray text in the Custom column is CFE offering potential results. If the gray text looks good, you click OK and lock in the results.

But look at it. Alice Damman in row 3 is showing as A. Dan. In row 9, L. Nelson Lightfoot shows as L. N. Lot. *GEEZ!*

Sometimes you can type in more examples, and CFE will eventually return what's wanted. In the next image I typed S. Sims for row 12.

Looks pretty good! Sometimes CFE can't find a pattern and will return nulls, signifying that it's given up and can't find a pattern.

One thing to note is row 6: Ann-Marie Dejesus. It's up to the user to determine if the desired result is A. Dejesus or A. M. Dejesus or another variation. This highlights the point that you need to know what's in your data and be clear about the results you need to see.

Column From Examples can be helpful with data that has a fair level of consistency. In situations where there's great inconsistency, it might help to divide the data into segments that are similar and handle them on their own—or isolate the entries that create the most complexity and modify them manually. For example, CFE won't be of much help with the following list of donors that includes business names, names that are in different formats, and entries like Violet & Courtney Kincaid. You'll need a multi-part strategy for working with such a list.

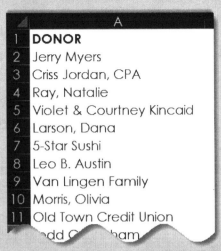

	A
1	**DONOR**
2	Jerry Myers
3	Criss Jordan, CPA
4	Ray, Natalie
5	Violet & Courtney Kincaid
6	Larson, Dana
7	5-Star Sushi
8	Leo B. Austin
9	Van Lingen Family
10	Morris, Olivia
11	Old Town Credit Union

Another thing you need to know about Column From Examples: It generates a formula based on your sample entries and refines the formula with additional examples. I won't get into the code, but I want to show you this.

After typing the examples S. Bur and T. M. Pye, the CFE-generated formula is:

```
= Table.AddColumn(#"Added Custom Column", "Custom.1", each let splitName =
    Splitter.SplitTextByDelimiter(" ", QuoteStyle.None)([Name]) in Text.Combine({Text.Combine
    (List.Transform(splitName, each Text.Start(_, 1)), ". "), Text.End([Name], 2)}), type text)
```

After then entering S. Sims, the resulting formula is:

```
= Table.AddColumn(#"Renamed Columns", "Custom", each let splitName =
    Splitter.SplitTextByDelimiter(" ", QuoteStyle.None)([Name]), splitName2 = List.Reverse
    (Splitter.SplitTextByDelimiter(" ", QuoteStyle.None)([Name])) in Text.Combine(
    {Text.Combine(List.Transform(splitName, each Text.Start(_, 1)), ". "), Text.Middle
    (splitName2{0}?, 1)}), type text)
```

Analyze Data (Formerly Known as Ideas)

Here is some course data. To dig into it with the Analyze Data feature: Home | Analysis |Analyze Data. (Note that in some earlier versions of Excel, this was called Ideas or Insights).

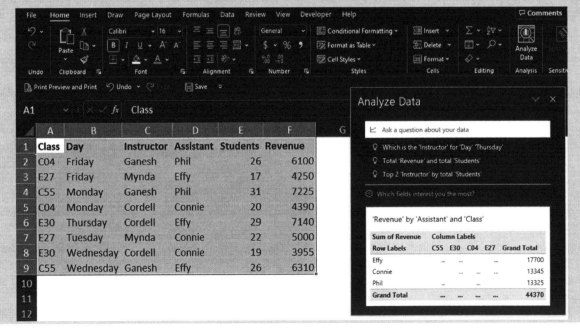

	A	B	C	D	E	F
1	Class	Day	Instructor	Assistant	Students	Revenue
2	C04	Friday	Ganesh	Phil	26	6100
3	E27	Friday	Mynda	Effy	17	4250
4	C55	Monday	Ganesh	Phil	31	7225
5	C04	Monday	Cordell	Connie	20	4390
6	E30	Thursday	Cordell	Effy	29	7140
7	E27	Tuesday	Mynda	Connie	22	5000
8	E30	Wednesday	Cordell	Connie	19	3955
9	C55	Wednesday	Ganesh	Effy	26	6310

Analyze Data

Ask a question about your data

Which is the 'Instructor' for 'Day' 'Thursday'
Total 'Revenue' and total 'Students'
Top 2 'Instructor' by total 'Students'

Which fields interest you the most?

'Revenue' by 'Assistant' and 'Class'

Sum of Revenue	Column Labels				
Row Labels	C55	E30	C04	E27	Grand Total
Effy	...			...	17700
Connie		...	...	...	13345
Phil	...		...		13325
Grand Total	...	...	...	...	**44370**

The Analyze Data pane opens, and Excel highlights the dataset. You're offered some ideas for details that you might want to know about the data, such as Top 2 'Instructor' by Total 'Students'. Scroll down and resize the pane, and you see some graphs and possibly useful insights.

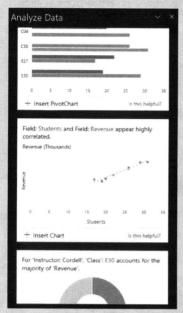

Click on Top 2 'Instructor' by Total 'Students'. Here's the result:

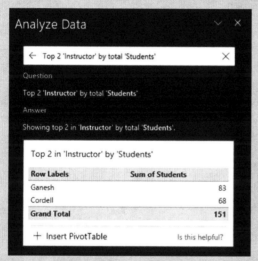

Cool. If this is what you need, mission accomplished! However, there's much more that's available in this data.

Analyze Data has a natural language feature. I'm warning you, though: This is where things get very scary.

Using Natural Language with Analyze Data

It's possible to type in a question to ask Analyze Data about your data. For the data shown above, it would be nice to know which class had the most revenue. If I asked you that question, you'd likely ask me for clarification. "Oz, do you want the summary of each class's revenue (class C55, $13,535), or do you want an individual class's revenue (class C55, Monday, $7225)?"

Analyze Data can't ask you questions for clarification. It returns a summary, as shown below. Is that what was needed? Maybe. Maybe not.

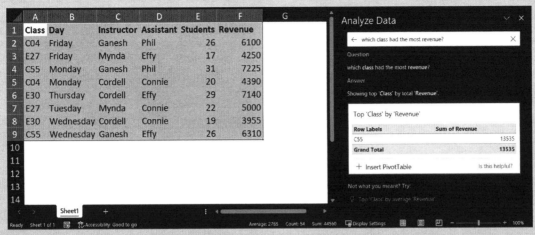

Here are a few more examples:

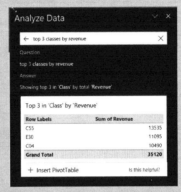

On the left, the question is: Which classes had less than 20 students?

Result: No match

Seems like a simple request, but Analyze Data bombed. You and I can eyeball the data and see two classes: E27 on Friday had 17 students and E30 on Wednesday had 19 students.

Center image: The request is for the top 3 classes.

Result: Analyze Data summarized each class by number of students. Maybe the need was for the top three individual classes, with C55 on Monday with 31 students. Or maybe we wanted individual classes by revenue, with C55, Monday, $7225.

What Analyze Data returned is indeed accurate. Class E27 isn't listed because it came in fourth place. But the question remains: Did Analyze Data respond with what was really needed?

On the right, the request is for top 3 classes by revenue.

Again, Analyze Data returned a summary. The good news is it's correctly looking at the revenue. What's uncertain is whether this is the desired result.

A Final Word on Machine Learning–Driven Features in Excel and Power Query

Analyze Data, Column From Examples, and Flash Fill can be extremely useful. I'm not here to trash them. Personally, I make great use of Flash Fill and Column From Examples. My biggest concern is the hype that surrounds artificial intelligence and machine learning. There isn't enough said about the extra vigilance that's required. That's our responsibility as guerrilla data analysts: Ignore the hype-makers. Machine learning and artificial intelligence are not omniscient.

Don't be a person who blindly trusts machine learning and passes along data that is either wrong, horribly wrong, or embarrassing.

We must know our data and know the strengths and shortcomings of our tools. Sometimes eyeballing, sorting, and filtering are more powerful than the slick titillating tools. We have to be strategic. Wherever possible, break tasks into pieces and use the tools for what they do well—minimizing work that requires complex solutions or just plain manual effort.

Chapter 23: Avoid Working on Your Source Data

I learned this the hard way. I'd get data and dive straight in, move things around, write formulas, delete extraneous details, and then ... *OOPS!*

At some point, I'd realize something was wrong:

- Things weren't adding up right.

- I'd uncovered something odd that hadn't been apparent when I started.

- I'd gone off in the wrong direction with the processing of the data and needed to backtrack.

I would then need to refer back to the source data or start all over again with the source data. But I had been working on the source data. *OMG!*

Getting back to the source data might mean waiting three days for the database admin to rerun the report for me and suffer his contemptuous eye rolls as he asked, "Didn't I send you that two days ago?" Or, if the data came from multiple sources, I'd have to compile, clean, and reformat it all over again.

You must be able to get back to your source data—for two reasons:

- If necessary, you can always get back to the starting point.

- You can verify where your results came from.

"How do you know this data is right?" is a common question folks ask analysts—especially when they don't like the results. Don't get defensive. Instead, sometimes it's helpful to take the person all the way to the beginning and say, "Here's what I started with." Show them the raw original data and walk through the process that led to the result.

One time I got word that a report was flawed, and I might have to redo several months' worth of work to get everything corrected. Fortunately, I had the source data that I'd used, and I could compare it against the updated data. It showed me the work that needed to be redone was minor: It spanned two months instead of eight months.

One suggestion: Copy the source data onto a new worksheet and label the sheet accordingly. This image shows a tab called SOURCE for the source data and another called Working for the working data.

709	CM-097331	8:45 AM
710	CM-107064	1:00 PM
711	CM-121074	2:15 PM
712	CM-127880	3:00 PM
713	CM-142479	10:45 AM
714	CM-144876	8:05 AM

SOURCE **Working** ⊕

Other tips:

- If the source data was an email attachment, don't delete that email.

- Keep the source data in a separate file or folder that's easy to retrieve.

Chapter 24: Using Slicers

Slicers have been around since Excel 2010, and they can be used with Pivot Tables and data that's formatted as a table. Slicers give you a way to filter your data without having to fiddle with the dropdown filters. Also, with a slicer, you can pick the fields that you want to filter by.

Using Slicers with Tables

Here we have the first few rows of data on 30 workshops, and it's formatted as a table:

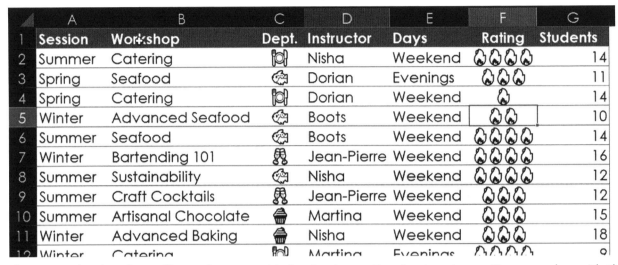

If you use the dropdown filters, they can add visual noise to the sheet and sometimes overlap with the column names:

Moreover, depending on your purpose, you might not want to filter for all of those headings. Time to add some slicers.

> **Note:** If the filter buttons show up on your table, you can toggle them off by clicking inside the table, then: Table Design | Table Style Options | untick Filter button.

With the cursor within the table: Insert | Slicer | tick the options Session, Dept., and Instructor | OK.

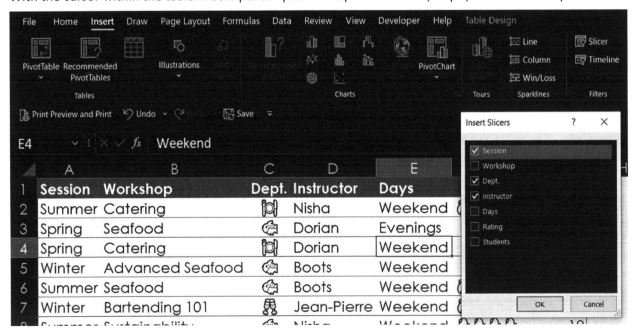

Now you have these three slicers and can easily filter for whatever you want:

In the image below, there are several things going on:

- The 🐟 department is selected.

- Notice in the Session slicer that the checkmarks icon next to the funnel is highlighted. When you click on it, you get the option to select more than one item. I selected both Spring and Summer, and they are highlighted, but Winter is not.

- **I did not make any selections in the Instructor slicer.** The three instructors that are highlighted are the only ones who taught courses in the 🐟 department in Spring or Summer. The slicer automatically grayed out the other instructors, removing them as options that can be selected. You can tell that a selection hasn't been made in this slicer because there isn't an x next to the funnel.

  To clear the filter on a slicer, click on the x that appears next to the funnel.

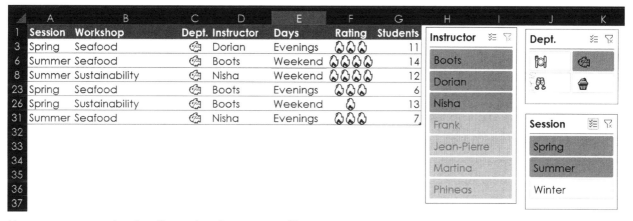

Now you can see the details on the six courses of interest.

Did you notice that the Dept. slicer is in two columns? You can set up a slicer this way by clicking in the slicer so the Slicer tab appears in the ribbon. Now you can change the Columns option to the number of columns you want.

In the image below, the table's total row has been enabled, showing a sum of 104 students and a count of 8 workshops for courses in the cupcake department.

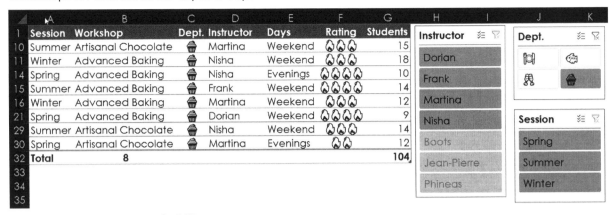

Pivot Tables and Slicers

To see how to use a Pivot Table with a slicer, create a Pivot Table, as shown in Chapter 6, and use the field list to configure the Pivot Table with:

- **Columns**: Days
- **Rows:** Instructor
- **Value:** Count of Workshops

To insert a slicer, click inside the Pivot Table and then: PivotTable Analyze | Filter | Insert Slicer.

Create slicers for Workshop, Dept., and Rating.

This image shows that Craft Cocktails and Mixology are selected. (I've changed the Pivot Table to Outline Form by clicking inside the Pivot Table, then: Design | Layout | Report Layout | Show in Outline Form.)

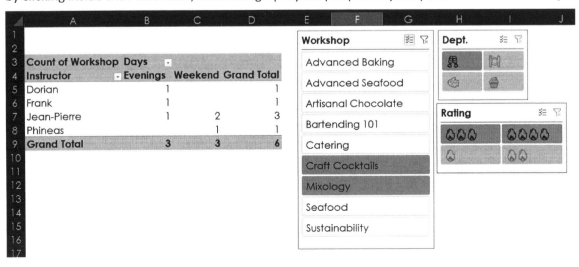

What can you see?

- Jean-Pierre has taught two weekend courses and an evening course.
- None of the courses have been rated less than three flames. So, they're pretty hot courses.

To see the one-flame workshops, select the one-flame icon in the Rating slicer. Fortunately, there are only two workshops with this lowest rating. You can see that they were both on weekends.

Chapter 25: Data Models and Relationships

Creating relationships is a fantastic way to leave data in place while treating the separate ranges as one range. The result is called a *data model*.

For example, the figure below shows a worksheet with the following datasets:

- Sales (85 rows)
- Sales reps and their sales assistants
- Sales regions and the directors over those regions

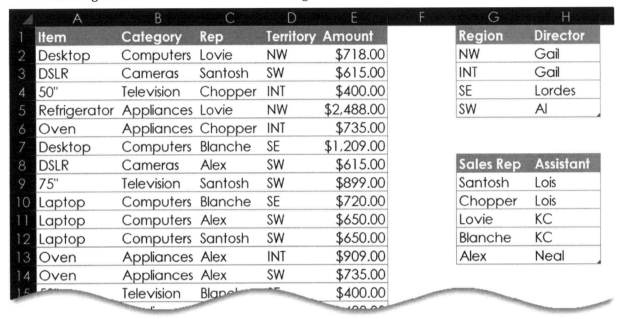

Here's the scenario:

- Your objective is to calculate bonuses for the assistants Lois, KC, and Neal, based on the sales in column E. (For example, Lois's bonus is calculated based on the sales where Santosh or Chopper is the rep.)
- You know that the CEO will be curious about sales by region and by director. (Notice that Gail is over two regions.)
- Sometimes a director will drop by and ask questions like, "How many televisions were sold in my region?"

Do you see the challenge? To answer each question, you need data from more than one table.

If you only wanted to calculate the bonuses for the assistants, you could do a SUMIFS and then do a SUM since Lois and KC are assigned to more than one sales rep. And, since you anticipate needing different configurations for the data, you could create a data model rather than employ a tangled mix of formulas and helper columns over several worksheets.

One more thing to point out: I've named the tables Sales, Regions, and Reps.

Here's how you create relationships between these tables:

1. Select Data | Data Tools | Relationships | New. The Create Relationship dialog appears.
2. In the Create Relationship dialog, create the first relationship by linking Territory in the Sales table to Region in the Regions table (see the next figure). Click OK.

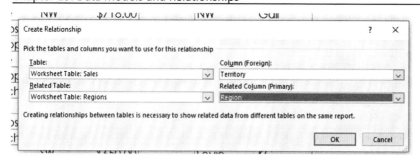

3. Repeat step 1 and then, in the Create Relationship dialog, create another new relationship that links the Sales table's Rep and the Regions table's Region. Click OK. You now have the relationships shown in the next figure.

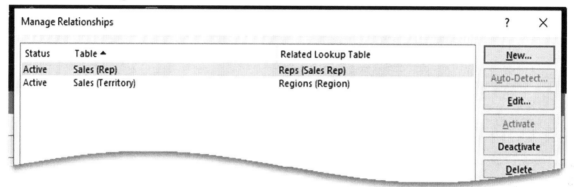

Next, you'll create a data model and tally the total sales for the sales assistants. Here's what you do:

1. With your cursor in the Sales table, select Insert | Pivot Table.

2. In the PivotTable from Table or Range dialog that appears (see the next figure), tick the Add This Data to the Data Model box and click OK.

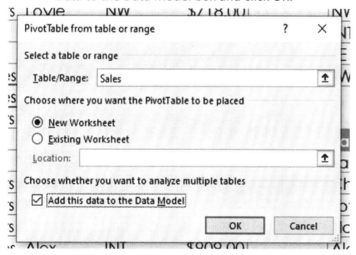

3. From here, in field list, select All so that all of the tables in the data model are available to you; and click on the arrows next to each table to expand and showing all of the columns in each table.

4. Configure the data in the field list as shown below.

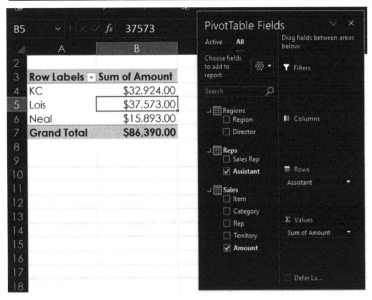

AMAZING!

Lois had the most sales. No formulas and no helper columns were used to find this information.

Now! With the data model all set up, you use the field list as you'd use it with a regular Pivot Table. Configuring the data as shown below, what do you see?

When Gail calls, you can tell her that her two regions sold five televisions.

Because the source data is in tables, it's easy to add, remove, and modify data and have those changes reflected in the data model. It's a matter of refreshing the data model after changing the source data by selecting any cell in the data model, right-clicking, and choosing Refresh.

Foreign and Primary Keys

In the Create Relationship interface, you saw some jazz about primary and foreign. What is that?

In order for the relationships between tables to work, you need one dataset that has no duplicates in the column. That will be your primary key, and it can be matched with a foreign key—which can have repeats. This is why the Territory column in the Sales table is in the Foreign section, and Region in the Regions table is in the Primary section.

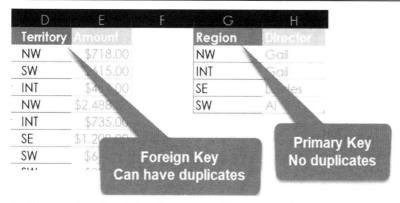

Territory	Amount		Region	Director
NW	$718.00		NW	Gail
SW	$15.00		INT	Gail
INT	$4...00		SE	L...les
NW	$2.48...		SW	A...
INT	$735.0...			
SE	$1.2...00			
SW	$6...			

**Foreign Key
Can have duplicates**

**Primary Key
No duplicates**

Why a Data Model vs. Power Query?

Power Query requires that every table be placed in a query, and with this setup, you have to create the requisite joins to make one enormous table. This is a legitimate alternative to a data model. You have to decide which strategy is best for your needs and comfort level.

If you don't have primary keys, then Power Query is the way to go. Let's say you have these two datasets and need to merge them.

Apt	Resident	email
A1	TJ	TJ@fake-email.com
A2	Skip	Skip@not-real-email.edu
A3	Irrfan	Irrfan @fake-email.com
B1	Chris	Chris @fake-email.com
B1	James	James @fake-email.com
B2	Carmine	Carmine @phony-email.com
B3	Ana	Ana @fake-email.gov
B3	Jekyll	Jekyll @fake-email.com
B4	Gigi	Gigi @fake-email.com
B5	Tobias	Tobias @fake-email.com

Unit	Maintenance Req.	Cost
A2	Bathroom Sink	$ 300.00
A3	Replace oven	$1,244.00
B1	Bathroom Sink	$ 300.00
B2	Ceiling fan	$ 213.00
B3	Bedroom door	$ 219.00
B3	Clogged toilet	$ 99.00
B3	Hole in wall	$ 186.00

You cannot use a relationship in this case because:

- You'd need to match or create a relationship between the Apt and Unit columns.
- Both tables have duplicates (in the Apt and Unit columns).

You'll need to do an outer join in Power Query to merge these two tables into a single dataset.

Chapter 26: People, Processes, and Tools

⚡When you're working with data, you have to remain cognizant of this trinity: people, processes, and tools.

Too often, Excel is treated like a magical portal where you can pour in data and then step over a few feet to another portal, slide open the door, and retrieve all the beautiful results. No. It doesn't work like that.

There are also the people who villainize Excel. They point to mistakes that were made by someone who used Excel and conclude that Excel needs to be banned from the workplace.

Actually, it's vital to think about this trinity of people, processes, and tools.

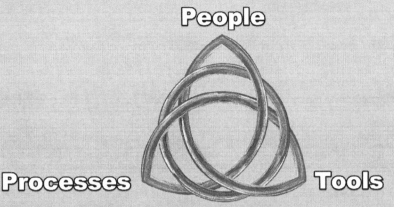

You are the *people* in this trinity. And it's important when you're working with data and you've got a problem. Do you have a tool problem? Do you have a people problem? Do you have a process problem?

Let's say that you bring in a lot of data from a website, and there's something wrong. Things aren't adding up. Some calculations are giving you really bizarre answers. Maybe in part of the process, you are aware that the form that people have to fill out allows people to put today's date in the birthday cell. That is a process problem. And in the trinity, a *person* has to be aware of such weaknesses in the *process*. The person needs a *process* to adjust for this broken process.

The Restaurant

One time I went to help a restaurant that was having problems with data. One example the owner gave was, "I bought $90 worth of salmon that disappeared, and no one could tell me where it went."

That salmon didn't swim away, and the owner wasn't concerned about theft. She wanted to know:

- How much was cooked and served to customers?
- How much fell on the floor and was thrown away?
- Was any used by the chef to explore new dishes for the menu?

Our conversation led me to conclude that I could not offer any help. I found out there are tools—expensive tools—that are dedicated for this purpose in the restaurant industry. But why weren't the tools being used? The owner said that everybody claimed to be too busy to input the data.

That told me they had a people issue. No one but the owner seemed to be interested in getting the data right. I had an instinct that people feel like they're running around, doing their jobs, and at some point they're supposed to sit down at a computer or a terminal and load data in. It was up to them to find the time to get this done. Thus, it was really a process problem.

Building something in Excel—taking their money and delivering this tool—would still leave them within a context of disinterested people and no processes.

The Caterers

In another case, the people in a small company wanted data, and they had a tool and processes. However, the tool was incredibly sophisticated, with key features buried in sub-sub-sub menus, and the caterer only needed a few of the features. They had a tool problem.

I was able to build them exactly what they wanted in Excel. ☺

Chapter 27: Keeping Your Data in as Few Places as Possible

Skirmish

🐉 One way that octopus spreadsheets emerge is when data is kept in several places. The image below shows data about gift cards that were purchased in four different stores.

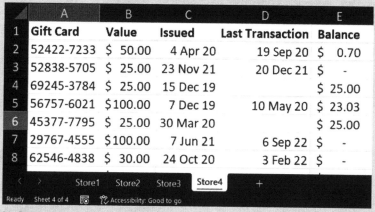

	A	B	C	D	E
1	Gift Card	Value	Issued	Last Transaction	Balance
2	52422-7233	$ 50.00	4 Apr 20	19 Sep 20	$ 0.70
3	52838-5705	$ 25.00	23 Nov 21	20 Dec 21	$ -
4	69245-3784	$ 25.00	15 Dec 19		$ 25.00
5	56757-6021	$100.00	7 Dec 19	10 May 20	$ 23.03
6	45377-7795	$ 25.00	30 Mar 20		$ 25.00
7	29767-4555	$100.00	7 Jun 21	6 Sep 22	$ -
8	62546-4838	$ 30.00	24 Oct 20	3 Feb 22	$ -

Store1   Store2   Store3   **Store4**   +

Ready   Sheet 4 of 4   Accessibility: Good to go

In Store4:

- Row 2 shows a gift card with a balance of 70¢, and there were 168 days from the date of issue to the last transaction.
- Row 4 shows a gift card that hasn't been used, and the full $25 value is still there.
- Row 7 shows a card whose $100 was expended over 456 days.

It makes perfect sense to keep this data separated across the four stores if you typically only look at one store at a time. But this creates a problem when you want to do analysis over all of the cards, regardless of the store. You might want to dig into questions like:

- How many cards haven't been used?
- How many cards have a balance less than $5.00?
- How many cards have ≥50% of their value?
- What is the most common purchase value?
- Of the cards that have 0 balance, is there something to learn about the time it took to go from full value to 0?
- What is the total value of cards that have not been used?

Answering these questions is hard to do when the data is across four sheets. You'll need Power Query to append the data, or you'll need to write formulas to summarize what you want. More formulas mean more areas where your calculations and analysis can break—and also flipping back and forth and scrolling through the sheets.

If your sheets have formulas, you could have four different places to make changes. If you make three changes, get up and go to the restroom, and come back and do your analysis, you might find ... *OOPS!* That fourth change wasn't made, and now the analysis is wrong.

Reserve that type of work and hassle for times when you have to work with someone else's data, and their data is sprinkled here and there.

In the image below, the data is all in one place, in the Overall sheet. This would be a better way to compile the data. With this format, it's not so easy to look at a single store, but you can get that information by sorting or putting the data into a table and using a slicer or Pivot Table.

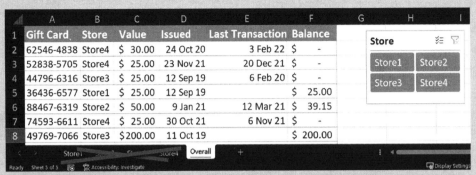

Setting up an Excel file this way requires thinking ahead: "Would I ever want to do analysis on all of the gift cards?" If so, keep the data in one place and add relevant columns that will let you easily peel out what you want.

The key here is to keep data in as few places as possible. You won't always want to pile data in just one place. If you have expenses and income, you might not want to put those in a single worksheet with an Expense/Income column. But, you could create just one sheet for expenses and one sheet for income with a Category column so that you can isolate, for example, auto expenses or rental income.

Chapter 28: Rough-and-Tumble Tips and Insights

This chapter includes quick tips, insights, warnings, and advice that can help solve problems that confound analysts. This chapter explores answers to questions like:

- How can I get a worksheet to print on a single page?
- Can I mix formulas and numbers in a single cell?
- How do I unhide column A?
- Can unnecessary zeros be hidden?

Unhiding Column A

This is one of the craziest things about Excel: If you hide column A, you can't unhide it like every other column.

Here's one way to get column A back. As shown in the following figure, type A1 in the Name box and press Enter. Excel sends the cursor to cell A1.

Notice in the formula bar that Start Date is the content in cell A1.

To get the column back, select Home | Cells | Format | Visibility | Hide & Unhide | Unhide Columns. As shown below, column A is back!

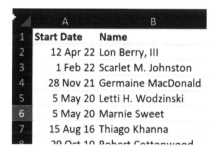

🐉 When Data Is the Start, Not the End

Skirmish

There's a lot of data floating around, but you have to be wary and ask questions about what is really being measured. Some folks at YouTube answered a question regarding video-length and watch-time data.

My question: Can YouTube tell if I watched a 1-hour video but I watched on three different devices over two days?

Their answer: No.

The analytics will show three different sessions, let's say, averaging 20 minutes each. Thus, leading to a conclusion that an hour is far too long for a video when the average watch time is just 20 minutes.

The point being: Data is not everything, and I say this as someone whose career is rooted in data.

It's vital that you know when you can and when you cannot rely on data and analytics—not because they're wrong but because they are extremely limited in what they can show about the real world, your context, and your purpose.

Here are a few more examples where analytics might be accurate in what they measure, but there are other critical details that cannot be measured.

YouTube Analytics

YouTube used to send out a report with analytics and the suggestion "do more of this," while highlighting videos that have been performing well.

One time I looked at the data and YouTube's suggestion, and I knew that one video did extremely well because it was a six-person collaboration ... NOT something that I can execute often:

- Coordinating six people is hard to do.
- The content was for fun and a departure from the regular content. My audience enjoyed it, but they wouldn't want a steady diet of that.

My Most Popular Blog Post

Years ago, I took some advice and wrote a blog post that continues to do well—according to the data. Personally, I regret having written it. The advice was to write something provocative ... voice a strong but unpopular position on something.

The result has been great analytics along with 10 years of comments with words like *stupid*, *wrong*, *idiot*, *crazy*.

Some people would be okay with the attention, the website traffic, search engine ranking, and possibly ad revenue, but that would be a whole different mission. This forced me to get really clear about my mission and who I am. I realized I was a blogger who wanted to share knowledge about data and Excel. Being a professional agitator wasn't part of my vision.

The Snail Mail Fundraiser

One time I was at a conference and a guy, Martin, chased me down to tell me about one thing he was able to do after reading the second edition of this book.

The nonprofit he worked for had mailed out letters requesting donations. After a few months, they analyzed the results and saw that very few donations were mailed back, even though they'd included an envelope with return postage. This led to conversations about dropping the snail mail fundraising campaigns in the future.

But Martin was suspicious. He gathered a lot of data, did some comparisons, and was able to show that a solid level of people who received mail did make donations, but they donated online. That changed the whole conversation away from dropping snail mail and opened an inquiry about how to do it better.

This is also a story about the power of having the right data vs. operating on hunches or the first interpretation of the data.

Formula Triggers

A formula trigger can be used to prevent a calculation from happening if the required inputs are incomplete, and the incomplete calculation will be problematic. In other words, a trigger tells the formula "Don't calculate something premature and crazy until you have everything you need!"

Calculating Candidate Evaluations

The image below shows two sheets from a workbook. On the Candidates sheet there's a list of candidates, and in the Score column data is being retrieved from the Program A sheet, using XLOOKUP:

```
=XLOOKUP([@Candidates],Scoring[Evaluations],Scoring[FINAL],"")
```

The FINAL scores are being calculated as a sum of the four scores (Portfolio, Application, Fundamentals, Interview):

```
=SUM(Scoring[@[Portfolio]:[Interview]])
```

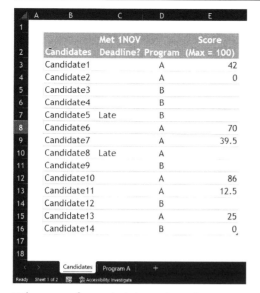

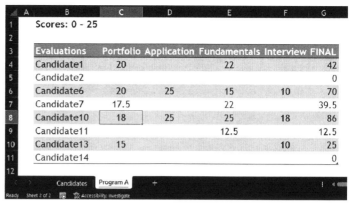

Why use a formula trigger here?

Let's say that Niles, the program coordinator, looks at the Candidates sheet and thinks, "Hmmm ... I thought Candiate7 would have done better than 39.5 out of 100." If Niles doesn't look at the Program A sheet, he doesn't know that some of the scores are incomplete, and Candidates 6 and 10 are the only ones with complete scores.

To prevent this misrepresentation and unnecessary alarm, wrap the FINAL in a trigger:

```
=IF(COUNTA(Scoring[@[Portfolio]:[Interview]])<4,"",SUM(Scoring[@[Portfolio]:
[Interview]]))
```

Since each candidate needs four scores, the trigger uses COUNTA to count the non-empty cells. If COUNTA is less than 4, the formula returns an empty cell. When COUNTA results in 4, the scores are added together.

The image below shows that more evaluation scores have been loaded. When Niles looks at the Candidates data, he can trust that the 70 for Candidate6 is complete.

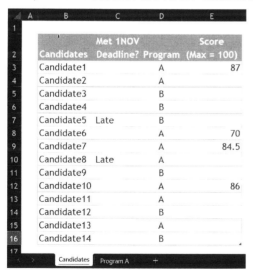

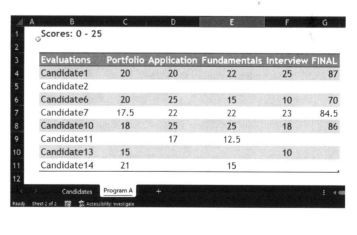

You can use formula triggers in creative ways. Rather than return an empty cell, the formula can be modified to return INC. for incomplete scores. And here it is:

=IF(COUNTA(Scoring[@[Portfolio]:[Interview]])<4,"INC.",SUM(Scoring[@[Portfolio]:[Interview]]))

Counting Invitee Confirmations

In the image below, the task is to count the number of invitees who are considered *confirmed* (i.e., the invitee has submitted proof of insurance and has paid at least 50% of the fee). The RSVP column is ignored.

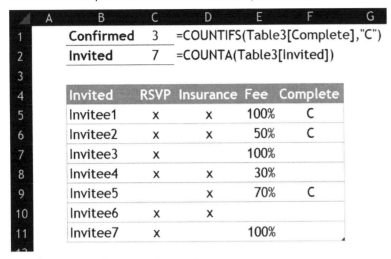

	A	B	C	D	E	F	G
1		Confirmed	3	=COUNTIFS(Table3[Complete],"C")			
2		Invited	7	=COUNTA(Table3[Invited])			
3							
4		Invited	RSVP	Insurance	Fee	Complete	
5		Invitee1	x	x	100%	C	
6		Invitee2	x	x	50%	C	
7		Invitee3	x		100%		
8		Invitee4	x	x	30%		
9		Invitee5		x	70%	C	
10		Invitee6	x	x			
11		Invitee7	x		100%		

The formula in the Complete column:

```
=IF(AND([@Fee]>=0.5,[@Insurance]<>""),"C","")
```

Observations:

- Invitee1, Invitee2, and Invitee5 are complete.
- Invitee3 and Invitee7 aren't complete because their proof of insurance is missing.
- Invitee4 has submitted proof of insurance but hasn't paid at least 50% of the fee.

Adding Emojis to Cells and Formulas

In a few sections throughout this book, you've seen emojis used. In Windows, to open the menu of emojis, use Windows key+. (period). For a Mac, use Ctrl+Cmd+Spacebar.

To add an emoji to a cell, place your cursor in the cell | Windows key+. | search for and click on the emoji that you're after.

To add an emoji to a formula, start typing the formula, and when you reach the point where you want the emoji, follow the steps above. When your emoji is in place, complete the formula. This formula, for example, uses COUNTIFS to count the number of sharks in D2:D22:

```
=COUNTIFS(D2:D22,"🦈")
```

One thing that's nice about emojis is they aren't dependent on the font being Webdings or one of the three Wingdings fonts. For example, if you type N into a cell and change the font to Webdings, you'll get an eye; if you change the font to Wingdings2, you'll get a hand. Let's say you want to change the font of an entire worksheet from Ariel to Tahoma. You have to remember that your Webdings eye will change back into an N when you apply Tahoma. You'll have to go back and change it to Webdings font.

Hiding Unnecessary Zeros

It's February 3, and a spreadsheet has been set up to tally the number of class registrations, by month, for the entire year. In the image below, the Summary sheet is all set, and it's pulling data from the Registrations sheet.

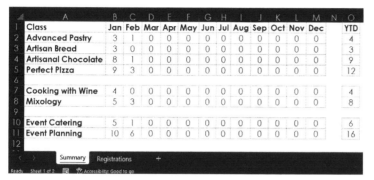

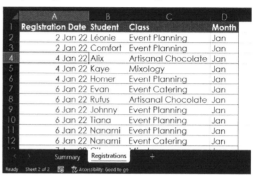

All of the zeros in the summary are making visual clutter. It would be nice to hide the zeros until there are registrations to count. To do so: File | Options | Advanced | Display Options for This Worksheet | Untick Show a Zero in Cells That Have Zero Value | OK.

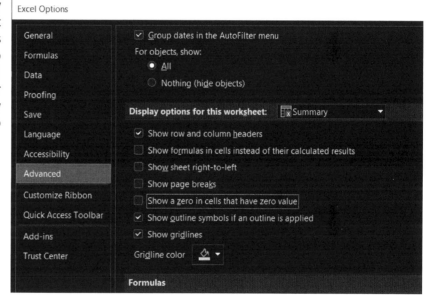

The image below looks much cleaner. The cursor is in F4, and the formula bar shows that there's a formula in the cell, and it's all set to start calculating when you get to May and people start registering for Artisanal Chocolate.

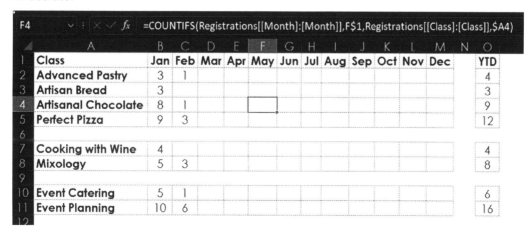

F4 =COUNTIFS(Registrations[[Month]:[Month]],F$1,Registrations[[Class]:[Class]],$A4)

Class	Jan	Feb	Mar	Apr	May	Jun	Jul	Aug	Sep	Oct	Nov	Dec	YTD
Advanced Pastry	3	1											4
Artisan Bread	3												3
Artisanal Chocolate	8	1											9
Perfect Pizza	9	3											12
Cooking with Wine	4												4
Mixology	5	3											8
Event Catering	5	1											6
Event Planning	10	6											16

Forcing a Report to Fit on One Page

Don't you hate it when you print your work, and most of your report is on a single page, but there's a second page with just two rows and a third page with only a column? Here's how you can force the entire report to fit on one page: Page Layout | Scale to Fit | Width: 1 | Height: 1.

You can limit a page to fit one page wide and one page high or whatever is suitable for the specific purpose. You can also change the printout to be a percentage of normal size.

The Page Setup dialog box has a lot of settings that you can adjust, including:

- Adding headers or footers to your document
- Adjusting margins
- Setting a page to print one page wide with no limit to how many sheets long

Setting the Print Area to Print a Section of a Worksheet

The image below represents an event that's being planned. The seating chart is being created, and there's a wait list, budget information, and a countdown to the event. How can you print the three graphics and the wait list?

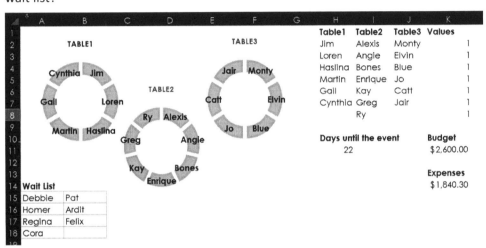

Highlight A1:G20 | Page Layout | Page Setup | Print Area | Set Print Area.

To ensure that the document will print properly: File | Print.

The print preview opens, and there it is!

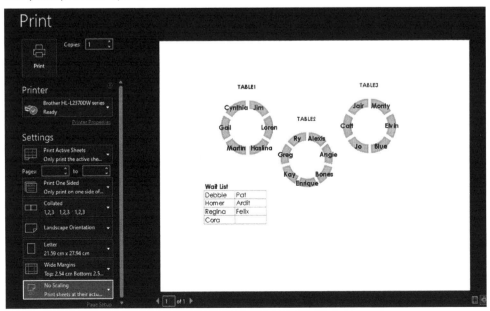

Notice:

- At the bottom of the screen you see 1 of 1. This tells you there aren't any other pages, and this is the only data that will be printed.
- In the Settings section, set the sheet to print in landscape orientation.

To center the printout on the page: Page Layout | click the arrow in the Scale to Fit group to open the Page Setup dialog | Margins | Center on Page | tick Horizontally and Vertically.

If you want to remove the print area and print the entire worksheet: Click anywhere on the worksheet | Page Layout | Page Setup | Print Area | Clear Print Area.

Alt+Enter for an Extra Line in a Cell

There are two main reasons to add an extra line in a cell.

Using Alt+Enter to Make Long Formulas Easier to Read

In the image below, a long formula has been written. It works. It's accurate.

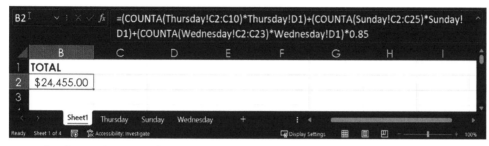

Now check out the same formula in the next image. It's been split into three rows instead of one long string that wraps wherever it wraps. Wouldn't this version be better to understand, troubleshoot, or modify? It's not *easy*, but it's better than that single string.

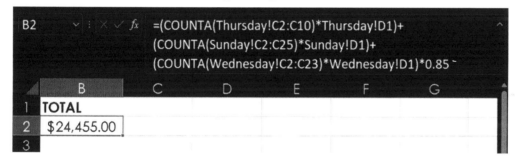

To break a formula into multiple lines: Place your cursor in the formula wherever you want the break(s) to happen | Alt+Enter | Enter.

Using Alt+Enter to Add New Lines Within a Cell

You can also use Alt+Enter to keep a list readable and prevent the cell contents from shifting around if you widen the column. Note that this also assumes that you won't need to sort or count those names because you cannot sort content that's within a cell. You can sort the column, but you won't, for example, be able to sort the four names in B2.

Handling Dates

Excel stores dates as the number of days since 1 January 1900. For example, 14 June 2024 is stored as 45457—i.e.., 45457 days after 1 January 1900. Excel stores time as a fraction of a day. Noon is represented as 0.5, and 6:00 a.m. is stored as 0.25.

Type the following into a cell in Excel:

```
12/17/2024 7:25 pm
```

Press Enter and format the cell as a number with 10 decimal places. The returned number is:

```
45643.8090277778
```

This equates to 7:25 p.m. 45,643 days after 1 January 1900.

Date-Handling Functions

Function	Purpose
=NOW()	Returns the present date and time.
=TODAY()	Returns the date (only) for today.
=YEAR(A1)	Returns the year of the date in cell A1.
=MONTH(A1)	Returns the month of the date in cell A1, as a value 1 through 12.
=DAY(A1)	Returns the day of the month in cell A1, as a value 1 through 31.
=DATE(Year,Month,Day)	Converts the date you use to a year, month, and date.
=DAYS()	Calculates the number of days between two dates.
=WEEKDAY(A1)	Returns the number of the weekday.
=EOMONTH(A1, Number of Months)	Returns the last day of the month. Use 0 for the current month, 1 for next month, and -1 for the previous month.
=NETWORKDAYS.INTL (Start Date, End Date, Weekend, Holidays)	Calculates the number of workdays between two dates, based on your weekends and custom list of holidays.

Caution: TODAY and NOW are volatile functions; i.e., they recalculate with every change in the worksheet. Be careful. If you use TODAY to calculate that a project ended today and took 34 days, the formula will recalculate if you come back 12 days from now. The formula will incorrectly tell you that the project took 46 days. In such situations, it's best to use actual dates and not formulas. Use Ctrl+; to insert the current date in a cell. Use Ctrl+Shift+: to insert the current time in a cell. For both date and time, use Ctrl+Shift+: followed by Ctrl+; followed by Enter.

Calculating Next Birthday/Anniversary

Date-handling functions are useful when you want to know when someone's next anniversary or birthday is coming up.

This image shows that today is 19 Aug 21, and Zahra joined on 30 Aug 20. There isn't a straightforward way to show that her next anniversary is 11 days away, on 30 Aug 21, because the year value makes everything messy.

F2			fx	=DATE(YEAR(E2)+DATEDIF(E2,$B$2,"y")+1,MONTH(E2),DAY(E2))			
A	B	C	D	E	F	G	H
1	**Today**		**Member**	**Join Date**	**Next Anniversary**		
2	19 Aug 21		Zahra	30 Aug 20	30 Aug 21		
3			Ahava	29 Sep 15	29 Sep 21		
4			Lee	23 Nov 18	23 Nov 21		
5			Vicenta	1 Jan 10	1 Jan 22		
6			Evi	5 Jan 21	5 Jan 22		
7			Pascale	6 Mar 21	6 Mar 22		
8			Lorna	7 Mar 15	7 Mar 22		
9			Chanda	13 May 21	13 May 22		
10			Malcolm	17 Aug 13	17 Aug 22		

Here's the formula that needs to be used:

```
=DATE(YEAR(E2)+DATEDIF(E2,$B$2,"y")+1,MONTH(E2),DAY(E2))
```

Handling Time

Times can be challenging when working in Excel. 60 minutes in 1 hour; 24 hours in 1 day; 12-hr clock vs. 24-hr clock; AM or PM; elapsed times; 7.5 hours vs. 7:30 … Excel can handle it all, but it takes extra effort on your part to provide the right guidance.

Take a look at the image below, where there are start and end times, and in cells E4:E6 the formulas are subtracting the end time from the start time to calculate the elapsed time.

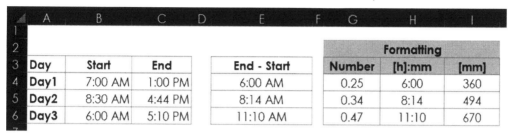

Day	Start	End		End - Start		Number	Formatting [h]:mm	[mm]
Day1	7:00 AM	1:00 PM		6:00 AM		0.25	6:00	360
Day2	8:30 AM	4:44 PM		8:14 AM		0.34	8:14	494
Day3	6:00 AM	5:10 PM		11:10 AM		0.47	11:10	670

Having an AM or PM in an elapsed time makes no sense, but the 6:00 is accurate for the elapsed time here because the difference between 7 a.m. and 1 p.m. is six hours.

Columns G:I in the image above show the results of three different formats for elapsed time. You set up the format in the Number column like so: Highlight G4:G6 | Home | Number | select Number from the dropdown list.

For Day1, the difference between 7:00 a.m. and 1:00 p.m. is 6 hours. The 0.25 is one-quarter of a day. That's great if you want to calculate days.

In cells H4:H6, Day3 shows 11 hours 10 minutes. This is a custom format that's done this way: Highlight H4:H6 | Home | Number | click the arrow to open the dropdown list | scroll down to More Number Formats and select it.

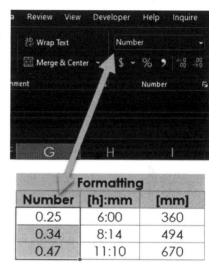

	Formatting	
Number	[h]:mm	[mm]
0.25	6:00	360
0.34	8:14	494
0.47	11:10	670

In the Format Cells dialog, select the Custom category | either type in or scroll down to select [h]:mm | OK.

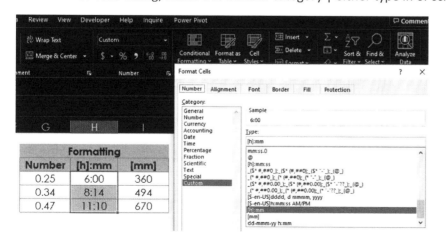

Note: Notice in the Format Cells dialog, below [h]:mm is [mm]. That's the format being used in I4:I6, and it's formatting the elapsed times in numbers of minutes.

If you calculate a sum of each column, the results are:

- 1.06 days
- 25 hours 24 minutes
- 1524 minutes

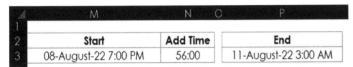

	Formatting		
	Number	[h]:mm	[mm]
Start	0.25	6:00	360
AM	0.34	8:14	494
AM	0.47	11:10	670
SUM	1.06	25:24	1524

What's the deal with the square brackets in [h]:mm and [mm]?

The square brackets tell Excel to do the addition, and it's okay if the result exceeds 24 hours. I invite you to change the formatting in H8 and I8 to formatting without the brackets. In cell H8 you'll end up with 1:24 instead of 25:24 because the calculation started from 0 after 24 hours.

Time formats without the brackets are used if you want the result to be a time. In this example, 56 hours is being added to 7 p.m. on 8 August 2022 to calculate the ending date and time.

Start	Add Time	End
08-August-22 7:00 PM	56:00	11-August-22 3:00 AM

The cells are formatted as follows:

Cell	Custom Format	Description
M3	dd-mmmm-yy h:mm AM/PM	No math is being done on this value. Here, the formatting only represents the preferred way of seeing the data. Note that the mmmm tells Excel to spell out the full name of the month. (mmmm … so YUMMY!)
N3	[h]:mm	The square brackets will allow a number greater than 24 hours. Without the brackets, the 56:00 will flip to 8:00 because Excel subtracts 2 full days (48 hours).
P3	dd-mmmm-yy h:mm AM/PM	Same formatting as cell M3.

Negative Times and Formatting

In the image below, row 13 has start and end times. In E13 and H13 Excel returned a series of hashes—basically an error saying that you can't start something at 3 p.m. and end 8 hours earlier. But there are negative values in G13 and I13.

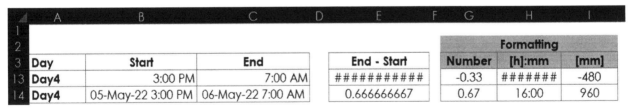

Day	Start	End	End - Start	Number	[h]:mm	[mm]
					Formatting	
Day	Start	End	End - Start	Number	[h]:mm	[mm]
Day4		3:00 PM	7:00 AM	###########	-0.33	######	-480
Day4	05-May-22 3:00 PM	06-May-22 7:00 AM	0.666666667	0.67	16:00	960

In row 14, Start and End are shown with both the dates and times, formatted as:

```
dd-mmmm-yy h:mm AM/PM
```

Excel can handle this! The results are:

- Two-thirds of a day
- 16 hours
- 960 minutes

Hours:Minutes and Decimal Hours

Say that CJ worked a total of 31:15 (31 hours 15 minutes). CJ's rate is $55.40/hour. If you multiply those values, you'll get $72.135, which is not just wrong, it's *horribly wrong*.

The time is formatted as [h]:mm, and do you recall what Excel does with that? It converts the value to a number of days. 31:15 hours is 1.29 days. And there ya go, the horribly wrong answer: 1.29 * $55.4 = $72.135.

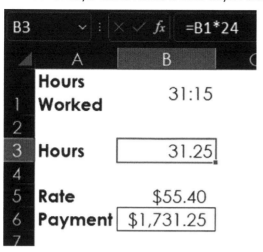

To make this right, the 31:15 must be multiplied by 24, as shown in the image in cell B3, where the time in B1 is converted to a decimal. Finally, the decimal version of the hours is multiplied by the rate in B5. *BOOM!* Pay CJ $1731.25.

Using the TEXT Function with Dates and Times

The TEXT function is useful if you have dates or amounts that need to stay as they are, but you also need to see the values a different way.

The following table provides an overview of the various ways the TEXT function can be used. All of these examples use the following values:

- **Date as a number in B1:** 45170.6
- **Date:** 1 September 2023
- **Time:** 3:50 PM
- **Full date and time:** 01-September-2023 3:50 PM
- **Value in B3:** 97333.47

TEXT Formula	Result
=TEXT(B1,"mmm")	Sep
=TEXT(B1,"mm")	09
=TEXT(B1,"mmmm")	September
=TEXT(B1,"dd")	01
=TEXT(B1,"d")	1
=TEXT(B1,"ddd")	Fri
=TEXT(B1,"dddd")	Friday
=TEXT(B1,"mmm dd")	Sep 01
="A Great "&TEXT(B1,"dddd")&" in "&TEXT(B1,"mmmm")	A Great Friday in September
=TEXT(B1,"yy")	23
=TEXT(B1,"yyy")	2023
=TEXT(B1,"mmm-yyy")	Sep-2023
=TEXT(B1,"dddd h:mm AM/PM")	Friday 3:50 PM
=TEXT(B1,"mm.s")	50.24
=TEXT(B3, "$0.00")	$97333.47
=TEXT(B3,"$0,000")	$97,333
=TEXT(B3,"$0,000.00")	$97,333.47

The image below shows a dataset of course completions. The actual completion dates in column B are important, but in your role, you only care about the cohorts based on month and year. That column was added using the TEXT function. In cell C2:

```
=TEXT(B2,"mmm yyy")
```

Putting the data into a table and inserting a slicer (as shown in the image), you can isolate the entire March 2021 cohort while retaining the granular detail that SZT completed on 1 March 2021.

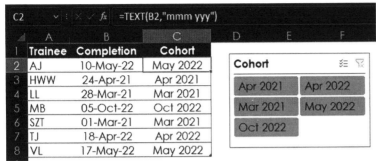

🐉 Breaking Down Tasks into Manageable Pieces

I'm including this skirmish as an example of real-world problems that aren't handled in a single, magical step. **This is your permission to iterate through a task** to get it done and get it done accurately.

Let's say you're faced with the list of product IDs and counts in the image below, and the list needs to be merged with the product names and then summarized. The IDs should be formatted like the value in B7: H-0005-3B. That is, H, a hyphen, four digits (including leading zeros), a hyphen, a number, and a letter.

	Product	Count		Product	Count
1	Product	Count		Product	Count
2	18-1b	30		H00053B	15
3	4441B	17		H02061V	10
4	-444-1B	54		H-0206-1V	29
5	53B	6		H-0311-1B	57
6	H- 4-V	55		H-0327-2V	42
7	H-0005-3B	49		H-0444-1B	8
8	H-0019-4B	2		H-1010-2V	45
9	H-0037-4B	75		H1050	14
10	H-0206-1V	13		H-1376-2B	52
11	H-0444-1B	11		H-18-4V	30
12	H-0515-2B	20		H-311-1B	28
13	H-1008-2B	87		H-5-3B	13

There are problems:

- B2 should be H-0018-1B.
- B4 should be H-0444-1B.
- E2 and E3 are missing the hyphens.
- The values in B6 and E9 are incomplete, and the corrections aren't obvious.
- B19, B20, and B21 are missing the leading zeros.

Solution: Iterate through the task.

1. Get the data into a single dataset with a single ID column and a single Count column.
2. Identify the IDs that are correct and move them to another column or sheet.
3. Identify the IDs that have similar problems—e.g., the ones that are missing leading zeros or the H in front. Break them into their respective groups and correct them.
4. Identify and correct the IDs that are missing leading zeros and fix them.
5. Identify the IDs that are missing the H in front. Get them corrected.
6. Set aside the values that don't make sense and research what they should be.

Connecting Cell Values to Shapes or Objects

Sometimes you have important data that needs to be front and center. Here, an event is being planned, and the budget is strict. Every new expense needs to immediately show how it's affecting the bottom line.

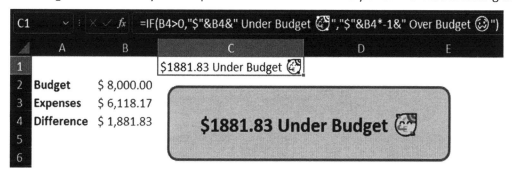

Here is the formula in C1:

```
=IF(B4>0,"$"&B4&" Under Budget ☺","$"&B4*-1&" Over Budget ☺")
```

After writing the formula, you need to add a shape: Insert | Illustrations | Shapes | pick the shape you want and adjust it to the size you want.

With the shape selected, type an equals sign in the formula bar. Then: click on cell C2 | Enter. Alternatively, type =C2 directly into the formula bar.

And here's the result when overbudget:

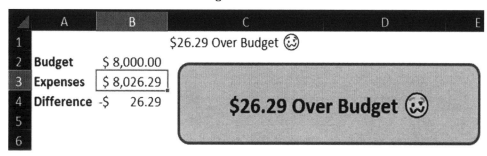

🐉 Asking Questions of Those Who Ask You for Data

Skirmish

An excellent question was asked during a Zoom conference with people training to be analysts. I was explaining that when someone asks you for data, you have to ask for details on how they need the data and what they want it for.

She asked: "They don't know what they want?"

Based on the tone in her voice, this seemed like a simple question, but she didn't know how deep and intense that question was. It went to the heart of what we as analysts face in this battle to get, maintain, and provide clean, useful data.

I replied: "No. Often, the people who ask us for data aren't data people."

Let's say you're called into the office of the director of classroom operations. She asks for revenue over the past three years.

Is this what she wants? It's literally what she asked for.

YEAR	REVENUE
Year1	$18.03M
Year2	$24.11M
Year3	$25.45M

But seriously! Part of your role as an analyst is to apply your expertise to help people get what they want from the available data. The director of classroom operations might have expertise in negotiating contracts with venues for holding classes, managing her teams, and managing the budget and cash flow.

In this scenario, you as the analyst need to know:

- How the business works
- How the data hangs together

You ask her: "Why do you want this data?"

She replies: "Ah! To see how online course sales are trending."

She is telling you something: The data you get needs to identify online vs. non-online transactions.

What else might you ask?

- Do you want only the online course sales, or do you also want the in-person course sales?
- Do you want:
  - individual transactions?
  - weekly summaries?
  - monthly summaries?
  - quarterly summaries?
  - all or some of those?
- Classes X and Y have a revenue share with another company. You only keep 30% of those sales. Do you want the total sales data or just the revenue that you keep?
- Do you want to see refunds? Or just totals?
- Do you want to see individual accounts? Maybe there's a story to be told if a few major clients are most of the sales compared to the general public placing order as individuals.
- Do you want to see individual classes or class categories—or just totals?
- Do you want a count of transactions in addition to the dollar amounts? Sometimes a huge dollar amount can mask either a single huge order or a lot of small orders.

It can feel uncomfortable asking these questions, but it shows that you're willing to take charge and be the expert. Also, it cuts down on a lot of back-and-forth in getting data, where the person who requested it says it's not enough or it's too granular or it's just plain not what was really needed … try again.

Shipping Costs

Someone once described his director asking for data because he sensed that the company was charging too little for shipping. Knowing the purpose changed everything the analyst had been thinking. That triggered questions like:

- Do you want to know how much was shipped via the U.S. Postal Service vs. FedEx vs. UPS?
- Do you want to know about regular shipping vs. priority vs. overnight?
- Over what period of time do you want this data?
- Do you want a summary of how much shipping was refunded or how much shipped for free?

Refunds and Policies

One time I was asked for a report of refunds.

There had been a complaint that customer service reps were processing refunds outside of the 90-day policy, and either they weren't getting approval or they weren't making the required notes in the system saying who gave them approval.

The report needed to show the rep's name and any notes the rep added to the order (or the blank space where a required note didn't exist).

Also, the report needed to show only the refunds that happened greater than 90 days from purchase. I had to pull all the refund transactions in a way that included the original purchase date. In Excel, I subtracted the refund date from the sale date and kept the results that were >90.

There was no need to capture what was purchased or customer details. We did, however, capture the sales amounts.

This report could tell the director how often these infractions were occurring, if specific reps were regular offenders, and the dollar value of unapproved refunds that had been processed.

Ad Hoc vs. Canned Reports

The examples in this skirmish are requests for ad hoc reports—that is, reports that are for one-time use or infrequent needs. A canned report would be one that's in your system and part of established processes—e.g., a report that is generated and distributed to those who need it every Wednesday morning.

Being able to create ad hoc reports is another example of where an analyst can be invaluable. You can get data whenever it's needed, in the desired format, with the desired level of granularity. You might not have to go through other people and depend on their schedules.

Useful Excel Functions

You've already seen a load of functions throughout this book. Here is a quick overview of a few functions that can help you get your data to cooperate and make life easier for yourself and the people who rely on what you do with the data you're in charge of.

TEXTJOIN

In this example, the original data was columns A through G. In your role, you want to keep the languages that each book was written in and translated into, but you'll never sort or filter for the languages. You can save space by putting all the languages into a single cell, as shown in column H. TEXTJOIN was used to get all the languages into one cell.

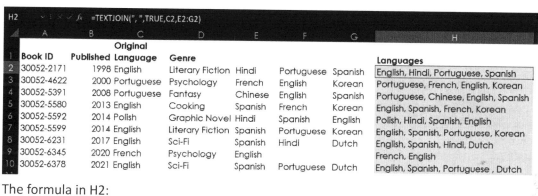

The formula in H2:

```
=TEXTJOIN(", ",TRUE,C2,E2:G2)
```

Syntax:

```
TEXTJOIN(delimiter, ignore_empty, text1, [text2], …)
```

- **delimiter:** In this example, "comma and space" have been chosen to separate languages. Note that the delimiter needs to be inside double quotes.
- **ignore_empty:** The options are TRUE or FALSE (or 1 for TRUE, 0 for FALSE). Use TRUE to ignore empty cells when you just want everything in one cell. In the next section we'll look at an example using FALSE.
- **text:** In this formula, C2 is the original language. E2:G2 joins the range of cells so you don't have to input each cell one at a time.

From here, you can copy and paste as values in the Languages column and delete columns C, E, F, and G.

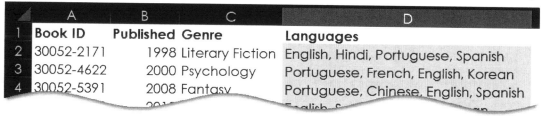

TEXTJOIN: Don't Ignore Empty Values

In this example, you and I are responsible for assigning shift leaders for columns Shift1, Shift2, Shift3, and Shift4. Someone else assigns the assistants. The way the data is set up, columns B:J are hard to make sense of. Thus, column K was added to make it easier to see what is most important to us.

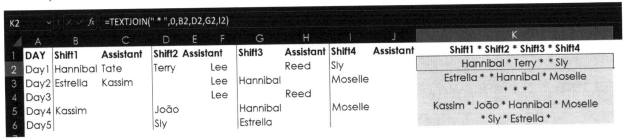

The formula in K2:

```
=TEXTJOIN(" * ",0,B2,D2,G2,I2)
```

In the *ignore_empty* part of the formula, a 0 is used because we **do not** want to ignore empty values. The empty values will leave holes that tell you that no one has been assigned and for which shifts. In K2 there's no name between Terry and Sly; thus, you need someone for Shift3 Day1. In K6 (Day5), Shift1 and Shift4 still need to be assigned.

Notice how the formula was built and that there's no confusion with shifts that have assistants but no shift leader. For example, Lee and Reed are scheduled to assist Day3, but no shift leaders have been scheduled.

New Functions in 2022: TEXTSPLIT, TEXTAFTER, TOCOL, TOROW, and WRAPROWS

In March 2022, 14 new functions rolled out to the Insiders channel of Microsoft 365. I am going to cover five of them here: TEXTSPLIT, TEXTAFTER, TOCOL, TOROW, and WRAPROWS.

TEXTSPLIT and TEXTAFTER

The TEXTSPLIT function allows you to do Text to Columns with a formula. It actually is a lot better than Text to Columns. The syntax for TEXTSPLIT allows you to specify a column delimiter and/or a row delimiter. The first example in the figure below specifies a hyphen as a column delimiter. Each word is split into a new cell in a row from A4 to G4.

The formula in A6 (but shown in A5) is not using a column delimiter, and it specifies a hyphen as the row delimiter. In this example, each word is split into a new cell in a vertical column from A6 to A12.

	A	B	C	D	E	F	G	H
1	=TEXTSPLIT(text,Col_delimiter,row_delimiter,ignore_empty,match_mode,pad_with)							
2	This-is-some-text-in-a-cell							
3	=TEXTSPLIT(A2,"-") ← **Split to columns**							
4	This	is	some	text	in	a	cell	
5	=TEXTSPLIT(A2,,"-") ← **Split to rows**							
6	This							
7	is							
8	some							
9	text							
10	in							
11	a							
12	cell							

But the next figure shows how you might really use TEXTSPLIT. The goal is to split each sentence into a new row and each word into a new column. There is a lot of trickiness that you have to deal with here.

	A	B	C	D	E	F	G
1	This is some text. This is another line. I am excited! Can, it handle a comma?						
2	=TEXTSPLIT(A1,{" ",", "},{".","!","?"},TRUE,TRUE," ")						
3	This	is	some	text			
4	This	is	another	line			
5	I	am	excited				
6	Can	it	handle	a		comma	
7							
8	column:	{" ",", "}					
9	row:	{".","!","?"}					
10	empty:	TRUE					
11	match mode:	TRUE					
12	pad:	" "					

How can you tell the end of a sentence? It might be a period, a question mark, or an exclamation point. To tell Excel that any of these punctuation marks should start a new row, you use an array constant of {".","?","!"}. In a similar fashion, the column delimiter might be either a space or a comma, so you use either " " or "," as an array constant.

But here is another gotcha. If you were to tell Excel that each comma or space should split to a new column, you would get Can in A6. Since A6 is followed by a comma and a space, B6 would be blank, and C6 would contain it. To prevent the comma-space from being read as two words, you need to specify TRUE for the *ignore_empty* argument. The Match_Mode treats "A" and "a" as the same. But since the is no "upper case" for punctuation, this argument is not important in this example.

And the final gotcha: Joe McDaid thinks that just because the last sentence has five words, each of the sentences should have five words. When row 5 only has three words, Joe wants to fill D5 and E5 with #N/A errors. There are nerdy reasons behind this. Just know that you have to specify the sixth argument, *pad_with*, as a space.

When TEXTJOIN debuted in February 2017, I began hoping for TEXTSPLIT. It took five years until TEXTSPLIT arrived. Every time I did a YouTube video that could have been 30% shorter with TEXTSPLIT, I would wonder when TEXTSPLIT was going to arrive. I was happy to finally see TEXTSPLIT among the functions recently released. However, in the few weeks since the 14 new functions arrived, the one that I find that I love is TEXTAFTER.

First, let's talk about the *instance_number* argument in TEXTAFTER. This formula would give you everything after the dash—in this case, 123:

```
=TEXTAFTER("ABC-123","-")
```

What if there are multiple hyphens in the text? You can use the *instance_number* argument to specify which hyphen. So this formula would give you B-C-D-E:

```
=TEXTAFTER("A-B-C-D-E","-")
```

But this formula would give you C-D-E:

```
=TEXTAFTER("A-B-C-D-E","-",2)
```

The *instance_number* argument is found elsewhere in Excel. It is in the SUBSTITUTE function. It is a very good way to get beyond a specific hyphen in some text.

Now for the reason that I love TEXTAFTER: It's because of an idea introduced by Excel MVP Charles Williams. Charles sells a Fast Excel add-in that includes 80 new Excel functions. In the Fast Excel add-in, he invented the concept that if you specify a negative number for *instance_number*, then you want Excel to count from the end. Imagine how cool it would be if =INDEX(A1#,1) would point to the first cell in the A1 array and =INDEX(A1#,-1) would point to the last cell in the array. Of course, INDEX doesn't do this, but TEXTAFTER does.

Say that you have a series of sentences in a column. Each sentence has a different number of words. You want a formula to find the last word in each sentence. Before TEXTAFTER, doing this was possible but convoluted. With

TEXTAFTER, you can say that you are looking for the text after a space and specify -1 for the *instance_number* argument. This formula will successfully return the last word in each cell, as shown below.

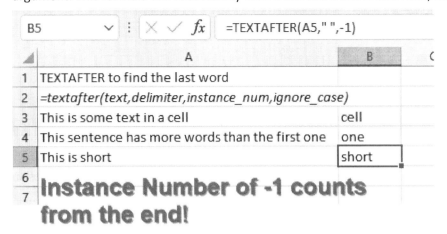

	A	B	C
B5	=TEXTAFTER(A5," ",-1)		
1	TEXTAFTER to find the last word		
2	=textafter(text,delimiter,instance_num,ignore_case)		
3	This is some text in a cell	cell	
4	This sentence has more words than the first one	one	
5	This is short	short	
6			
7			

Instance Number of -1 counts from the end!

TOCOL, TOROW, and WRAPROWS

Several useful new functions are for array shaping. In the image below, you have 16 names in A2:D5. To unwind this to a single column, use:

```
=TOCOL(A2:D5)
```

To unwind it to a single row, use:

```
=TOROW(A2:D5)
```

> **Note:** I've truncated the results of both of these in the screenshot below. More words continue where the red arrows point.

	A	B	C	D	E	F
1	Unwrap and re-wrap					
2	Andy	Barb	Chris	Diane		
3	Ed	Flo	Gary	Hank		
4	Ike	Jared	Kelly	Lou		
5	Mike	Nan	Otto	Paul		
6						
7			=TOROW(A2:D5)			
8	=TOCOL(A2:D5)		Andy	Barb	Chris	Diane
9	Andy					
10	Barb					
11	Chris		=WRAPROWS(A9#,3)			
12	Diane		Andy	Barb	Chris	
13	Ed		Diane	Ed	Flo	
14	Flo		Gary	Hank	Ike	
15	Gary		Jared	Kelly	Lou	
16	Hank		Mike	Nan	Otto	
17	Ike		Paul	#N/A	#N/A	
18	Jared					
19	Kelly					

Once you have a single column or single row of data, you might need to wrap it back into a rectangular range. In the image above, WRAPROWS takes a vector and wraps it into a range that is three columns wide. Note that if the last row is not completely filled in, the function fills the last cells with #N/A. Prevent the #N/A by specifying " " for the optional *pad_with* argument.

PMT

You are finally buying a new car to replace that hunk-o-junk your coworker loaned you. In the image below, the formula in C5 is used in B2 to determine that $682.59 will be the monthly payment on a loan of $23,200 at 3.77% over 36 months.

Notice that Excel shows the result as a negative number.

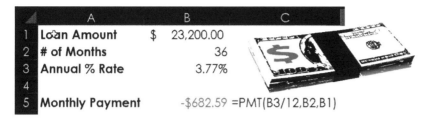

Drive safely. 😁

FORECAST

In the worksheet in the following figure, you have to generate a budget for year 5. You can use Excel's FORECAST function to make predictions based on actual sales and based on orders from the previous years.

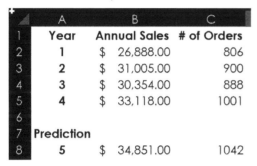

Formula in cell B8:

```
=FORECAST(A8,B2:B5,A2:A5)
```

Formula in cell C8:

```
=FORECAST(A8,C2:C5,A2:A5)
```

CEILING.MATH and FLOOR.MATH

In the next figure, the values in column A represent the cost and markup of several products, but they'd look odd on a price list or menu. CELING.MATH is being used in column B to round up to the nearest 50¢.

The syntax:

```
=CEILING(number to round, [significance to round up to], [mode])
```

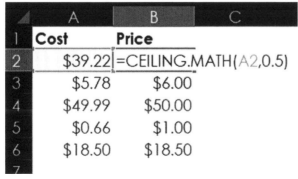

The optional *mode* argument to the CEILING.MATH function is used if you have negative numbers. A *mode* value of 1 will round negative numbers away from 0; leaving *mode* blank will round toward 0.

FLOOR.MATH works the same as CELING.MATH but in the opposite direction.

Compatibility (Deprecated) Functions

If you type in a function and see a warning triangle (like the one next to the CEILING function in this image), that means the function has been replaced with one or more functions and exists for compatibility with old versions of Excel.

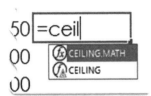

Functions are sometimes replaced to improve how they perform or to give users more control. As described in the previous section, the *mode* argument to CEILING.MATH lets the user pick how negative numbers are handled. The old CEILING function does not offer that option.

Here are a few other functions that have been replaced:

Old Function	Replaced With
CEILING	CEILING.MATH
CONCATENATE	CONCAT
FLOOR	FLOOR.MATH
FORECAST	FORECAST.ETS
	FORECAST.ETS.SEASONALITY
	FORECAST.LINEAR
	FORECAST.ETS.CONFINT
	FORECAST.ETS.STAT
RANK	RANK.AVG
	RANK.EQ

For a full list of deprecated functions: Formulas | Function Library More Functions | Compatibility.

For the most part, the old functions still work for very basic needs, but it's strongly recommended that they be avoided.

MAX, MIN, LARGE, and SMALL

You often want to find the largest or smallest number in a range. These four functions can all help you do this:

- MAX returns the largest value in a range.
- LARGE returns the *n*th largest value in a range.
- MIN returns the smallest value in a range.
- SMALL returns the *n*th smallest value in a range.

The image below shows the times for a competition that had six competitors over five days. In this case, the lowest times are the best.

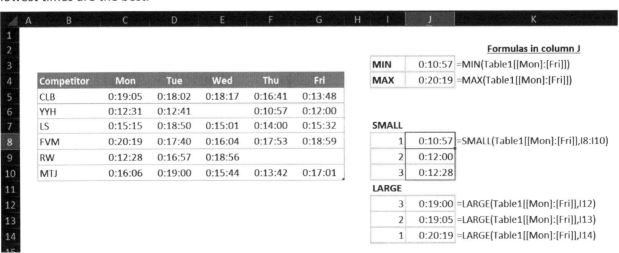

J3 shows the minimum (fastest) time. J4 shows the maximum (slowest) time.

In J12:J14 the three slowest times are being retrieved with three different formulas using the LARGE function. To retrieve the three fastest times, a single dynamic array formula using the SMALL function is being used in J8:J10.

Note one thing that's very interesting and important: Cells E6, F9, and G9 are empty. However, SMALL and MIN don't read those cells as 0:00:00. A distinction is being made between not showing up and being extremely fast and finishing in less than one second.

LEN

The LEN function counts the number of characters in a cell.

Using LEN to Check for Accuracy

In this example, the original data had the headers Transaction, Product, and Count.

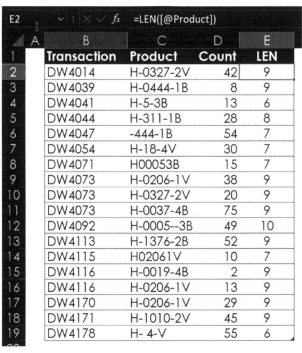

In this example, what's known about the product IDs is they should have nine characters each—e.g., H-0037-4B.

The LEN column was added in order to flag product IDs that have anything other than nine characters so they can be corrected or researched. This is the formula in E2:

```
=LEN([@Product])
```

   Caution: If LEN yields 9, check it because it could be wrong.

Using LEN to Check Acceptable Title Length

LEN can be used to check if values are within acceptable parameters. In this example, LEN is checking for titles that are too long or too short.

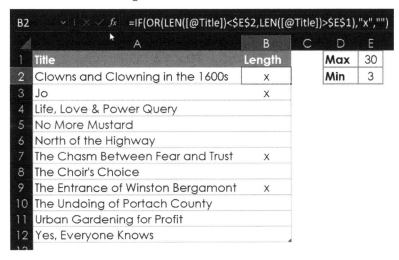

These proposed titles are being checked for acceptable length. D1:E2 shows that a title can be no shorter than 3 characters and no longer than 30 characters. This formula uses IF, OR, and LEN to check the length and flag errant titles with an x:

```
=IF(OR(LEN([@Title])<$E$2,LEN([@Title])>$E$1),"x","")
```

COUNTA

This is my favorite function ... so underused. ☺

Plainly stated: COUNTA counts the number of non-empty cells in a range. The usefulness of COUNTA is vast! Let's look at ways this function can help when you're under fire.

In this example, the Attended column is populated if a person did attend. The formula in E2 gets a count of all non-empty cells: You don't have to count X, x, Y, or Yes, and you don't care that Simon was 15 minutes late. You know that if there's **anything** in the cell, the person attended.

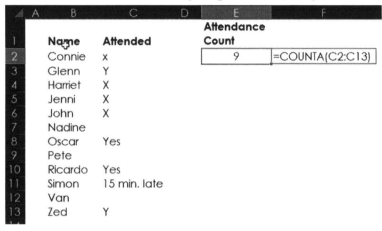

	Name	Attended		Attendance Count	
2	Connie	x		9	=COUNTA(C2:C13)
3	Glenn	Y			
4	Harriet	X			
5	Jenni	X			
6	John	X			
7	Nadine				
8	Oscar	Yes			
9	Pete				
10	Ricardo	Yes			
11	Simon	15 min. late			
12	Van				
13	Zed	Y			

Using COUNTA to Determine the Size of a Job

In this example, you're faced with collecting data and filling in the attendance matrix. X indicates that no class was held. The numbers represent the numbers of students who attended. Observations:

- Jerrod didn't lead a class on Day7.
- Sadiya had 56 students on Day1.

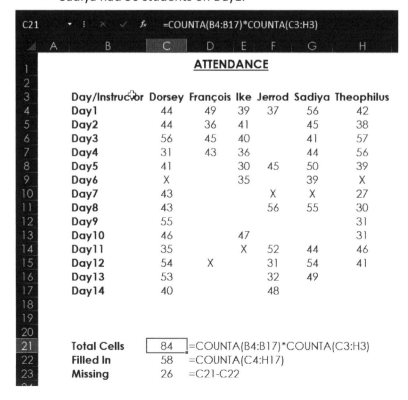

C21   fx   =COUNTA(B4:B17)*COUNTA(C3:H3)

	Day/Instructor	Dorsey	François	Ike	Jerrod	Sadiya	Theophilus
1	**ATTENDANCE**						
4	Day1	44	49	39	37	56	42
5	Day2	44	36	41		45	38
6	Day3	56	45	40		41	57
7	Day4	31	43	36		44	56
8	Day5	41		30	45	50	39
9	Day6	X		35		39	X
10	Day7	43			X	X	27
11	Day8	43			56	55	30
12	Day9	55					31
13	Day10	46		47			31
14	Day11	35		X	52	44	46
15	Day12	54	X		31	54	41
16	Day13	53			32	49	
17	Day14	40			48		
21	**Total Cells**	84	=COUNTA(B4:B17)*COUNTA(C3:H3)				
22	**Filled In**	58	=COUNTA(C4:H17)				
23	**Missing**	26	=C21-C22				

The goal is to fill in each empty cell with either an X or the number of students.

There is a lot of missing data, but before diving in, how about getting a count of how many total data points are required. How many do you have, and how many are missing? You need to get some idea of what you're up against.

The formula in C21 uses COUNTA in two ways: It counts the number of rows in the matrix and the number of headers. By multiplying them together, you see that 84 total data points are needed. COUNTA is used in C22 to tell how much of the work is done. Simple subtraction in C23 reveals that 26 data points need to be filled in.

This is a small example. Imagine, however, if there were 5000 data points and 300 of them were missing. Knowing this ahead of time would give you the opportunity to ask how important those missing 300 points are and maybe get someone to help.

True story where COUNTA could have helped: I was contacted by someone who'd assigned two people to fill in data on a spreadsheet consisting of 2000 rows and 3 columns. The duo jumped right in and after two days, they were frustrated by how slowly things were going—all the scrolling around ... typing ... copy and pasting ... mistakes they had to correct. They didn't know a few important details:

- How many data points were missing when they started and needed to be filled in
- How many data points they were able to fill in over the two days
- At their current pace, how long it would take to finish

Had they known the size of the battle before they started, they might have reached out for help before they got started.

CONVERT

The CONVERT function offers several dozen conversions in areas including volume, temperature, time, weight, energy, force, and pressure. Its syntax:

```
CONVERT(number, from_unit, to_unit)
```

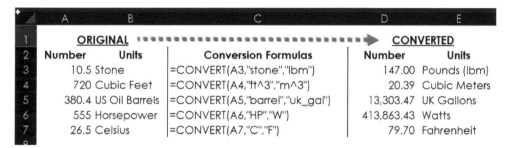

| | ORIGINAL | | | CONVERTED | |
Number	Units	Conversion Formulas	Number	Units
10.5	Stone	=CONVERT(A3,"stone","lbm")	147.00	Pounds (lbm)
720	Cubic Feet	=CONVERT(A4,"ft^3","m^3")	20.39	Cubic Meters
380.4	US Oil Barrels	=CONVERT(A5,"barrel","uk_gal")	13,303.47	UK Gallons
555	Horsepower	=CONVERT(A6,"HP","W")	413,863.43	Watts
26.5	Celsius	=CONVERT(A7,"C","F")	79.70	Fahrenheit

One recent improvement to CONVERT is that it no longer allows strange conversions. Previously, CONVERT would give you the options to convert, say, feet ("ft") to hours ("hr"), and you'd get an #N/A error. However, this image shows that converting 96 tons ("ton") is now limited to reasonable options. It can't be converted to light-years ("ly") or meters per second ("m/sec").

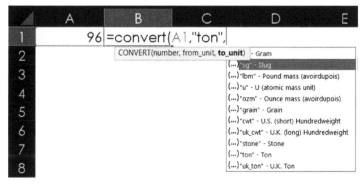

ABS: Comparing Variations in Absolute Terms

Sometimes you just want to know the difference between two values and don't care if the difference is positive or negative. Thus, you need to calculate the absolute value of a number.

In this example, 65 is the ideal reading. What's acceptable is 65 ±3, meaning values 62 to 68 ... no problems.

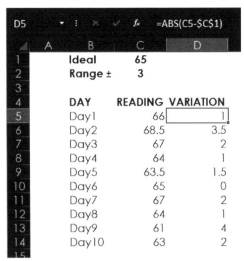

Using ABS, the result in the VARIATION column reveals that Day2 and Day9 were outside the accepted range. Being above or below doesn't matter. It just matters that *something was wrong!*

NETWORKDAYS.INTL

You're part of a market that's only open 1 February 2022 through 31 August 2022, and you want to know how many days your shop will be open. Here are more details:

- The market is open Tuesday through Saturday; it's closed Sunday and Monday.
- You'll be closed for four days for inventory.
- You'll be closed specific holidays.
- You'll be closed on your birthday.

The following image shows:

- The market start and end dates
- The dates you'll be closed (and the reason for each closure)
- How many total days there are between 1 February and 31 August
- The number of days you'll actually be open

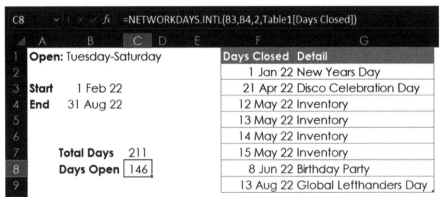

NETWORKDAYS.INTL syntax:

```
NETWORKDAYS.INTL(start_date, end_date, [weekend], [holidays])
```

The formula in C8:

```
=NETWORKDAYS.INTL(B3,B4,2,Table1[Days Closed])
```

NETWORKDAYS.INTL includes the [*weekend*] component, which is useful if your weekend is something other than Saturday and Sunday. The image below shows the various options. This example uses option 2 because your weekend is Sunday, Monday.

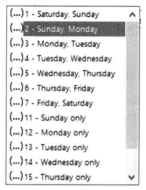

=NETWORKDAYS.INTL(B3,B4,

But, what if the given weekend options aren't what you need? Say that your assistant, Cyrus, is only needed on Wednesdays and Fridays. NETWORKDAYS.INTL will let you customize his weekends:

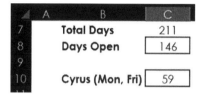

Formula in C10:

```
=NETWORKDAYS.INTL(B3,B4,"1101011",Table1[Days Closed])
```

In the *weekend* argument, you must use a string of seven 1s and 0s, with 1 = day off and 0 = day working. The first value is Monday, and the string must be in double quotation marks. Thus:

Weekend String	Workdays
"1101011"	Wednesday, Friday
"0011100"	Monday, Tuesday, Saturday, Sunday
"1110001"	Thursday, Friday, Saturday

Note: Excel has a NETWORKDAYS function, but it does not include the weekend argument.

Integrity Checks and Troubleshooting

Errors are a reality of working with data. A formula could be wrong, a sloppy cut and paste can throw things off, and Excel may show an error when you aren't sure what it's referring to. Here are a few ways to check your work.

Quickly Checking Sums, Counts, and Averages

Sometimes you need information about a range of data quickly. In the figure below, how do you know that the right sum is in D1? To find out, highlight the range. Notice that the status bar at the bottom of the Excel window provides you with SUM, COUNT, and AVERAGE formulas. You can see that yes, the 78.67 in D1 matches the 78.67 in the status bar. New in 2022: left-click any number in the status bar to copy it to the clipboard.

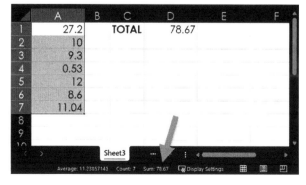

Tip: If you have a dataset that isn't contiguous, highlight one range, hold down the Ctrl key, and use your mouse to select the other ranges.

Tip: If you right-click the status bar, you'll see a long list of other customizations you can make, including minimum and maximum values, sheet number, and whether to turn the zoom slider on or off.

Using Ctrl+` to See Underlying Formulas

In the United States, most keyboards have a tilde (~) and grave accent (`) on the same key. While it is easier to say "Control tilde" than "press Ctrl and that weird backward accent symbol in the upper left that most Americans cannot name," it is important to note that outside the United States, many keyboards have the tilde and the grave accent key on two different keys. Thus, you have to press Ctrl+`, not Ctrl+~, in order to toggle into Show Formulas mode.

This key combination provides one handy way of troubleshooting when there's a problem and you don't know exactly where it is.

The data below shows the number of building permits that have been issued, with a summary in rows 13:16. The totals for Angel Park and Kincaid do not match!

	A	B	C	D	E	F
1			**New Building Permits**			
2						
3		**City**	**January**	**February**	**March**	**Q1 Total**
4		Angel Park	100	76	111	296
5		Bariston	40	72	80	192
6		Chase	76	43	40	159
7		Kincaid	100	101	91	283
8		Middleton	24	39	17	80
9		Mt. Patten	190	100	93	383
10		Winters	183	170	131	484
11						
12						
13			**Permits**			
14		**Angel Park**	287			
15		**Kincaid**	292			
16		**Middleton**	80			
17						

You can press Ctrl+` to make the spreadsheet show all formulas. Now you can see the story:

	A	B	C	D	E	F
1			**New Building Permits**			
2						
3		**City**	**January**	**February**	**March**	**Q1 Total**
4		Angel Park	100	76	111	=SUM(C4:E4)+9
5		Bariston	40	72	80	=SUM(C5:E5)
6		Chase	76	43	40	=SUM(C6:E6)
7		Kincaid	100	101	91	=SUM(C7:E7)-9
8		Middleton	24	39	17	=SUM(C8:E8)
9		Mt. Patten	190	100	93	=SUM(C9:E9)
10		Winters	183	170	131	=SUM(C10:E10)
11						
12						
13			**Permits**			
14		**Angel Park**	=SUM(C4:E4)			
15		**Kincaid**	=SUM(C7:E7)			
16		**Middleton**	=SUM(C8:E8)			
17						

Someone manually added 9 in cell F4 and subtracted 9 in F7. This commonly happens when an inexperienced person has good reason to make a correction. Or ... something shady is going on.

Crossfooting

Crossfooting isn't an Excel feature or function; it's a concept that you need to know because crossfooting is a huge help in staying out of trouble. Simply put, crossfooting is calculating something several ways—expecting them to be equal, and checking to see if they are all equal.

Below, the sales for the SW and SE regions are in, and summaries need to be created, by rep and by region.

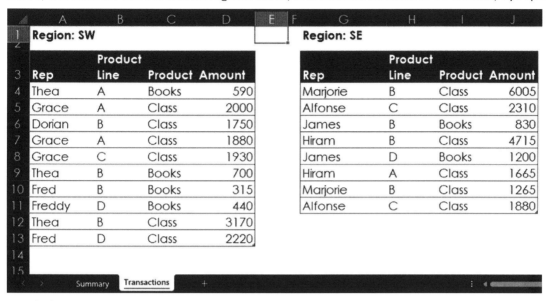

Here's the Summary sheet with calculations for items, reps, and regions:

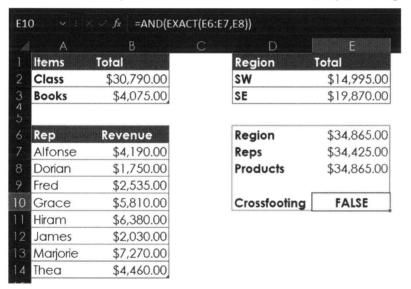

The Region, Reps and Products data should all be equal, they've just been calculated in different ways. The data in range D6:E10 is the section where the crossfooting is happening. E6 is the sum of the Region data; E7 is the sum of the Reps data and E7 is the sum of the Products data. (They are not hard-coded values.)

The formula in E10:

```
=AND(EXACT(E6:E7,E8))
```

This formula checks to see if E6, E7 and E8 are all equal. If they are, the result will be true. However, there's a FALSE. Something is wrong, and without the crossfooting, this would be hard to catch. Now that you see that there's a problem, STOP! Do not send this on to the VP of Sales.

Go back to the Transactions sheet. In A11, Fred is entered as *Freddy* and wasn't captured by the formula that was summing the sales by *Fred*. This is why the Reps data is $440 lower than the Product and Region summaries. This also tells you that something strange happened in the process before you received the data because it allowed an inconsistent entry.

Note: If you can't influence an improvement in the process, in the future you'll need to check for these types of inconsistency goofs as part of YOUR process.

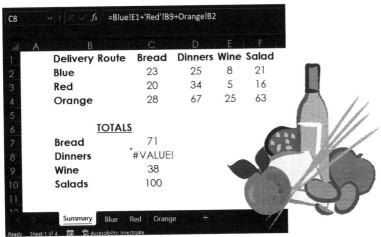

To wrap up, change Freddy to Fred. All calculations will update; the FALSE will change to TRUE in E10 on the Transactions sheet, and the data can be forwarded on to the VP of sales.

Using Evaluate Formula

Note: The Evaluate Formula feature is not part of Mac versions of Excel.

In the image below, the formula in C8 has bombed out with a #VALUE! error ... but it used to work. What's wrong? Time to troubleshoot!

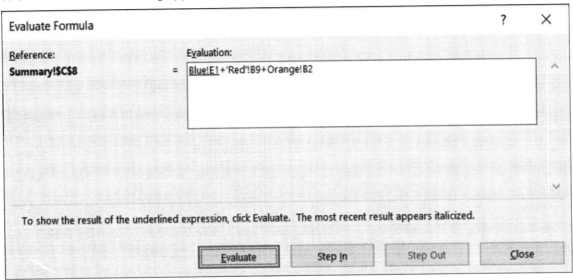

With your cursor in C8: Formulas | Evaluate Formula.

The Evaluate Formula dialog appears, showing the raw formula:

Click Evaluate. Each time you click it, another step of the calculation happens.

Step 3 shows 59+Orange!B2, representing 25+34 dinners ordered for the Blue and Red routes, respectively. The next step shows the value in Orange!B2.

The image below shows the result after four steps. Do you see the problem?

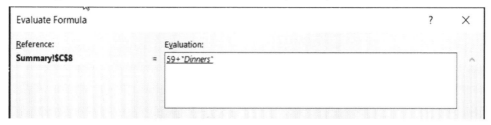

In step 5, the formula is going to try to add the word *Dinners* to 59.

No. Text and a number cannot be added together. Thus, the next step shows a #VALUE! Error.

Go over and take a look at B2 on the Orange sheet, and you see the problem:

Orange!B2 is the word Dinners. It should be on Orange!C2, which is the sum of the dinners that were ordered.

Evaluate Formula helped guide you in where to find the problem.

Troubleshooting by Checking Highlighted Ranges in a Formula

In this image, there is no earthly way the dinners for this event costs $16,620. The formula should count the number of people invited, add that to the number of guests, then multiply by the $26.50 in C2.

Troubleshoot by placing your cursor in E2 and then clicking in the formula bar (or double-clicking E2). Excel highlights the components in the formula/calculation

There should not be a highlight around C3, which is the cost of the venue. This can be corrected by dragging the highlight to the correct cell: C2..

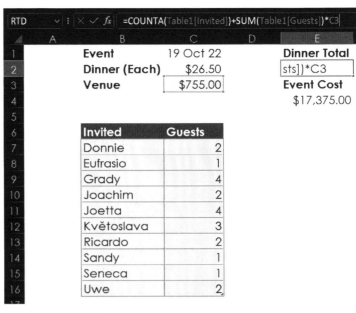

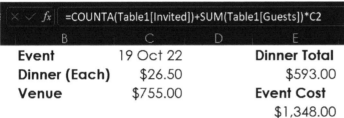

$593 for dinner and an event cost of $1348 make sense! ☺

> **Note:** Apologies to those who are reading the printed book and can't see the colors!

Error-Handling Functions: IFNA vs. IFERROR

IFNA allows you to work with formulas and errors—specifically #N/A errors—in a very granular way.

Let's say you have a list of ID numbers and need to use VLOOKUP to retrieve item names from a comprehensive list. You also know that some item numbers don't exist on the comprehensive list because they were discontinued. When VLOOKUP doesn't find an ID number, you don't want the #N/A error; you'd like for the formula to return "discontinued."

IFERROR can help, but if you don't use it carefully, it can mask too much. It masks #REF, #VALUE, among other things. Here's an example:

```
=VLOOKUP(A5,$I$2:$K$7,w,FALSE)
```

This formula results in #NAME? because w makes no sense here; it was possibly a user typo. You need to see the #NAME? error because something is wrong with the formula. If you nested the formula in IFERROR, like this, it would hide the blunder and incorrectly tell you that all of your parts are discontinued:

```
=IFERROR(VLOOKUP(A5,$I$2:$K$7,w,FALSE),"discontinued")
```

However, wrapping the formula in IFNA, like this, gives you control over lookup values that are not found:

```
=IFNA(VLOOKUP(A5,$I$2:$K$7,3,FALSE),"discontinued")
```

The formula will still show the other types of errors.

> **Note:** While IFERROR works in Excel 2010 and later, the IFNA function was introduced in Excel 2013 and will not calculate in Excel 2010.

One reason to get familiar with XLOOKUP is that it has the built-in component *if_not_found*.

Row Counts

My friend Robin Hunt of ThinkData Solutions, Inc. often talks about row count as a way to maintain data integrity and check if everything has been accounted for. In this example, there is a list of teams on the Teams sheet. On the Conferences sheet, the teams are split by Lower Valley, Northeast, and Other. But is it accurate?

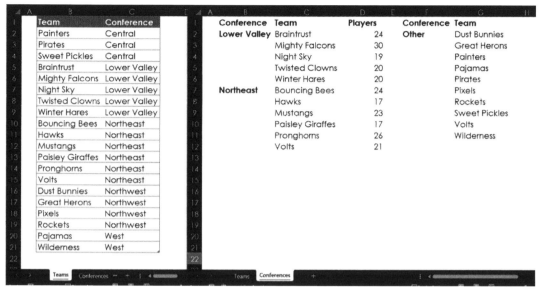

If there were a row count, the data would be easier to review, as shown below:

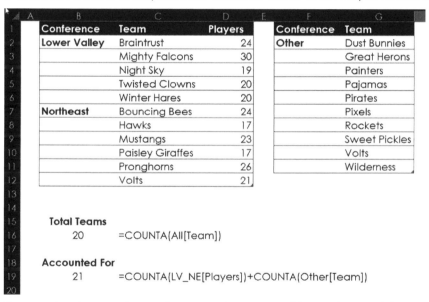

I've put the data on the Conferences sheet into tables and named them LV_NE and Other.

The formula in B16 is counting how many total teams are in the source data. The formula in B19 is counting the number of teams in LV_NE and adding it to the number of teams in Other.

Something is wrong because 20 ≠ 21.

Problem: The Volts are counted twice, in cells C12 and G10.

> **Caution:** Going by row counts isn't perfect. You could end up with 20 = 20 and still have something wrong. But row count is a simple indicator that can be put in place for a rough overview.

Imagine starting with 2000 rows of data that need to manually be moved to five different groups.

	A	B
1		**Row count**
2	Source	**2000**
3		
4	**Unassigned**	728
5	**Group1**	145
6	**Group2**	511
7	**Group3**	96
8	**Group4**	219
9	**Group5**	400
10		**2099**
11		

This image shows that the source data has 2000 rows. Note these details:

- 728 of the 2000 have not been assigned.
- Of those that have been assigned, there's a count for each group.
- Cell B10 is calculating a sum of the unassigned plus Groups 1 through 5.
- If 1 record is moved to Group3, that tally will increase to 97, and the Unassigned count will drop to 727.
- Currently, B10 shows a total of 2099 rows—99 more than the source.

Before assigning any more of the 728 unassigned, **STOP!** Figure out where the extra 99 came from and get rid of them.

Checking row counts and using crossfooting (see page 253) are just two alerts that you can build into your worksheets to identify goofs before crap data capitalizes on them and you find yourself defeated and embarrassed or the subject of an international scandal. Next thing you know, you're wearing a wig and have a new name, hoping no one recognizes you.

Chapter 29: Spreadsheet Layout and Development

Up to this point, we've covered a lot of technical topics. We've gone through slicers, a lot of functions and formulas, and Power Query. The examples have tended to be standalone solutions.

This chapter gives a quick overview of the importance of good spreadsheet layout.

Here's an event-planning scenario. On the Overview sheet, there is a lot of information that you need to keep track of.

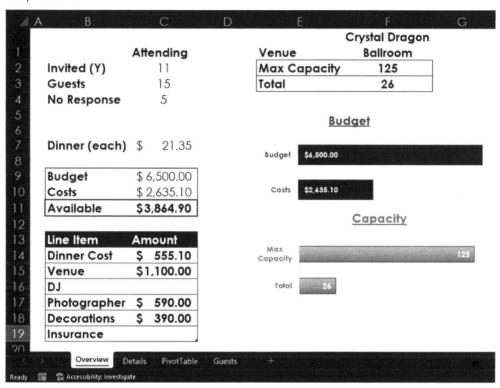

Note these details:

- The Budget graph is an easy visual that lets you know how close you are to the budget. That graph is tied to cells B9:C10.

- The values for the budget are in the table in B13:C19. Because the dataset is in a table, when more data is added or when changes are made in the data, the budget graph will automatically update.

- The Capacity graph keeps you out of trouble with the fire marshal and insurance company. The room holds 125, and so far 26 are expected to attend. That data is tied to E2:F3.

- The dinner price (C7) and decorations costs (C18) are coming from the Details worksheet via XLOOKUP.

Both of the datasets shown below are in tables reflecting the various tiers and price changes.

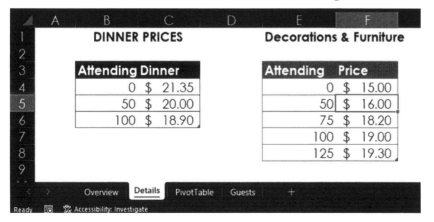

The Guests sheet is where all of the invites, responses, and guests are managed. It is also where the Overview sheet is pulling data from to count people who are coming, how many guests they're bringing, and who hasn't responded.

There's even a slicer to make it easy to see who's coming, who's not coming, and who hasn't responded. (Notice that the slicer is not case-sensitive.)

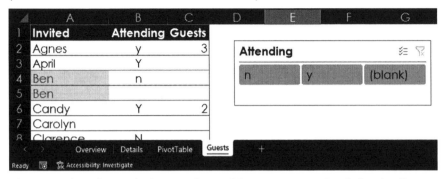

The guest list also includes conditional formatting to check for duplicates. You can see that Ben is in here twice. And because everything is integrated, when the duplicate is removed, all of the calculations and graphs will update accordingly.

There is also a Pivot Table on the PivotTable sheet for a quick peek and summary from the Guests sheet.

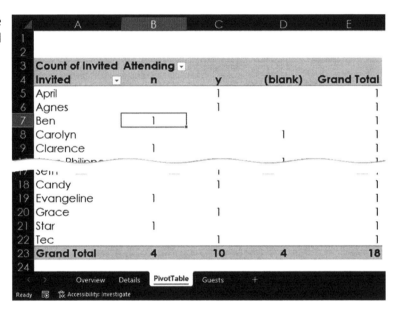

When the guest list changes and with every individual update, all relevant calculations update. Here's a revised overview:

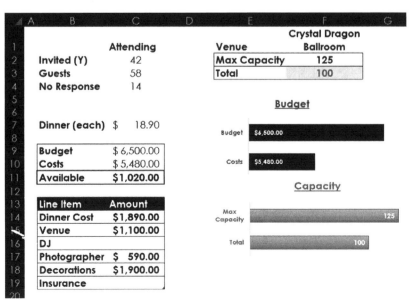

Note these details:

- The total number of invitees who are attending, plus their guests, is 100.
- The cost of dinner has dropped from $21.35 to $18.90.

But wait! Why is F3 shaded?

Answer: There is conditional formatting to warn that capacity is being approached.

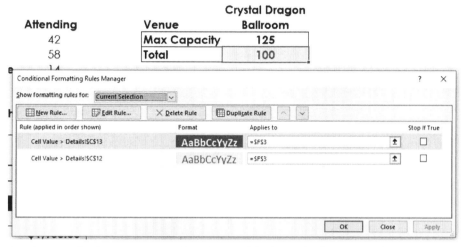

On the Details sheet, a section has been added to calculate 77% of capacity and 90% of capacity. Overview!F3 is highlighted yellow because 100 attendees is between 77% and 90%.

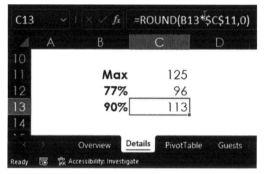

A Final Word About Spreadsheet Layout and Development

Poor spreadsheet layout and development creates lots of headaches. Poorly developed workbooks can be expensive to fix, and sometimes they never get fixed. There's too much going on, there are too many disconnected pieces, and crap data is deep in its fetid cave, having a great victorious laugh at your expense.

To claim victory over crap data and satisfy your job as the hero for people who have to live with the consequences of your work, it all starts with forethought as you begin to lay out your spreadsheet.

The original layout won't always be the final layout. Good layout includes anticipation of moving things around, adding new pieces, and deleting things that you realize you didn't need. A number of measures can help you safely move graphs, formulas, and datasets:

- Put your data into tables.
- Keep data in as few places as possible.
- Be comfortable with absolute and mixed cell references.
- Be familiar with Pivot Tables.
- Do not use hard-coded values.

Index

Symbols

39% zoom trick 161
#FIELD! error 185
@ for Implicit Intersection 158
[h]:mm 235
@Mention 44
[mm] 235
#N/A error 52
#REF! error 12
#SPILL! error 162
symbol 150
& to Concatenate 12

A

ABS 249
Absolute versus relative 4
Accounting underline 23
Ad hoc vs. canned 241
Advanced Filter 146
Alt+Enter 24
Analyst role 48
Analyze Data 212
AND 8
Anniversary, next 234
Anti Join 114
Aquarium data 163
ARRAYTOTEXT 186
Artificial intelligence 207
  Analyze Data 212
Asking questions 239
AVERAGEIFS 50

B

Barboza, Carlos 266
Bassist 20
Beck, Billy 180
Begins with 32
Birthday, next 234
Blog post, popular 228
Bottom up lookup 55
Breaking Down Tasks 238

C

Candidate evaluation 228
Cascade Cigar & Tobacco iii
CEILING.MATH 245
Charting 190
  Chart Title 192
  Column width 194
  Data Labels 197
  Gridlines 197
  Histogram 190
  Markers 196

Prevent resizing 193
  Title from cell 197
  Y-axis 196
Checkmark
  P as Wingdings2 9
Chesapeake, VA 188
Christian, Raymond iii
Clemons, Clarence 188
Collaborating 43
  Sheet Views 45
Column from Examples 210
Column quality 201
Comments
  @Mention 44
Compatibility functions 246
Concatenating names 11
Conditional Formatting 139
  Icon sets 140
Contextures 159
Contiguous, selecting non- 252
CONVERT 249
COUNTA 8, 248
Count distinct 82
COUNTIFS 50
Crossfoot 253
Ctrl+` 252
Ctrl+; for date 234
Ctrl+Shift+: for time 234
Currency exchange rates 180
Custom list 27
Custom Views 48

D

Data in 1 place 225
Data Model 220
  vs. Power Query 223
Data needs 239
Data Profiling 200
Data quality 28, 163
Data Type 180
  Custom 189
  Data Card 186
  Drill down 188
  Extracting data 182
  Extract to Grid 188
  Sort by hidden field 183
Data Validation 39, 165
Date filters 33
DAY 234
DAYS 234
De-duping
  Advanced Filter 146
  Assembled ID 149
  IF 149
Deprecated functions 246
Distinct 158
Distinct Count 82

Diving In 198
Don't Move or Size 194
Drill down 70
Dropdown list
  Dynamic 38
Dropdown Lists 166
  Autocomplete 166
Duplicates, find with CF 139
Dynamic Arrays 150
Dynamic spreadsheets 10
Dystopian genre 57

E

Elapsed time 235
Emery, Ann K. 7, 195
Emoji 230
Ends with X 31
Energy conversions 249
EOMONTH 234
Error-Handling 256
Error list 4
Escobar, Miguel 86
Evaluate Formula 254
EXACT 253
Excelapalooza 81
Excel.CurrentWorkbook(). *See* CurrentWorkbook()
Excel encyclopedia 180
Excel on Fire channel viii
Exchange rates 180
External links 17

F

F4 to toggle references 6
Fast Excel add-in 243
Filter 28
  between numbers 32
FILTER 153
FIND 6
Fit to Page 232
Flash Fill 207
  Two rules 208
Flattening data 84
FLOOR.MATH 245
Floyd, Maere iii
Force conversions 249
FORECAST 245
Foreign Key 222
Formula
  Higlight used ranges 255
  Notation 3
  readability 205
  Triggers 228
FREQUENCY 190
Fuzzy Matching 135

G

What Others Are Saying About This Edition

Wouldn't it be great if all data was clean and if you had received comprehensive Excel training so you knew exactly what to do when faced with a spreadsheet? Please do send me an invitation to that corner of DisneyWorld when you find it. If – as happens in the real world - your data is less than perfect and you are facing into a daunting data world, and all you have is the equivalent of a spoon and a fork – this book is for you.

If you need to go into the data trenches – be sure to bring this book by Oz du Soleil and Bill Jelen (AKA Mr Excel) with you. They've got your data back – in all sorts of ways.

You have a data problem: misspelled multiple entries, linking data sets together, octopus spreadsheets, what formula to use - they've got a solution. There is a chapter on Power Query – Excel's best kept data secret or as Oz du Soleil calls it: "Power Query =EmPOWERment" . You've got the "usual suspects" of vlookup/ xlookup – when you need to hook up data sets together.

It's not just all data – there is lots of guidance on how to ask better questions from your users to help clarify what the person – "really really wants". Practical sane guidance and advice. Read this book and become a data freedom fighter...It's like the "The Art of War" for data..

Anne Walsh – The Excel Lady – author of Your Excel Survival Kit – your guide to surviving and thriving in an Excel world.

Be aware: this is not just a technical book about spreadsheets but arguably a dense treaty on how to get yourself out from data conflicts, end unnecessary misery and make something happen with powerful Excel sorcery (Power Query, Pivot Tables, Dynamic Arrays, & more!). May this book lead you to begin the endless joyful journey of going from a "crude Excel user" to a "bona fide Excel beast", and more importantly, may this book also help you claim victory over crappy datasets and become the hero for the people the data is connected to.

Carlos Barboza, Guerrilla Data Analyst & bilingual Excel & Power BI developer

Reading through and asking myself, what is not in here? This book showcases a lot of key excel features (pivots, dynamic arrays, LET function, PowerQuery) every modern data guerrila should have in their arsenal. It does not get into excessive details, but provides just enough for the reader to step-up their data game. Some chapters are short, in length, but not in impact. A good book, worth every penny and every second of your time.

Victor Momoh, Microsoft Excel MVP/Excel Enthusiast